THE BOY WHO COULD TICKLE CLOUDS

STEPHEN BRIGGS

To Jean and Gerry for this wonderful life.

The Australian outback is a *magical* place… to find yourself.

1 PARABURDOO, RED DIRt WONDERLAND

Darren Bignell stood at the bottom of our driveway, and called me *a choker*. "If ya pants were any higher you'd choke," he said. "What's wrong with ya? For Christ's sake pull 'em down a bit."

I was totally shocked. I'd always thought I wore my shorts at a reasonable height. After all, just under my armpits was the height Mum told me to wear *everything* at. I couldn't believe that only two days earlier I had my fifth birthday on that very driveway, where I'd felt the sheer jubilation of riding my tomboy friend Sarah's bike without training wheels, or at least without them touching the ground. I didn't even really know Darren. He was just a kid with hair as white as toothpaste, who lived up the road and always looked like he was grumpy about something, but didn't know what. That didn't make it any easier though. I can't explain why I felt like I did. There was just this sickness in my tummy like I had gorged myself stupid on musk sticks and Easter eggs.

I stood and stared straight at him, secretly hoping that if I smiled long enough he would say he was only joking. But Darren didn't take well to this silence — his fists forcing down my shorts as he punched me in the nose and barked in my ear, "You're a fuckin' little poofter aren't ya Choker?"

The ground around Paraburdoo was like nothing I had ever seen. Altogether covered in thick red dust, with a continuous slide show of different colours, textures and shapes splattered on top. And it was *big*. Everything stretched out to the fuzzy, flickering horizon. We came to Paraburdoo because someone stubbed their toe on a rock that turned out to be Iron Ore. But I don't think the desert liked being dug up. No matter what you were doing, something from the ground would try and get ya. Whether it was flies, dust, King brown snakes, centipedes, pollen, huntsmen, scorpions, death adders, red backs… or heat. The *heat* was dry like morning breath. It was as if you were standing in a microwave oven with a million hair dryers going full bore at you. The temperature reached 42 C plus, nearly every day in summer. A friend of Dad's got lost without water and was dead in five and a half hours. Dad always told that story, but never spoke about it.

It must have been a huge change from the English countryside my parents were used to. I was too young to remember Yorkshire. The only pasture I knew was the pongy mountainside spinifex that the entire Hamersley Range wore like a spiky yellow shawl.

After the Darren Bignell incident, I kept pretty much to myself. I would hop on my pushbike and head for the bush that cuddled the town. I don't think my Drag-Star was actually *designed* for off-roading, but I didn't let that stop me. I had three gears and I was going to use them. The training wheels were a bit of an encumbrance though. I asked Dad to take them off but he said, "Jesus Bludy Aitch Christ. Where did a little lad like yer learn a word like 'in...come...brunce'? "

"I read it in *Reader's Digest*," I told him, "I like words." But he wouldn't take them off. "It's betta to be safe than sorry. Maybe when yer six," he said.

Anyway, so long as I watched out for the big river rocks I was fine. But one day I missed one. Well missed seeing it. I was riding through a quartz field, which was as big as the main footy oval, covered in sharp, shiny, jagged white stones the size of golf balls. I used to change down to second gear when I was on quartz patrol, but I thought I had seen a bunyip down at Bill's Billabong and I wasn't changing down for no-one. Riding over quartz was really bumpy. Not big bumps, just hundreds of little ones that made you shake like you were cold. I had just about made it to the path, when I looked over to see if the bunyip was following me. As I turned back to see where I was going, I realised I was about to hit a whopping big river rock. I couldn't lock up the brakes cos I would skid and stack it and end up with quartz rash, which hurts far more than gravel rash and carpet burn put together. I couldn't turn around it. There wasn't enough room, not with training wheels. I had no choice. If the bunyip wanted to chase me again, it would protect me. So I aimed my tyre at the middle of the river rock and closed my eyes. I knew I'd go over the handlebars, so I told my legs to jump as I started to go and I got a clean take off. For three or four delicious seconds, I was tickling clouds, riding the thermals of the Pilbara desert… Suddenly my ride ended. Well not so much ended, more like, sided. I smashed into the side of a half-decomposed cow. It caught my shoulder with its rump, as I went whizzing by, and it pulled me into the safety of its pus-filled guts. It must have been the bunyip's idea of a cushion. It was *pretty* comfy compared to a tree or a ditch, but it sure did stink. The kind of stink that won't rub off once you've touched it. But I sure was grateful. I didn't even get a flat tyre. That bunyip liked scaring the shit out of me.

When I got home, Dad tried to get the pong off with petrol and a rag. He said that I smelt much better, but we both knew that he was lying. He couldn't believe that I had landed in a cow. There hadn't been cattle seen around Paraburdoo for years. I told him about the training wheels, and he took them off as his dinner went cold. I wrapped it in alfoil and put it in the oven, but I must have put it up too high because I burnt it to a cinder. Dad didn't mind cos he got to have kippers. He loved them and we hated 'em, but that night their smell didn't bother me as much as usual.

What I could salvage of Dad's meal I took out to the smartest pet that ever lived in the whole state of Western Australia. Kimba the white guinea pig! I was going to call him Snowy, because he was pure white, and I thought Snowy would remind Mum and Dad of England and the snow they used to get at Christmas time, but then I thought it might just rub in what they were missing.

Now Kimba he was talented. A really gifted guinea pig. I never actually *saw* him do it, but I certainly heard him. Kimba used to sing Frank Sinatra songs. You could always hear him when Dad played *Strangers in the Night*. He didn't have a loud voice, but you could definitely hear a shrill voice singing in the background. Mind you, every time I'd go out to check he wouldn't do one bar. He was very humble. He lived in a converted tea chest in the middle of our patchy back yard. I used to move it around every few days to ensure he always got nice fresh grass to munch on. Not that the grass was really luscious, or green, or anything. It was patchy, yellowy brown couch.

When we first got to Paraburdoo, Dad tried everything to make it go green and thicken up. He put fertiliser on it, he tested the soil for trace elements, he even took me up to the clearing behind the school after the Perry Brothers Circus had been to town. We shovelled every type of manure you could think of. It was great fun working out which was the lion's and tiger's. I needed a hand with the elephant's, one mound was bigger than my spade, and when I tried to lift it, it lifted me and flung me around into what I think was the zebra's, on account of the stripes. We brought back an entire trailer load and scattered it about until way after dark.

"That's not a vege patch. That's Noahs Bludy Ark," said Dad. "All we need now is a good shower." But as it didn't rain until Christmas the following year, Dad had to run the gauntlet of strict water restrictions, and use his tea pot as a watering can after he thought the neighbours had gone to sleep. Eventually he gave up, "This bludy garden's just like my 'ead," he said, "It won't grow nought." I suggested we should rub some of the left over elephant manure on his bald patch, but Dad wasn't too keen to try it.

The sun was extremely strong at our house, even first thing in the morning. I was a real good sleeper, but not good enough to escape the sun. I'd always go to sleep on my back and wake up lying on my side with the pillow wrapped in my arms. Then the sun would bend around the corner of the blind and onto the back of my neck. Once I woke up with the hair on my neck starting to singe. It sure made a good alarm clock, got you up nice and early. I didn't mind though, cos as soon I woke up I'd rush out the back and play with Kimba. He told me he loved the mornings too. He didn't actually use *words,* he used twitches of his nose to tell me. Every morning before breakfast we'd hop on my bike and go for a burn in the easement next to our house. Kimba was a great rider, he'd sit with his paws hanging out of the basket at the front and he'd lean from side to side when we went around corners. His favourite was the bunny hop over the kerbs. Boy could he jump high. Sometimes right out of the basket, but I was always there to catch him. After breakfast, if we were really lucky, Dad would let us go to work with him. Mum would only let him take us if he was going on a short trip, usually to see how his boys were going. And Dad had to promise Mum we weren't going up any really big hills.

When we arrived in Paraburdoo there were six half finished houses. Our place had all of its walls, but only three quarters of its roof. The town was only a few months old and Dad had come to help put up the power lines and give the town a regular electricity supply. It was his job to drive up the steep mountains and make sure his team were putting in the power poles correctly. He didn't just watch though. He always got into the action when he had to. You know, when one of the guys slipped and the pole started to fall or something. And those poles were always doing something they shouldn't. Particularly when you consider the terrain they were going into. Sometimes they had to stick them right out the side of a cliff, hundreds of feet above the scrub. Kimba and I were really proud of him, especially when we'd ride past one of his powerlines, we'd both look at each other and say, "our Dad did that."

I spent a lot of time with Dad in the few months before I started school. I was always helping him with something. When we finished our jobs for Mum, we'd sit on the verandah and have a drink. When Mum wasn't looking, Dad used to slip me a shandy. Mum liked shandies too but she didn't like me having them. Some days Charlie Crabbe, our next door neighbour, would come over for a game of pool. We must have been the only family in Paraburdoo to have our own pool table. Dad had bought it off an ex-publican in Perth, and had it shipped up on the back of a truck carrying power lines. It was a great table with a lovely soft green fur on top of it. When no one was around, I used to lay my head on it and with one eye look at the table and the other look at the yard. Dad was really excited when I showed him how to do it. He said, "Yer done it son! I've finally gota green lawn t' be proud of. People might think I've gone round twist though when I get 'em to go all cross eyed and lay on table."

When we first got the table I couldn't actually see over it to play, so Dad built me a little stool to stand on. It was a bit of a hassle moving it each time I had a shot, but after a while I just did it with my feet. I used to spend hours on that pool table. I'd make up games like having to sink three balls in a row or the bunyip was going to get me. Sometimes when I missed the second or third ball I'd chuck a spack sprint into the house and hide under my bed. If I was having a bad day and missing a lot, I would have taken the precaution of already hiding Kimba under there. Then once I'd said "balese" three times, the Bunyip couldn't get me. I must have got pretty good at pool, cos one night when Dad had his boys around for a barbie, one of them called Pablo, asked me if I could play. I told him I was *ok* at it, if I could use my stool. Twenty four games later, I had beaten all of the boys three times. Pablo didn't mind, because after I beat him in two shots, he started betting the other guys I would beat them. The other guys hadn't really seen me beat Pablo because they were still dizzy from crossing their eyes and staring at the grass.

2 OWNING UP TO THE YELLOW TIDE

I didn't realise going to school was such a big deal, until Mum started crying at dinner. She kept saying, "He's too little. He's growing up too fast." I hadn't really given school a second thought. I just thought it would be a *mint* ride because it was at other end of town, and to get there I'd have to go through the shops. Just thinking about how many times I would be able to get into third gear gave me goose bumps. And everyone knew the shiny concrete up at the shops was perfect for skids. But seeing Mum taking funny breaths filled with wails really upset me, and the night before school was the first sleepless night of my life.

I started to think, if it's got Mum that upset, school must be *really* scary. Each time I slid off to sleep I would wake with a snap and think the bunyip was coming to get me. Two or three times I saw it sitting in the shadows at the end of my bed.

The next morning at breakfast, Dad told me to make sure I listened to what my teacher told me and Mum did lots of reminiscing about when we first got to Paraburdoo and how the town had a pet Emu called Hooky. I wish she hadn't mentioned Hooky cos I really liked him. He got run over by a two seater Cessna, as it was trying to take off from the airstrip.

I begged her to change her mind, but Mum wouldn't let me ride on my first day. She insisted that she take me in the car so she could introduce herself to the teacher. Thing was, by the time we got to the school Mum could hardly say 'hello', she was blubbering so much. In the end I had to say, "Hi I'm Stephen and this is my Mum; Mrs Briggs." Mum shook hands, blew her nose and left. When I turned around, I saw 24 sets of eyes, staring, straight at me. I searched their faces to see if they had just endured a similar separation. But if they had, they weren't showing it.

Miss Jessop was a strange looking teacher. I thought she'd be like Mum but she looked much younger. Her face was blanketed by two red triangles, the skin around her eyes was coloured shiny green and her denim shorts were so small that when she sat down you could see her knickers. She was nice though. Weird looking but nice. She gave us all nametags, which we had to stick on our shirts after we told the class a bit about ourselves. I told everyone that I was really annoyed because I wasn't going to get to skid on the way home. And of course I told them about Kimba. The teacher said, "Oh he sounds fascinating, maybe one day we could hear him sing."

"Well today's your lucky day!" I said as I pulled him out of the secret compartment in my bag. The class went mad-everyone wanted to pat him and give him a tickle. Everyone, except a little boy called Jimmy Walker. He screamed and Kimba got stage fright. We had to sing songs cross-legged on the carpet, until Mum came back and took Kimba home. I don't know how she knew I had him because I didn't tell her. It turned out for the best though, because second time around Mum didn't cry at all, she just said, "Wait till I get yer home." I was a bit sad without him at lunchtime. I was sitting by myself for most of it, until Jodie O'Grady, a girl from my class with the reddest hair I had ever seen, came over and told me she liked me. I said, "That's nice," and asked if her hair was redder than the dirt at the mine. She said she didn't know because she had never been to the mine. She sure knew her way around the playground though. She took me to the water fountain, the monkey bars, and the wire fence near where the older kids played. Jodie asked me, "Have you ever played with doogs?"

"Oh yeah, our next door neighbour Charlie Crabbe's got a cocker spaniel," I replied.

"Not dogs, doogs silly," I was stumped. It was obviously important to know what doogs were but I didn't have a clue.

"It's all right, I didn't know what they were either," she said. "They're marbles. The older kids play two sorts of games with them, one is called, Set 'em Up. That's where you set up your best doog and they have to hit it three times to win it. And if they roll 10 marbles at it and miss each time, they lose 10 marbles. The other game's name... I can't remember, but you dig a hole and you have to flick all your marbles into it." Jodie sure could talk. She asked me if I had a girlfriend and I said, "What would I want one of those for? I've got Kimba!"

I kind of enjoyed the walk home, as my head was spinning with all the learning I had just done. Miss Jessop told us that this was just the beginning of ten years of learning, maybe more if we went on to university, whatever that was. I was just coming to terms with that and deciding whether I should say something about her knickers poking out of her shorts, when someone grabbed my legs and threw me to the ground.

"I thought I told you to pull those shorts down. You little choker! "Darren Bignell and two of his mates had snuck up behind me and sprung an ambush. "Well, what have you got to say for yourself?"

"Nothing," I replied, possibly with a little too much spirit, spirit that Darren Bignell decided he had to douse.

"Regular little poofter aren't ya? You know who wears their pants up that high?" He said, towering over me as his scaly mates held me down.

"Dick wacks like you," I said. He must have found it *really* insulting to be called a dick wack because he pulled my hair up to his face.

"Little babies are chokers. And you know what little babies do don't ya? They wet their pants." With that he let go of my hair, pulled his shorts down and sprayed hot wee all over me.

As I walked up the driveway, I couldn't believe that he'd managed to squirt it up my nose. It must have looked pretty bad, because one of his mates said I really *was* choking and they got off me quick smart. If only I hadn't been thinking about Miss Jessop's *knickers*, if I'd seen them coming I might have been able to run away. All that ducking into the house so the bunyip couldn't get me, had made me pretty fast on my feet. I was a mess by the time I reached the end of our street. What was I going to say to Mum?

Fortunately it was a very hot day and most of the wee had dried on my shirt. My shorts were still pretty damp though. When I walked in the door and Mum started tearing strips off me for sneaking Kimba into class, I couldn't cope. Even when I told her Kimba had begged me to take him, she wouldn't calm down, "And look, yer've got yer *uniform* all wet. Take it off, hop in the shower and I'll hang it out." Boy was I packing it in the shower. I didn't want Mum to think I had wet my pants and I sure didn't want her to know that dick wack Bignell had wissed on me. Somehow it seemed to go unnoticed, that was, until Dad came home from work.

I was out the back playing with Kimba, pretending that it was his coronation as Mayor of Paraburdoo. I'd found a nice shaped twig to be his staff, and a silver milk bottle-top to be his crown. I don't know how he did it, but he'd really got carried away with the *occasion* and given his coat a bit of a perm. He looked like one of those judges

21

with the wigs. As I sat there and read a list of Kimba's good deeds to the townsfolk, my Dad sat on the verandah trying to work out what he was going to say to me.

"Stevie, can yer come 'ere for a moment?" he called.

"In a minute. I'm just giving Kimba the key to the city."

"Now son please." Dad didn't use that tone very often, so Kimba suggested we take a rest from proceedings so he could check his perm. "Would yer like a shandy son?"

"What about Mum?" I whispered.

"She won't grieve what she don't know. 'ow did yer first day at school go? "he inquired, as he filled my shandy, with a little more beer and a little less lemonade, than usual.

"Gee, thanks Dad. Oh school was ok," I bluffed.

"Did yer make lots of new friends?" he asked enthusiastically as he lifted me onto his knee.

"I met a girl called Jodie O'Grady. She said she liked me and she showed me how to play doogs, which are really marbles."

"Jodie O'Grady? She's Paddy O'Grady's daughter. Yer'll be doin' well if yer get on with 'er. 'er dad's mine manager. Oh rather," Dad said with a hint of pomp and ceremony. Then Dad pulled a serious face, that told me he knew something about this afternoon. "Son do yer remember when yer were little and yer used to wet the bed."

"And you used to put the plastic sheet on," I said, finishing his sentence. He liked it when I finished his sentences, it was like I could read his mind.

"Well son, sometimes, people can start wettin' their beds again, and sometimes they don't even wet their beds, sometimes, it's themselves. Son, Mum smelt the wee wee on yer shorts. We don't want yer to be embarrassed. It's just somethin' that 'appens to some people. If we *know* that it's 'appenin,' we can go to doctor's... and 'e can fix it. Now don't get embarrassed, I just need to know if yer, 'ad a little accident today?" I sat terrified, I couldn't lie to him but I couldn't tell him the truth either. "Stevie I can't do anythin'... unless yer tell me. Did yer wet yer pants today?"

"No," I whimpered.

"Don't lie to me Stephen," Dad said firmly.

"I'm not lying Dad."

"Well 'ow did the stink get there then? Son, look, it really isn't a *big* deal, just tell me yer wet yer pants."

I burst into tears and blurted it out, "But I didn't... Darren Bignell did."

"Yer what?" said Dad.

"Two of his mates held me down and he wissed all over me, even on my head," I wept.

"That fuckin' little bastard. Piss on my son? We're going to 'ave words, with that prick's father. Jean! Bruce Bignell's twat of a son pissed on our lad." By the time Mum made it out the back, Dad, was in a lather.

"I've never liked that arsehole, or his fuckin' son."

"Now calm down Gerry. What are yer going to say? Yer can't just, barge in there and say, stop yer Darren pissing on my Stephen," she argued. But Dad wasn't going to give up that easy, "Why the bloody 'ell can't I? Jesus H Christ woman! I've got to defend his dignity."

"Well do as yer like but I think it's a mistake. Bruce Bignell is a very respected member of our community. If he gets that promotion, he could be yer boss, "said Mum, adopting the tone that usually wins her arguments and gets her appliances.

"Well I've got do somethin'... Poor defenceless bugger... I know! I'll teach 'im 'ow to box. I'll get a punchin' bag and I'll teach him 'ow to defend 'imself with 'is fists."

Once I was older, I'd *thank* Mum for not letting Dad go round and take revenge on the Bignells. In the Doo, reputation was everything. And if you were going to survive, you had to be prepared to fight your own battles and wear your shorts pulled down a bit.

I think Dad had done two weeks worth of training and three years worth of brawling, in pubs and taverns all over the world, when he was in the Royal Navy. He didn't really have much technique, but you sure wouldn't want to be on the wrong side of one of his punches, that 'bag,' sure took a pounding. I think Dad really enjoyed teaching me how to punch, as *he* used to look forward to the sessions a lot more than I did. I just thought the whole thing was a bit stupid, but you couldn't tell him that. Every other day, after he finished work, we would go into the shed and punch that old hessian bag filled with rags. Eventually Dad caught on that I wasn't *really* interested, mind you, it took a bit of hinting.

"Now son, come in close and punch *really* fast, to the body. Just like this. Yer see? Are yer watchin'?" Dad said, with sweat vaulting off his nose.

"Yes Dad," I agreed, half-heartedly.

Dad went up a gear, "Now look what I'm doin' to 'im. I'm workin' 'im downstairs. Look 'ow badly 'e's takin' it. 'e's crumblin'. There's no way 'e's goin' to go the distance. Now the left, right, combination and pow 'e takes an upper cut and 'e's 'istory."

"Dad, *he's* a fertiliser bag filled with your old socks and Mum's ripped knickers. Don't you think you're getting a bit carried away?" I pointed out sincerely.

Dad's voice quivered a little, as he said, "What do yer mean son?"

"Well it's just…" I tried to find the words but they wouldn't come.

"No. Come on Stevie. Are yer tryin' to tell me, yer don't *like* boxin'? I 'ope yer not, because we are doin' this for yer bloody benefit yer know."

"I know Dad, and I appreciate you teaching me. It's just… it's just… Stupid. Bloody stupid… And brutal, and boring. And if you want to keep training and win those yellow, I mean golden, gloves you keep talking about, that's great. But I don't… At all."

As soon as the last word hacked out of my mouth, I saw hurt, for the first time in my father's eyes. I finally understood what it was to be absolutely honest, and my father had been knocked out by his own corner. He looked at me as if I had cut out the centre of his spleen with an apple corer. The combination of heat and smell in the tiny tin shed forced me to tears and within seconds I was sprinting for my sanctuary under the bed. As I reached the back door, I had already got one glove off and paused as the second lost its grip and fell to the concrete floor. Dad saw me toss those special red gloves he had driven 80 kilometres on the dirt road to Tom Price for, and he wasn't happy, "Stevie those gloves cost a fortune!"

"Well take them back then, I don't want them! I never did!" I snapped, as my right leg involuntarily twitched and kicked the glove half the length of the back yard and straight into my father's questioning hands.

3 toEPUNtS, DICKS AND tAILS

The following Sunday, I found myself sitting in the car with Dad, on the collar of the main oval.

"You'll like it Stevie... It's the world game," Dad assured me as he opened my door. I was feeling a bit nervous as I walked out to the group of boys sitting in the middle of the oval. But just as I was about to retreat, an enormous thundercloud passed directly over my shoulder and I started to smile. I liked clouds. They rarely brought rain but they certainly were good company. Sometimes thousands of feet wide and high, they were the only things that could, if they wanted to, blot out the Pilbara heat and scorching light. I loved the colours they would bring.

I didn't know what colour was, until the first time I saw a thunderstorm. Normally, the sun stoops so close to the desert that it bleaches *everything* it touches. Nothing has a chance to show off its colour because it is drenched in a heat haze so strong, that the amount that falls on one strand of spinifex in a moment, could power the lights at the Melbourne Cricket Ground for a month. When the clouds come, Paraburdoo germinates in front of you. The spectrum of flowers, the red and yellow ochres, the silver gravel, the white cockatoos, the pink galahs, the green twenty-eight parrots, the brown bungarras, the yellow goannas, the jarrah frilly necked lizards, the black crows, and the molten blue bitumen. As Dad drove off in our Torana, I was again reminded what *purple* really was.

A middle-aged Scottish man in a singlet, whose nose was too large for his face and legs were shaped like crescents, approached me, "You must be young Steve. I'm Mr Mac. Your Da said you might be coming down. Come and have a seat with the other lads. Everybody, this is Stevie. Introduce yourselves as we go," he said, as he dotted large orange witches hats all over the grass. I looked around at the scattered, puzzled faces. Some I recognised from school like Jimmy Walker, some I'd seen riding around town and some were older, not particularly friendly-looking boys, that I didn't know at all. "Ok let's have you in two lines. Now, I want you to weave in and out, along the line of hats. Both feet, if you can manage it," he said with a hopeful expression. I stood nervously in line. The witches' hats didn't look too close together but from what I was seeing the other boys do, I was going to have my work cut out for me. I kinda thought the coach would go easy on me cos I was new, but the first time I touched the ball, he blew his whistle and came over, "Have you ever kicked a soccer ball Stevie?"

"I've kicked a boxing glove but not a real ball," I said in a big voice. He put his arm on my shoulder, as the other kids gathered around.

"I see. Well I don't know about boxing gloves but I can tell you the easiest way to kick a ball and that, is to use the *side* of your foot. Like so," he instructed, as he slowly nestled the side of his foot against the ball. "What you're doing, and it's a common mistake, is using your toe. The common, garden variety, toe punt. Apart from being a very ugly looking kick, it's also, very hard to control the direction in which you want the ball to go... So have another go." I had listened very hard to what Mr Mac said but as I brought the side of my foot up to the ball, Jimmy Walker laughed, my leg spasmed and a toe punt resulted. Mind you, it would be fairer to call it a toe rocket... that ball was going so fast when it finally stopped you could hear it skidding. Mr Mac came over.

"I'm sorry Mr Mac. I really did try," I said meekly.

"Don't worry lad, it's only your first training run, and besides, your natural kick may not be the most beautiful one I've seen, but you certainly get some power out of it," he said with a hint of respect. I sure did a lot of running that afternoon. Every time I touched the ball, it would go a mile and I would have to chase after it. Mr Mac said he was starting to think my toe was made of rubber.

It *was* frustrating though, especially when we started playing a scratch match. I would try and kick it softly but even when I did, the ball would go half the length of the pitch. Then I'd just have to sprint after it and hope that I could get to it before the other boys. Quite a few times I could, but then I'd just boot it a mile again, even when I was really close to the goal. I could see that Mr Mac was a very wise man because he was right, you couldn't control that ugly toe punt. Added to that, my gym boots sure made it tricky when I had to stop. The time I didn't spend toe punting and chasing, I spent stacking it and getting up again. Some of the older boys had proper soccer boots with metal studs. I only realised after one of them slid into me and left a perfect indent in my shin. It *really* hurt but I didn't let on.

"There's plenty more where that came from… useless," he said. By the end of the training session everyone was calling me "useless." I thought it was *great,* cos I'd never had a nickname before and every one was calling me it, apart from Mr Mac; no one ever used it when he was close enough to hear.

After we finished training, I was busting for the loo, so I went into the shed next to the oval to find the toilet. When I got in there, there was only one cubicle and it was being used by one of the older boys and when I say used, I don't mean number ones. The smell was so bad, I had to take tiny breaths so I didn't throw up. After about 10 minutes of waiting, I thought I better knock on the door and make sure he hadn't passed out.

"Are you all right in there?" I asked, after tapping lightly on the door.

"Yeah I'm fine. Who's askin?" he said, sounding a bit annoyed.

"It's Stevie, I mean, Useless. I really need to do a pee," I said pleadingly.

"Oh well, you'll have to piss off and piss somewhere else. I'm reading a stick magazine," he barked.

"What's a stick magazine?" I asked.

"Shit, you really are useless, aren't you? A stick magazine is full of dirty pictures," he shouted, as the door flung open and he thrust the open magazine in my face, his pants still draped around his ankles. The pictures were really scary. There was a man and lady in the nude, they were both on their hands and knees and the man was *stabbing* the lady with something which I couldn't quite work out, it looked like his tail. It *was* his tail! It sure looked different to mine.

"What's happened to his tail?" I screeched.

"His what?" he spluttered, in disbelief.

"His tail!" I said, in a dare devilish way, signalling to him that I knew we were about to discuss something *naughty*.

"That's not a *tail* that's a dick, a cock, or maybe even a doodle but it's definitely not a tail. Where'd you learn that?" he whined, gagging on his laughter.

"Oh. That's what my Mum and Dad call it. But they're English. I guess it must be called a tail over there," I reasoned.

"Well I got news for ya and it's all bad. We're not in England, we're in the Doo and round here, it's called a dick. Fuck you sure are useless. No wonder everyone calls you it," he said with a trace of compassion. It was then that I realised my nickname wasn't exactly the nicest one I could have hoped for. I didn't realise they really *meant* that I was useless, I thought it was just a joke.

Some time later, I found myself day dreaming on the footpath as I made my way home. Dad hadn't come to pick me up like he promised he would, so I had to walk home. But far worse than that... I was a young boy searching my heart to find a way to forgive my parents for telling me the wrong name for my tail. I mean dick.

As I rolled Kimba onto his back for a scratch, my curiosity really got the better of me and I couldn't help but take a peek and see if *he* had a dick. It was pretty hard to say, I couldn't really see anything under all that fur, so I foraged around a bit.

"Steady on," twitched Kimba, "What are you playing at?"

"I'm sorry Kimba. I shouldn't have been looking, but I just had to see if you had a... a... you know." I stammered.

"Oh you mean a dick," he said knowingly.

"You call it a dick too?" I questioned.

"Well what else would I call it?" he twitched again. At that moment, Dad appeared from the house carrying a box wrapped in fancy paper.

"Stevie, I've got somethin' for yer," he said hiding the box behind his back.

"How could you Dad? How could you?" I squeaked in a sort of angry disillusionment.

"Yer said yer didn't want the gloves, so I took 'em back," Dad retorted defensively.

"Tails Dad. Tails! Or should that be... DICKS?" I blurted.

"Stevie, I think yer got a bit too much sun at soccer trainin'. That or yer need to wash yer mouth out with soap," Dad frowned with bewilderment.

"I found out at soccer, quite by accident, that in Paraburdoo the tail is called a 'dick.' And I know that you come from England and over there it might be fine to say 'tail' but we're not in England any more and from now on I think we should call a dick, *a dick*, not a tail. OK?" Dad looked like a wombat that had been run over by a road train.

"Well um… if, that's what yer want Stevie?"

"Yes dad it is," I insisted.

"All right Stephen… but I will say this. *Tail*, 'as been used by the people of my village in Yorkshire, to describe that part of a man's body, for 'undreds of years. It's what my father, my grandfather and all the other men in the Briggs family 'ave called it; but if it will make you 'appy, I'll break with my tradition because I love yer and yer 'appiness, is very, very important to me."

I think that embracing 'dick,' was one of the hardest things Dad did. He was a very proud Englishman, who on a daily basis found himself stretching and remoulding his skin to fit this new, red land. After a few moments of silent memorial for what he had just lost, he handed me the package.

"This is for you son. I'm sorry I weren't there, to pick yer up, after soccer. I 'ad a little errand to run."

"Dad, I didn't mean to ruin your tradition," I said, feeling a little guilty.

"It's alright… It's alright son. Yer right, we don't live in England anymore, we're Australian now. Anyway, we've said our respective pieces and now we can carry on. Mr Mac just called and said yer 'ad a lot of natural ability, which makes me think I may 'ave done the right thing." I opened the box, to find a brand new, size five, all leather soccer ball, then I realised that Dad must have driven all the way to Tom Price to get it and that's why he couldn't pick me up.

"Oh Dad, thank you so much, it's a ripper! I promise that I'll practice and practice and make you proud of me."

"I already am proud of yer son," he whispered, as my arms reached up around his neck. "Ok, we can 'ave a kick, once... I've put box in shed. We may be livin' in a new country but I'll never stop 'oardin' stuff like an Englishman. 'ang on a minute! What's this?" he puzzled, looking into the bottom of the box.

"What Dad? What's in there?" I sniffed. He held the box up to his face and out of my reach, "I don't really know son, I think yer better 'ave a look, your eyes are better than mine." Inside the box was a note saying, 'Yer pillow ain't what it used to be.' Dad was always playing these kind of tricks and I raced inside to see what he'd been up to. When I ran into my bedroom, my pillow wasn't there at all, in its place were a pair of Adidas soccer boots. They fitted perfectly and came with screw in studs *and* a silver spanner. I couldn't help myself and leapt into the air yelping, "Bonza!"

Dad and I played kick to kick for hours and even though Dad had done a whole days work, he still managed to fetch all the balls I thumped past him, with a smile. It got dark pretty quick that night but we said we'd keep playing until the ground cooled down. Sometimes it would still be like a toasty jacket potato way after eight. Eventually Mum put her foot down and gave us five more minutes. We were just about to go in, when Kimba came up with a brilliant idea. Everything Dad and I had tried to make me kick softer had failed, apart from when I just brushed the ball and made it go a centimetre. Kimba said that his idea was pretty silly, but as we *were* playing by the light of the swollen new Kimberley moon, it might just work. He suggested, that I try kicking… with my *left* foot. And you know what? It worked. Right from the very first time I tried it; a perfect pass to my wonderful, puffing Dad. That night I slept like a champion. I had worked out the stuff about dicks and tails, I had got a new soccer ball and boots, and I had learnt to do little kicks, even if they were left footed and toe punts. It was really nice in bed that night, I felt a warm-furry-scamper nuzzle at my chin and then scuttle past my neck.

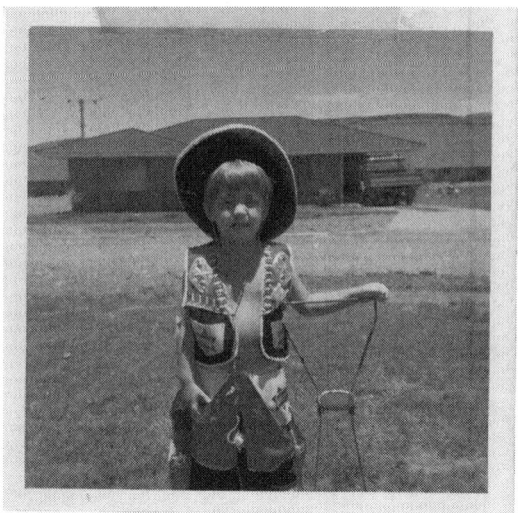

4 KIMBA'S WHITE COAT

The next morning, the sun didn't wake me up as usual because it was overcast, and it's never overcast first thing in the morning. I jumped into my tracksuit and ran down the passage. It would be a great day to look at all the colours I thought, and Kimba sure would be excited. As the screen door swung back, I was greeted by something *strange*. I realised Kimba's tea chest wasn't where I had left it. "Someone's playing silly buggers again," I said loud enough for him to hear me. But my mouth went dry and my fingers tingled, his chest was upside down. I ran the fastest five metres of my life, which still seemed to take hours. I only wish it could have taken longer. Kimba wasn't playing silly buggers and hiding somewhere trying to conceal his twitching nose. He wasn't staring up at the glorious palate of colours the cloud cover had provided. He was leaning on the mayor's staff I gave him for his coronation, at least most of him was.

I had never seen his beautiful white coat shimmer like it did in that light and I had never seen a red like the one that was splattered all over it. Someone had *gutted* him. They had torn him in half, put his guts in a pile and skewered the rest of him onto his Mayor's staff, which had then been planted into the ground. If *only* I had snuck him into my sanctuary under the bed that night, instead of giving it to my stupid new soccer ball and boots. As my tears caught the sunlight and made tiny rainbows, I lay down beside my dearest friend. I couldn't stand the sight of his intestines splayed across the grass, yet I couldn't look away. And then, as I made a sound so deep that it must have come from the balls of my feet, I made the *cruelest* discovery of all. Even with his guts torn out of him and his chest pierced right through, Kimba's eyes were still moving, though only slightly, as death was coming; but hadn't arrived yet. He looked up at me, his eyes coming into focus as if he had just walked into a dark room.

"I'm a gonner Stephen. We had some great times didn't we?" he said, as his coat burned even brighter. I tried to speak but the tears rained all over my words.

"You look after yourself. Don't forget to wear your shorts nice and low and remember to kick with your left foot," he whispered, as the twitch seeped out of his nose and he surrendered to the stick that impaled him. I yelled so loud and long that everyone from the surrounding houses came rushing out to see what had happened.

I threw myself as hard as I could into the ground, hoping that it would crack open where he lay and take me too. My Dad picked me up and held me with all his strength, so I couldn't hurt myself again. But he couldn't restrain my screams, which sliced straight through the trees, houses, cars and anything else that got in their path as they hurtled toward the continent's dead heart. I screamed and kicked and sobbed, for what seemed like hours, each reaction to the machete in my chest as intense as the last, until finally the land must have got annoyed with my sounds and sent pollen to clog my lungs.

As Mum and Dad rushed me to the hospital, I was convinced that my time in this hell called the 'Doo' was over and somehow Kimba had planned all this so we could escape together. However, a needle in the bum, a nebuliser clamped to my face and a night under observation in ward G, saw to it that Kimba left without me.

The next two years of my life were not so much sad, but still ones. I found it difficult to get either happy *or* upset. Unless of course I actually thought about how much I missed him. Then I would cry for hours. Especially just before I went to sleep. I lay in bed thinking about the things we used to get up to, like the time I snuck him into school, and the time we made him a balsa-wood glider so he could be the first guinea pig to fly across Bill's Billabong. Mum was desperate to find a way to snap me out of it. She offered to get me a new guinea pig heaps of times, but I wouldn't hear it. "All I want to do is read *Reader's Digest* and play soccer," I told her. And even though Kimba was gone, I still used to talk to him, or at least his grave. I buried him under the roots of the old ghost gum in the back of the yard. It was a favourite place of Kimba's; he used to love foraging around in all the decomposing leaves, sometimes he would set up twigs and branches and do hurdles and pole vaults over the top of them. "A fit guinea pig is a happy guinea pig," he used to say.

Other than not having my special little friend, things seemed to go pretty well in my first few years at school. I was the year two 'times tables' champion and the top of my class in everything except maths. In fact, when I got to the end of grade two, they put me up into grade four. I felt pretty stupid having to hang around with the older kids but I liked it when Darren Bignell had to repeat a year. I think Dad liked that too, especially as Bruce Bignell *was* now his boss. I liked going to school and I liked the way my teachers would always give me gold stars and special homework that no one else got to do, but it wasn't my favourite thing. That was unquestionably, soccer.

I was so annoyed with everyone calling me 'useless' at the first training session, that I spent every spare minute I had, and didn't have, kicking my ball. When Dad was working and I couldn't find anyone to play with, I would play with the brick wall at the side of the house. I'd come up with all sorts of challenges. At first, the biggest one was being able to control the bloody ball. But after thousands of kicks and rebounds off the wall, I started to know exactly where the ball was going to go and which minute part of my foot would be the perfect shape to stop it. Sometimes it was the bottom of the arch, others the top left hand side of the heel, and occasionally the tip of my little toe. I can't remember *when* it happened but at some time, I even made the transition from toe punting to legitimate kicking. Mind you, there was a lot of toe punting in between. At least a season's worth anyway.

And what a season it was. For the first six weeks everyone called me 'useless,' and if I'm honest I can understand why. I *was* pretty terrible. Not that I didn't try, I always tried, in fact I think I probably tried too hard sometimes. But I'm glad I went through that humiliating stage, when every time I went to kick the ball I'd miss and fall on my bum. One of the older boys—Jamie Roper— started calling me 'bum' but it didn't catch on. I was 'useless' and that was that… until that inter-town game against Tom Price that is. These 'friendlies' were anything but, because town pride was on the line and in Paraburdoo, town pride was everything. I had been practicing really hard and steadily getting better but I wasn't good enough to be in the starting team, especially because this game was open to under 12's as well as under 8's.

So I started on the bench, and I expected to remain there for the entire match, but fate would not have it. Twenty seconds into the game, two of the defenders from our team collided as they tried to head the ball. Mr Mac hadn't really covered headers, and it definitely showed because those guys had to be carted off to hospital for stitches. Anyway, it meant that we had to send on two reserves and we only had two, so I suddenly found myself as 'left back,' instead of left right out. Everyone's parents and teachers and brothers and sisters and dogs and cats and budgies were at the match. The Doo Beer Belly Club was even there. And as I ran on to the field, I swear you could hear a collective moan of despair.

Now I don't know if it was this, or the fact that I had just confronted Mum and told her that for the last 18 months, as soon as I left the house, I had been adjusting my shorts to a height deemed respectable by my peers. But whatever the reason, I was about to experience what *Reader's Digest* called 'a quantum leap.'

I had no sooner stepped onto the field, than I was in the thick of the action, and I do mean thick. We found out later that Tom Price had slipped a couple of under 18's into their team and I was marking one of them. Time after time, I would find myself face to belly-button with a bloke *twice* the size of me, who seemed totally intent on making me bleed with his three day growth.

The first time I looked up and saw him rushing at me, I packed my dacks like a kangaroo caught in a spotlight, and literally fell over right in front of him. As luck would have it, at the same moment he tried to kick the ball around me, which resulted in me blocking the ball and tripping him up, which to anyone watching would have appeared to be a pretty handy tackle. The sideline went mad, even the budgies were cheering, and didn't the celebratory slap of those colliding beer bellies make a huge crack. The next time he came barrelling at me I was about to fall over again, cos I knew this time he would be really angry. But just before I did, I realised that he was dribbling the ball a little too far in front of him, and as I'd just been reading about Bullfighters in Spain, I thought why not? With the poise of a matador, I stepped in front, stole the ball, and flicked him on the rump as the bull went flying past. I even held up an imaginary cape as I did it and yelled, "Tore! Tore!" Well, the sideline was wetting itself. Which was great, but it didn't help me with the little problem of having the ball at my feet. For a few terrifying moments I really didn't know what to do with it, but then I heard a familiar little voice… the voice of a fluffy white angel, "Run, Stephen run! No one can catch you. Not even a bunyip!" I looked up, and to my amazement there was Kimba, well, it wasn't actually Kimba, it was a ball of light shaped just like him. He took off up the left wing and yelped, "Follow me!" So I did.

Whenever a bloke from Tom Price tried to tackle me, I would just kick the ball past them, and then run around them. Kimba was going so fast that sometimes I left the ball behind trying to keep up, but I always managed to go back and get it. This kicking and running lasted the entire length of the pitch, until suddenly the ball of light was gone, and the soccer ball was in the back of the net. The guys on the sideline were pulling up their singlets and banging their bellies into each other again. I didn't even realise I'd had a shot. I was just kicking past and running around. I must have done that to the goalkeeper as well. The guy with the sandpaper beard said it was just a fluke, and I suppose he was right. Mind you, I fluked *three* more goals that day.

We ended up losing that game five goals to four. Everyone was disappointed, particularly the sideline. Strange thing was, as we squatted around the coach taking off our boots, people started talking to me. Not just a few people, *everyone* did. They were asking me all sorts of questions, about almost everything. And they stopped calling me 'useless' and started calling me Briggsy. It was all a bit too much to bear. Dad was thrilled to bits when we got home. He was dancing and skipping around the house saying, "Did yer see my lad? 'e's a champion! A champion! Four bloody goals and no one could get within coo-ee of 'im. And fast? 'e's like a bloody spitfire taking off on black ice."

It was around this time that Mum and Dad started to talk about boarding schools in Perth. Mum liked the sound of Aquinas, and Dad *Scotch* College because Scotch Finger biscuits were his favourite. They asked me what I wanted and I said I liked the sound of Paraburdoo District High.

"Son, we would love yer to stay in Paraburdoo and finish yer education but the school only goes up to year 10. And there are no opportunities here. Other than working in the mine," Mum said, as she gently dabbed mercurochrome onto the graze old beard face gave me, when the ball was up the other end.

"But the mine's good enough for Dad," I whimpered.

"Stevie it's very 'ard for yer to understand at yer age but we want yer to 'ave the things we never 'ad the chance of. We were dirt poor when we were kids." Dad argued.

"You grew up in the Great Depression," I added, "I've read all about it."

"Opportunities were nought when we were yer age. And we didn't 'ave yer brains neither. We want yer to 'ave the best possible chance," Dad explained, with a shiny film in his eyes, "But don't think we don't want yer round, because nothing',' and I mean nothin,' could be further from the truth." And that was that. One day when I was old enough to be in year eight, I'd be going to boarding school in Perth.

When I got to school on Monday, some of the older guys from the soccer team were hanging around near the front gate. "He's coming," I heard one of them say as I walked up towards them. I could tell they were up to something, so I swung my backpack around in front of me. I just hoped that they weren't going to do anything to me while Mum was still watching, as she had just dropped me off. She was taking me to the doctor after school on account of my wheezing. I was taking tiny steps and looking at the Torana out of the corner of my eye, but it wasn't moving, and the boys were getting closer. I really didn't want her to see me get picked on, cos she would spend the next week worrying. But it sure looked like she was going to, when all of a sudden, the boys split into two lines, joined their hands, and held them up in the air for me to walk under.

"Four goal Briggsy… Four goal Briggsy," they chanted. I couldn't believe that they were giving me a guard of honour and Mum's smile was brighter than the sun's reflection on the Torana's windscreen. When I sat down in my class, I felt strangely different. I didn't feel anxious but I certainly didn't feel relaxed either. It was like everyone being so nice to me freaked me out as much, if not more, than when everyone treated me with indifference. During question time that day, Jodie O'Grady asked my teacher how old you had to be to get married and then she asked if it was possible for a human to run faster than a racehorse goanna, cos she had seen me run at soccer and she was convinced I'd give the goanna a licking. For the rest of the morning, every time I looked up, Jodie was smiling at me and doing little bendy finger waves.

I realised, during gulps from the recess water fountain, that those four goals had set my life down a totally new, fast-flowing and unexplored creek. Without setting out to, I had accidentally taken a wrong turn and found myself half way to becoming popular; and I wasn't sure if I liked it. I suppose my teachers had always liked me because I only had to hear something twice to remember it. My parents had always liked me because I loved them, and never forgot to brush my teeth. But the other kids at school had never really thought that much of me, and although that made me pretty nervous, at least it was what I was used to. Mind you, that's not all together true, cos Jodie O'Grady certainly thought I was ok. But most importantly, I didn't know what I thought of myself. I guess I just felt like I… didn't belong in Paraburdoo. It was such a hostile place, and the kids were as unforgiving as the burning bright red dirt. I was ok when I could talk to adults, so long as they weren't thickos, and there were certainly quite a few of those, but kids didn't really interest me. If I had the choice, I would much rather hang around with my parent's friends and grill them to find out whatever it was they were passionate about. This of course didn't *always* net results, try as I might, I just couldn't share Charlie Crabbe's *lust* for model train sets, but generally speaking, about a third of the guests at any of my parent's gatherings, did have interesting hobbies and passions. And I used to love wandering around inside them.

It didn't take long to get used to people liking you though. Somehow, it made my deep uneasiness seem farther away. If everyone thought I was all right, then I must be. And after a couple of years of scoring goals, topping grade four, and being adored by Jodie, I was feeling the best I ever had, and even if I did have days when I felt insecure, so long as I didn't show anyone, no one would know. Of course I wasn't able to please everyone, but I had a bloody good go at it.

There was a boy in the grade four class called Trevor Barkla, he was the butcher's son, and everyone looked up to him. He wasn't smart, he wasn't really all that good at sport, but he had two things going for him. His brother Troy was the toughest kid in the school and Trevor was cool. He looked, acted and most of all walked, like The Fonz from *Happy Days* and don't ask me how anyone knew what *Happy Days* was, cos we didn't get Television until I was in grade six. But regardless, everyone treated him with absolute respect and when I was made to sit next to him, to help him with his English, a funny thing happened.

I was so keen to make him and his group of followers think I was all right, that his English improved and mine got worse. I actually started to make deliberate mistakes so I would think like he did, and word by word, *my* vocabulary started to be replaced by Trevor's. I applied less effort to my study and more to my walk. It wasn't so much that I was idolising Trevor; I just wanted to understand everything that made him tick. It did get pretty tricky though, especially trying to do the walk when you're dribbling a soccer ball. And it was really exhausting stuffing up tests to be cool and please him, while still trying to work out how many marks I could afford to drop and remain the top of the class, to please my teacher. In fact, I must have dropped a few too many, because half way through the year I was told I would be repeating year four again next year. I would still get advanced work but I would be with kids my own age.

Eventually, Trevor and his family moved to Tom Price and I was able to cut down on my use of 'The Fonz Strut' and halve my slang count, which made my neck a lot less painful and my Mum a lot happier. Mind you, he didn't move away until after the school sports carnival… and what a carnival that was. Talk about colours. They were all there; Red, Green, Gold and Blue. I was in Green and Mum had bought me a new Bonds t-shirt especially.

5 A GREEN T-SHIRT AND BROWN Y-FRONTS

When I woke up the morning of the sport's day, I was nervous, and I didn't feel too good because I'd slept really badly, worrying about the 50 metre sprint. I'd got myself so worked up the night before, that I'd snuck out my window and crept up to Kimba's grave. His shining halo was propped up against the root of the old gum tree, staring longingly up at the stars as usual. He was even wearing the blue paper-maché cap that I made him in art, with 'coach,' written on the front of it.

"It's only natural to be nervous," he said, "the trick is, to *use* your nerves to your advantage. Let them give you an explosive start."

"But what if I'm too sick to run?" I whimpered.

"Don't even think like that Stephen. You must run. You owe it to yourself and you owe it to me. What have we spent all that time and effort and training for? I haven't been leading you all over soccer pitches for nothing have I? It's all right for you, you've got big legs. Try reaching those speeds with legs the size of mine. Stephen I can't… rest… I won't rest until I know you are on the right track to making something of your life. You can do it. I know you can. Please Stephen, do it for me," he barked almost loud enough to wake up the house. He could be very persuasive when he wanted to and as I slipped back into bed, I tried to talk my nerves into working for me, instead of against me. I knew I would do ok in the 25 metre, but the 50 was as long as the town pool, and I wasn't sure I could make it to the tip of the diving board, let alone the end.

This was my first carnival, because we weren't allowed to compete when we were in grade one and two, and as I sat with all the other grade fours, I kept thinking that a teacher was about to come up and tell me that even though I had gone up a grade, I wasn't technically old enough to race, and would have to wait until next year. My stomach was having quite a rumble, when Mr Sereni the grade seven teacher (whose wife taught grade one and was nicknamed 'bazookas' because of her large boobies) tapped me on the shoulder.

"Stephen, I'm afraid we have a small problem with the running," he said, staring at his clipboard as a nervous spasm looped around my tummy.

"What's wrong sir?" I blurted, "I hope I can still run, cos I promised my dead... Uncle... on his death bed... dear old Uncle Kimba that I would run for him today and I have to." I felt quite bad telling a lie, but it was a white one, the same colour as Kimba, and I had promised I would run for him and I didn't want to let him down. Mr Sereni stared at me without saying anything. For a second, I thought he knew that I had called his wife 'bazookas' in my head, then luckily he spoke.

"Look Stephen, I've got you down for the 50 *and* the 25, and I think you'll only be able to run one. You see, Barkla and Bignell want to run as well. Now Bignell is our fastest runner, so he'll get to do both, and you and Barkla can do one each." I was devastated and spoke without thinking, "Please Mr Sereni, look, I'll do anything if you let me run. I promise... I promise I'll never say... 'bazookas' again. I won't even think it. I've just *got* to run for Kimba!"

He looked at me, as if suddenly I had something on him, "Ok Stephen, look, I can slip you into the year four 25 dash, and there's a space in the year six 50 metre dash. Ok? Now that's the end of it." He said, curtly, as he stamped off to his wife down near the finish line.

The grass felt particularly spiky that day, as I stood in the marshalling area behind the start of the year four 25 metre sprint. As I leant forward at the start, my head was buzzing, and I couldn't stop thinking about how scary 50 metres would be against grade sixes, even with Kimba's coaching, and how much I wanted to beat Darren Bignell, who was at the other end of the heat. My mind was so swollen with revenge plotting, that I didn't hear Mr Bolton clap his hands and I didn't know the race had started, until Mrs Sereni's bazookas bounced me along my way as she told me to, "Run, run for Green!" When I did snap out of it and look up, the rest of the field was half way to the finish and I was ready to give up. But without any conscious thought, my legs started spinning, so fast you could hardly see them, and I began running and reeling in the nearest of my rivals. My bare feet felt somehow liberated without the weight of soccer boots, and the yellow brown couch seemed determined for me to win, as it catapulted me along my way.

I swear I'm not exaggerating, when I say that Darren Bignell's hair was blown forward as I rocketed past him. Then just as independently as they had started, my feet slowed and a sea of Green converged around me. I had beaten my nearest rival by about 15 metres and my team was ecstatic! Well, as ecstatic as a group of Paraburdoo kids standing in full sun, with bare feet, on patchy grass reaching about 39 degrees Celsius can get.

It would have been very easy to spend the rest of the carnival coasting around on the emotional high of that win; that *was* if I didn't have to run in the grade six 50. By the time I was leaning into the starter's hands, my guts were scrunched up like a Twisties packet that'd been shrunk under a grill, and it took all my strength not to throw up. But this time I heard the starter's clap, and I, and more importantly Kimba, would not be denied. Even though most of the other guys in the race had already *started* their arc into puberty and were consequently longer and stronger than I was, they didn't have my invisible leg spin. At 10 metres I was 8 metres in front, and at 20 I was 15, and that's about where my lead stayed until near the end, when my legs decided to really open up and send the Green shirts into a whiz, not unlike the spin cycle of Mum's Simpson Top Loader. If I was really worried about being popular, then I had blown it big time, cos every one was talking about 'Speedy Stephen Gonzales.' Trevor Barkla's followers had abandoned 'The Fonz Strut,' and were wandering around behind me trying to copy my invisible leg spin.

As I gloriously gulped gallons of water from the Green team esky, I momentarily pushed my anxiousness aside and stood squarely in the moment. And what a moment it was: I had run, I had won and in doing so I had repaid all the hope, time, and effort, that Kimba had instilled in me. Seeing as there were another couple of hours of high school races to go before the end of the carnival, I thought I would sneak off and do some celebrating with the coach.

Mr Sereni's finger, tapping on my shoulder, made me turn around faster than the physics of my newfound confidence bubble would allow. Consequently causing it to burst. "Stephen," he said with a look that suggested both new respect and an imminent favour, "How would you feel... about running another race?" I looked up at him, with water still seeping into the space between my teeth and tongue, "I'm pretty tired sir."

"And I can certainly understand why," he pandered, "The thing is, we're short a runner and no one has been able to get anywhere near you all day. The team needs you Stephen, *Green*, needs you," he said stirringly, "You're not going to let us down are you?" This Green thing seemed to be quite contagious. After a couple of seconds deliberating, I put the esky down, looked Mr Sereni in the eye, imagined what he would look like with his wife's Bazookas and nodded my head, "I'll do it."

"Good boy," he said, as he marched off to register my name at the marshalling stand.

"But sir, which race is it?" I yelled after him.

"The Open 200 metres!" he sang back.

My old friend anxiety, a little pissed off at being banished earlier, returned with so much venom that I had the first heart palpitation of my life, there and then. My mind felt like it was being blasted by sand, as a Pilbara dust storm enveloped it. My legs became invisible again, but this time they weren't spinning; I was, and I fell like a kangaroo that had come just face to nuzzle with a 303 rifle. All I was aware of was the ground encrusted with jagged quartz rushing at my face, and just as I was about to hit it, Kimba caught me, laid me down gently, and nuzzled at my ear.

"You can do it," he said, "Good luck… with everything Stephen." And then he was gone, and replaced by hundreds of peering faces.

"Is he all right?," one said.

"He's still breathing," said another.

"I'm fine," I retorted, climbing to my feet, "I just tripped over, that's all."

"Oh, you dear dear boy," said Mrs Sereni, as she plunged my face into the valley of her chest. She took me over to the tin shed where I had been shown my first stick magazine, and for a while it looked like this was turning into one of the dirty stories you get inside them. I don't know how many times she pressed me into her cleavage and bounced my head from boob to boob. After I assured her I had only stumbled and I was all right, she told me to rest here until the 200 metres. That's right, the *200* metres! What with the dust storm and refresher breast feeding course in the jumping castle, I had completely forgotten about it. Oh my God! I was running in the open, that meant year 10's, 15 year olds! Didn't anyone realise that I was only eight?

As the dry desert wind poked about the shorts and shirts of the competitors over in the flag race, my stomach started making strange loud noises. I was glad I was out of the sun, and appreciated what relief the tin shed could provide. I felt like I needed to do a two but whenever I sat on the loo, the only thing that would come out was a noise that sounded like those fireworks that keep low to the ground, go off in numbers, and kinda go zum zum. I must have tried to go about 16 times. I was actually in there, when Mr Sereni came to get me for the 200.

"Are you all right in there champ?" he inquired, tapping lightly on the door. Champ? I thought that tag was reserved for Darren beaten-by-15-metres Bignell.

"I won't be a minute sir," I heaved, as I tried one last time to exorcise the demon in my bowel, but to no avail, the only thing I succeeded in forcing was another battery of fireworks noises, and a little blood to Mr Sereni's blushing face.

As Paraburdoo District High School was a civilised place, the girls ran before the boys, which meant I had time to size up the opposition and see how far 200 metres really was. And it was a long, long, way, not only was it four swimming pools, half of it was round a corner. I looked down at my feet and wondered if they would start spinning again, when I chanced upon the most delicious, sweet smelling, scent. Surely God himself, had harvested the tears of angels, infused them with bush honey and called it *IMPULSE* Wild Gypsy Rose.

The rapturous vapours were still tickling the passages in my nose, when I looked up and saw the most gorgeous girl I had ever seen in my life. She had yellow hair, tanned skin, white baby teeth and a sparkle that could start a bush fire. Her name, was Veronica Chrystal. She was wearing a little blue skirt and a gold t-shirt that stretched across the emerging bumps on her chest. 'Oh why couldn't she be in Green?' I thought. I went to speak but my stomach got in first.

"You got a real noisy stomach don't ya?" she commented, with the breath of an angel, well, actually it smelt a little bit like peanut butter sandwiches and brown bread, but peanut butter was my favourite.

"Yeah… I'm a bit nervous," I said, shocked that I could speak so easily.

"Don't be silly, I saw both your races today. You're faster than all of these guys," she said, as she walked over to the starting line.

"What grade are you in?" I gushed, desperate to know if I had a chance.

"Year eight," she replied, just before the starter clapped his hands. And she was off. If I'm honest, her style wasn't all that pretty, and at half way I didn't think she could

55

win. But then all the other girls started to get tired and slow down, but she kept going, at exactly the same pace she had started at, and by the end's blanket finish, she just managed to get her gold shirt across first and win by the narrowest of protruding bumps.

My mind was on a seesaw. I was so happy for her. And so sad for me. Year eight! She wouldn't be interested in me, but she'd seen all my races and she'd see this one. I *had* to win, and as I got into my starting lean, I was half convinced that I could. Until I noticed Troy Barkla, Trevor's brother, lined up next to me. He was the fastest kid in the whole school and the toughest. Even if I could beat him, I wouldn't want to, cos he'd probably beat me up for doing it. But I couldn't help myself, that sweet smell was still racing around my body and I had to try if I was going to have any chance with Veronica.

The starter told us to get on our marks and just as he went to clap, my stomach spasmed, and I let out an enormous fart that sounded like a camel that had just been branded. It came out with so much force that the other competitors looked around to see if there was anything behind them and it took all my strength to stop myself from being rocketed forward, into a false start. The starter told us to stand up. Then on your marks, and then, clap.

The start was pretty even but within three strides, the orchestra in my shorts started up again, and every step I took was accompanied by a huge, slushy cacophony of gas. I wondered if I did win, would I be disqualified for jet propulsion? As I rounded the bend, my rectal trumpet heralded my imminent arrival. My legs didn't seem too bothered though, as they started to spin faster and I moved up on Troy Barkla. At half way I could hardly believe it; I was level with him and my biggest problem was containing wind, not running like it. Troy glanced over, with a 'don't even think about it' look on his face, as he started to pull away a little. I was so tempted to just sit in there and pick up a second, but something about his look typified my feelings about Paraburdoo, its brutal inhabitants and the bucketing I used to get before people discovered I could play sport and I became half popular. And I thought, 'you can stick it up your bum Troy Barkla! I'm going to beat you,' and with that, I really tried to open up and mow him down, but something was wrong, something was blocking me. I tensed up really hard and moved a little closer but I knew I could go faster, so I squeezed every muscle I had, harder than the designer had *ever* anticipated. What resulted, was simultaneously the most triumphant and embarrassing moment of my life. My enormous muscular contraction did see me almost double my speed, surge forward, win by metres and collect the title of fastest runner in the entire school at the tender age of eight. But it also saw my underpants undertake a role that they were never really intended for… shit catching.

As I crossed the line, I must have looked like a lawn mower with a filled to over-flowing catcher on the back. Needless to say, my 200 metres turned into 340 metres, as I wasn't going to stop until I was safely locked behind the cubicle door in the tin shed. The only issue being the door didn't actually lock, so I had to lean against it as I frantically tried to come up with a solution. I must have been so absorbed in plotting the disposal of the shit catcher, that I didn't realise I was leaning too hard on the door, subsequently losing my balance and falling head first into Mr Sereni's knee length socks.

"You little bloody ripper Briggsy!" he bellowed, as he picked me up and hoisted me over his shoulder.

I thought this was pretty weird cos he should have seen the stain on my shorts, and then suddenly I realised why he hadn't. Ever since I could remember, well as far back as kindy, my friends had always worn flimsy, French style jockette underpants, whereas I, had always worn big white English y-fronts. Dad had often joked that they were bullet-proof and it looked like he was right. I knew every second was precious. "Actually Mr Sereni I'm feeling a bit sick. I think you'd better put me down," I said feigning dizziness.

"That's no good champ! What's wrong?" he asked. Once back on the ground I made a bee-line for the cubicle, "I'm going to throw up. Do you think you could mind the door please sir?"

"Of course Stephen. Are you sure you're all right? Do you need any help?" said a concerned Mr Sereni, as he held the door shut.

"No. I'll be fine. It's just all the excitement and too many sweets," I claimed, as I removed my shorts and checked them for stainage. Those jockey y-fronts were incredible, the shorts didn't have a mark on them. They didn't smell too crisp, but they had survived the rigours of a slippery sprint without so much as a dot. I wish the same could be said for the inside of the jockeys. It would have probably been a good idea to start dry retching at that point, to make it more convincing for Mr Sereni. But I didn't have to pretend, because as I pulled the elastic aside and peered down to assess the damage, my insides wrenched like a hose that'd just been turned on full bore and wasn't attached to a sprinkler.

Somehow, possibly via the now very faint smell of Veronica Chrystal and my desire to be crowned king of the 200 next to her queen, I managed to fight through my throttling convulsions and delicately remove the offending y-fronts, without spilling any of their cargo and after some gentle manoeuvring toward the bowl, I let out a huge vomiting noise, to cover the sound of the diarrhoea tumbling into the water. Then, all I had to do was take the jockey's clean outer side, wipe the remaining sludge from my legs and bottom, and flush everything down the s-bend. Which I did. Well at least most of it. I didn't know the y-fronts would block everything up.

As I stood on the box and took in the cheers of the crowd, the warm wind swirled through my shorts and blew away any remaining odour. A guy from soccer called Kevin Warren came third, so he got his medal first, then Troy Barkla got his, and finally, I was presented with mine. I've got to say, it felt pretty good up there, and it must have showed because five minutes later they asked me up there again, to get the Junior boy trophy and this time I wasn't alone. This time, I had to stand next to Veronica Chrystal, in fact the junior, intermediate and senior boy and girl champion all had to stand on the three boxes at once. I was supposed to stand next to the junior girl winner, but just as the local paper's photographer went to click her button, I jumped up next to Veronica and she held me against her so I wouldn't fall off.

Funny thing happened up on those boxes. As the photographer changed film, we all clung onto each other and the loose pyramid we were forming. But the senior girl sneezed and the senior boy, who incidentally was Troy Barkla, got such a fright that he fell off the podium and took the rest of us with him. And that's when the strange thing happened. I was closest to the ground so I fell first, then Veronica fell right on top of me and then the senior girl fell on top of her. It could have just been because I wasn't wearing underpants but for some reason Veronica lying on top of me made me feel funny, it made me *throb*, somewhere I'd never throbbed before and although it was scary, it was also kinda fun.

I could have laid there inhaling her sweet smell and feeling her protruding bumps on my chest for hours, and I probably would have, if the photographer hadn't managed to reload the camera and ask us to get back on the boxes. Which we did and then Veronica and I, standing so close it was almost rude, were immortalised on the front page of *The Paraburdoo Times*. And just when it seemed our fairytale reign as king and queen of the 200 would never end, a black Monaro, with tinted windows and GTS stripe, locked up its brakes and skidded to a halt in front of us. An old man, who I thought must be Veronica's Dad, stepped out. He had a three day growth as black as his muscle shirt and matching footy shorts and he said nothing, he just pointed at the passenger seat. Veronica hopped into the car, and every body had to duck for cover as the Monaro sprayed dust and gravel everywhere. In my haste to be next to Veronica I had almost forgotten what I had just accomplished, and after a few minutes staring at the Monaro's impression of a vanishing black dot, I grabbed my bike and burned home to tell Kimba what I had done and celebrate with him.

The back yard was strangely quiet as I made my way up to the ghost gum, a swag of medallions clinking in my hand. I had expected the usual flock of deafening sulfur crested cockatoos, getting high off the Eucalyptus leaves, but for the first time in months they were somewhere else. 'Maybe Charlie Crabbe's been shooting at them with his air rifle again,' I thought. At first, when I sat down and shouted that we did it and Kimba had been voted the greatest coach in the history of the sports carnival, well by me at least, I thought he was just too overcome with emotion to speak. I kept expecting his shimmering face to come scampering around the base of the trunk. But the longer I sat there in silence, the more I thought about what he had said on the oval, and the larger the waterfall down my cheeks became. Kimba wasn't coming out because Kimba wasn't there. He had moved on to somewhere better. When he said, 'Good luck with everything,' he was saying his last goodbye. The more I thought about it, the more I wept, and eventually I found myself hugging the gum tree and wailing at the sun. I was crying because I was happy for him. I was crying because I was so lost without him. And I was crying because I knew I would never know anyone like him again. He was gone, and I had never ever felt so alone.

A few days later, after a lot of detective work and smashing my piggy bank, I was consumed by two things. The first was a broken heart, after discovering that the

61

man in black was actually Veronica's boyfriend and professional roo shooter Clinton Lewis. Which meant he not *only* had a Monaro, he also had a gun. How could I possibly compete? And the second thing, which almost sent me broke, was a wall full of front page photos of me and my sweet, sweet, athletics queen.

It took me a real long time to come to terms with not being able to have Veronica. I suppose up until that time, I had mostly had whatever I wanted, and it was hard. Especially when Mum and Dad asked me what was wrong and whatever it was it couldn't be that bad and if it was, they would do everything they could to fix it. But that was just it, they couldn't do anything and I couldn't do anything. It was hopeless. After many hours lying under my bed, counting the springs and securing each one of them to a single twist-pile of carpet with a laser that came out of my finger, I realised that I was too young to be day-dreaming my life away. And besides, shooting Roos would be a very smelly business, and sooner or later Veronica would tire of that stink and the countless hours Clinton would be spending with his tailed girlfriends, and she'd realise she'd be better off with me. And I didn't care if I had to wait until the next solar eclipse for her, because I would, and one day, we would tell our children how fresh smelling 'Speedy Gonzales Briggsy,' triumphed over a pongy black car, muscle shirt, and three day growth.

These defiant kind of notions were, I suppose, pretty crucial in getting me over my first brush with unrequited love — but I guess the real saviour was soccer and a friendship I made through it. I had absolutely no idea that the set of boxes at the sports carnival would have such a lasting effect on my life. You see, the guy who came third in the 200, Kevin Warren a kid from grade 5, ended up becoming my best friend in Paraburdoo. It's amazing how you can spend seasons of soccer playing in the same team with someone and not know them at all. Then one day, they play a scratch match in the position next to you and you discover you really get along.

Our friendship started early in the first half. Our team was defending, I had about four players trying to take the ball off me and things were looking pretty grim, when all of a sudden, Kevin appeared. I passed it to him, he passed it back in a one two fashion, and we were away. I'd never realised just how good a soccer player he was, we combined together heaps that day.

After the game, we discovered we both lived near each other and both had the same type of Drag-Star, although his back tyre was a lot more nobbly than mine. We rode home together, skidding and talking soccer all the way and then, just as we were about to split down our respective paths for the small remainder of our journeys, Kevin went to do a controlled power slide that went awfully wrong and he ended up stacking it in a ditch. When I climbed down after him, I saw he looked pretty bad.

"Are you ok? Shit! Look at your arm. That's one hell of a graze!" I said, feeling a little giddy at the sight of blood, and there was a fair bit of it too. Kevin didn't seem too worried by it though. He wasn't a fat kid, but he was a lot more solid than me, and he didn't seem to care about blood at all. That was, until he held up his arm and actually had a good look at it, then he burst into tears.

"Oh no, my Mum's gonna kill me!" he shrieked.

"For grazing your arm?" I questioned.

"No, for ripping my new scoops!" he pointed down at the gaping hole in his shorts, I hadn't noticed them before but they were real beauties, with a fake money pocket *and* a sports stripe.

It would have been pretty risky for me to admit it, especially in the Doo, but I liked the fact that Kevin had been able to cry in front of me and tell me that he was scared about his Mum. It showed me that not only were we brothers in soccer boots, we were also brothers in sensitivity, and sensitivity was as rare as y-fronts in that neck of the woods. As Kevin rubbed dettol on his wound, I decided to tell him about the most fragrant flower north of the tropic of Capricorn; Veronica Chrystal. It was a huge step forward in the foundation of our friendship. I could be ruined if he were to tell anyone else how I felt. But I had to tell someone. Weird thing was, when I went to explain my feelings, my precious friends and favourite pastime, words deserted me. I just kept going over and over about how beautiful she was, and how great she smelt, and how she was all that I could think of.

Anyway, when I got to the end of my lovesick rant and finally drew breath, I became aware that Kevin had wandered off. If I'd had enough conviction to actually look him in the eyes while I'd been speaking, maybe he wouldn't have gone walkabout. But nonetheless, I hadn't and Kevin wasn't anywhere to be seen.

"Oh no! He's probably been on the phone, spreading my stupid crush around town. All those years of wearing my shorts around my knees, ruined, in one sentimental, gushing, torrent. Funny how the words come back to me now," I moaned to myself, as a beaming Kevin came out of his room. 'He'll have his pick of the seats at the next drive-in,' I thought. Everyone wanting to hear first hand, about useless's love for Veronica Chrystal.

As he sat down next to me, I noticed he was carrying a large folder crammed with clippings. "I know what it's like… to want something you can't have," he said, as he opened the folder and took out a photo, "Come, feast your eyes my friend. Ain't she a beauty?" he said, with a slight quaver in his voice. I thought he was taking the piss and really rubbing it in but as a little tear formed in the corner of his eye, I was relieved and amazed, to see that he was sincere.

"It's a… car Kevin?" I said slowly.

"It's not just a car. It's a Camaro!" he uttered indignantly. I could sense, that just as I had gone out on a limb telling him about Veronica, he was going out just as far by declaring his lust for this strange-looking motor car, and not wanting to disrespect him confiding in me, I jumped in up to my shorts.

"Oh, a Camaro! Gee I've heard all about those but I never thought I'd see one." I gushed.

"Well enjoy the perve, Steve mate, enjoy the perve," he insisted, as he ceremoniously placed the photo in my hands. I just stared at it, ummed and ahhed and hoped that would be enough.

"So, what have you heard about them?" asked Kevin innocently.

Oh my God, what was I going to say? I didn't know the first thing about cars. I decided to hand this one over to my brain and let it say the first… "Sponges!" I barked.

"What?" said Kevin, incredulously. Oh my God! Was that the *best* it could do? Five years soaking in *Readers Digest* and it comes up with sponges?

"Sea... sponges," I replied, in a slow, deliberate manner, convinced, that if I *sold* it right, I wouldn't have to go any further, but the look on his face suggested I would, "Just... think about it... You know the Camaro. You know sea sponges. Enough said."

With that, I got up to leave but Kevin insisted that I stay and have a game on his new Atari, and what a game it was! I had never seen anything like it. You could actually play tennis on a TV screen! It was so realistic, *you* had a small line that went down one side of the screen and your *opponent* had a line on the other side and you whacked a white blob back and forth to each other. It was incredible, and we played it for ages, until Mrs Warren told me it was probably time for me to go home for tea. Kevin said, "just one more game." I don't know if he was letting me win, or if he was just preoccupied — anyway, when I did go to leave, I noticed a real sadness in his eyes and I felt responsible.

My lie had made Kevin feel like he didn't know everything there was to know about Camaros. Imagine how I would feel, if he knew something about Veronica and he wouldn't tell me. I had to let him in on it. The only problem was, I didn't have a clue what *it* was.

"I've had a great time Kevin. Thanks for the game of Atari tennis, so realistic," I said genuinely, "Look, about the sea sponges. I'm sure you already know this but I'll tell you anyway. It's... all about... the inside?"

"The interior?" he questioned.

"Yeah! The interior," I repeated, pulling an interior kind of face. "Well, the designer of the Camaro's interior… loved sea sponges. In fact, he was mad about sponges. A certified sponge nut. Apparently, he had even tried to join Jacques Cousteau's ship once but they turned him down for… *mental* reasons. Anyway, he asked his boss if he could make the interior look like it was covered in them," I said matter of factly.

"What, all lumpy?" he asked.

"Yeah exactly. All lumpy. Well no one would want that would they? So his boss said 'No.' And the designer was gutted. It was like Cousteau, all over again. Anyway, he was so in love with sea sponges that he did it anyway. He made all the seats and dashboard and ceiling out of sponge, but he put special stuff on them so they wouldn't rot. And then, later that month, when they unveiled the Camaro for the first time at a motor show, the big big boss… and all the newspapers… and stuff… were shocked to find, the car's interior was made up of about 600 sea sponges," I gasped, carried away by the momentum of my own tale.

"So what happened then?" Kevin said, with eyes as wide as tyres.

"Well, they had to take it back and put a normal interior inside it and launch it again a few weeks later. And of course, the designer got demoted to the ash tray installer, but he still got his own back because whenever he could, you know when he was working late and there was no one else around, he would sneak a Sponge into work, dip it into green paint and then he would put a Sea Sponge print over the entire cream interior. And it used to look beautiful. Anyway, one night his boss caught him as he was just putting the finishing touches on one of his masterpieces and he got such a fright that he had a heart attack and died there and then, with the dripping sponge in his hand. There's only 17 Camaros with that special interior in the world and they cost double what the normal ones do." As I rode off on my bike, I was totally exhausted and entirely bamboozled, by the length and breadth of my little white lie.

Over the following months, Kevin and I became inseparable, riding, talking and skidding about the place. The only time we weren't together was when we were asleep and when we were in class.

And, as Dad loaded up the car for the 1500 km trip down to boarding school, no one was waving harder than my best mate Kevin. Of course, there were other people there. Actually there were lots of them. Mum, flanked by Mrs Crabbe and Mrs Spencer, was bawling her eyes out. Mr Mac and the whole soccer club were shoulder to shoulder with shorts around their knees, down the driveway and a selection of Mum and Dad's friends (most of whom harboured secret passions and hobbies that I had conducted forensic tests on, at one time or another) were milling around the car.

When Dad finally put the three on the tree into reverse, we edged past the congregation and I saw the emotion scrunched all over their collected faces, it's true to say, without any exaggeration that I was leaving the Doo as one of its heroes.

Despite my anxious beginning in this hostile punishing place, somehow I had managed to conquer my inner fears and triumph. I guess I'd probably put it down to toe punts and *Reader's Digest*. Anyway, as Dad opened up the throttle and the footpath started to blur, I shuffled backwards into the vinyl seat until everything but my neck and shoulders sat snugly in the hole worn by Mum's bottom. I felt like a snail with its house on its back and as I imagined my antennae unravelling toward the windscreen, I was actually optimistic about what the future held.

6 ONE KILOMETRE AT A TIME

My Dad sure could fart. Real stinkers, so loud that they drowned out the noise of the engine, and considering we were on a dirt road, that sure was something. It was on the journey down to Perth Grammar School, (which incidentally ended up being the school that I was enrolled in because all the others were full) that I had my first out of body experience.

This was something that over time, would become a regular fixture in my life. It could have been the heat, the emotional strain of being separated from my Mum and friends, the potency of my Dad's wind, or maybe it was just the right time for it to happen. Whatever the reason, it was like I spent a large section of the car trip lying in a hammock in front of the windscreen, watching my Dad and I talk, laugh, reminisce and stare.

The first 276 kilometres of our journey was on gravel. Dad reckoned it must have just been graded because the road was the smoothest he'd ever seen it. Mind you, that doesn't mean it wasn't bumpy, cos it was as bumpy as hell. It just means there weren't too many potholes. Which was great, cos potholes are the things that you can't see until you've driven over them and they've snapped your axle. We'd been driving for about an hour when I realised that in all the commotion of leaving, I hadn't had a chance to pay my respects at Kimba's grave. I begged Dad to take me back, but he said we didn't have time cos we had to make Carnarvon by nightfall, as we had a reservation at the Flag motel there.

From my vantage point in the hammock, I could see that Dad was agitated, in a way I'd never seen before. I think he really did want to turn back and let me pay my respects at the foot of the gum tree and maybe put off boarding school for a few more years. But his body was stiff like a robot and wouldn't let him turn the car around. Instead, it drove the car faster through the gravel and farther and farther away from the Doo.

When I was younger, I must have travelled that road a hundred times on our way to holidays or soccer championships. Every time I travelled it, it was a different shade of yellow or purple, but this time it was green. The rains hadn't made it to Paraburdoo, but they had sure made it here. There was life wherever you looked, and it made me feel like the landscape was happy that I was going off to Perth, and escaping the Doo. I think the excitement of leaving, combined with a sleepless night and the soothing green plateaus sent me off into a very bumpy sleep.

The road was dirt and gravel all the way to The Nannutarra Roadhouse and for some reason, it always made me sleepy. As I *was* asleep, I didn't see the hill we were climbing, I didn't know the road was snaking around it and I had no idea that Dad was looking directly into the sun, just as the road took a sharp bend. I think when I woke up, the Torana must have already left the road and become airborne. I thought I was still asleep and tried to nuzzle against Dad's arm as he braced it against my chest. The landing in the creek bed certainly woke me up though, especially as my neck whiplashed forward, sending my face into Dad's arm, and my front teeth into my lip. I went to scream but no words came out; in fact, the only sound you could hear was the gentle idling of the Torana's engine. Dad grabbed me by the shoulder.

"Are yer ok son? Stevie! Are yer all right?" I thought for a moment, as if internally checking each of my vital systems. I was just about to issue the all clear, when I tasted the unmistakable nothingness of blood and looked down to see a torrent of red, doing its impression of a lava flow on the front of my Paraburdoo Junior Soccer Club t-shirt.

"I'm bleeding Dad!" I screeched.

"It's only yer lip Stephen. Is there anythin' else wrong?" Dad inquired, in a very serious tone.

"No, just my lip. It hurts," I cried, as I looked out of the window for the first time. We were enveloped in a huge cloud of dust, which is extremely rare, only found in really big creeks and is softer and finer than icing sugar.

"Look Dad — bull dust," I said, pointing at the fast settling mist.

"Yeah, I think that's what people will say lad, when we tell 'em what just 'appened," said Dad as he looked up and retraced our path, "It looks like we must 'ave come off road… all the way up there, flown right over those gum trees and landed 'ere in creek bed. Jesus Aitch Christ… we're lucky to be alive."

"What about you Dad? Are you all right?" I asked.

"I'm fine son, bit of a cut from where yer bit me, after yer bit yer lip, but that's 'bout all," he assured.

As he watched the remainder of the dust vanish, I took a peek at the cut in his arm; my teeth had left a perfect impression.

"I guess that means we must be blood brothers?" I smiled, knowing how much Dad liked cowboy and Indian films.

"Yeah, I guess we must be. But I thought Pale Face were supposed to speak with fork tongue not bloody sharp teeth," said Dad as he got out of the car and checked it for trouble.

Remarkably, the only damage was underneath. A piece of dead wood from one of the gum trees had pierced the petrol tank and luckily broken off in the hole. Dad pulled it out and quickly plugged up the leak with chewing gum. He sure was clever, and he must have done a real good job because we did another 200 kilometres of bumpy dirt and it didn't shake loose or anything. Mind you, that piece of gum was about the only thing that didn't. The road was so corrugated that every few minutes the clasp on Dad's Seiko would fly open, and the rear vision mirror would shake violently as it tried to stay stiff, but sooner or later it would fall limp and Dad would have to stop and tighten it up with a screw driver again. He was a regular James Bond, fixing this and tinkering with that. But all the improvising in the world couldn't do anything about the bloody road. Dad and I were totally shaken and very stirred. My kidneys were like those balls on strings, that Jimmy Walker spent hours clacking together in the playground. Dad didn't mention it because he wouldn't want to alarm me, but secretly I knew he was longing for the beautiful blue bump-free bitumen, just as much as me.

By the time we reached The Nannutarra Roadhouse with it's sign saying 'population 20, 2 humans and 18 emus', I was starting to get a little homesick. I tried to get out of my seat and follow Dad's exaggerated demonstration of leg stretching but my skin had become one with the vinyl and it took quite a bit of kicking before the seat would give me an inch of my flesh.

Sunday afternoons, were normally spent watching *Countdown* and eating leftovers like Shepherd's pie. I used to get a bit sick of the pie but I never got sick of *Countdown* and Molly Meldrum. He was great, and I loved all the music, you know like KISS and Racy. I used to spend half the show dancing around the lounge room and pretending the settee was a huge piano. A kid in my class called Richard Pike was the biggest KISS fan in town, until one night when he was lying in bed, a poster of Gene Simmons started rolling its eyes and poking out its huge tongue at him. Dad said it had something to do with a kind of herb Mrs Pike liked to cook with. Anyway, the next morning Richard's father took his entire KISS collection, which included records, posters, tapes and dolls to the dump and burnt it while yelling at the top of his voice, "Knights in Satan's Service be gone from my three bedroom house." Then he spent the whole day, driving around town in reverse and bellowing, "My pergola was tailor-made by Jesus Christ," into a megaphone. I organised a dump salvage mission with Kevin, but by the time we got there the fire had really got hold, and all I could grab was half a tube of fake blood from an official make-up set.

Countdown kept Paraburdoo in touch with the outside world, and it started all sorts of fads, like The Knack and The Village People. Gee, The Village People were huge and that YMCA group formation dance was really big. All the women in town had the hots for the Indian Chief, and for a while there were two or three single blokes dressed up as him, wandering around on weekends.

I'll never forget the time Molly interviewed Prince Charles. Shit it was funny. Molly actually wore a tie, sat up straight, and spoke all posh. He did a really good job of talking to him though and finding out if he had a favourite group. Some of my Mum's friends said that I would come back from boarding school talking all posh like that. But I told them to *pull* the other one, cos I was 'Doo' born and bred, which wasn't entirely true, seeing as I was born in England but they weren't to know that.

When I did manage to get out of the car and join Dad at the petrol bowser, I found a solitary tear trickling down his big ruddy cheek. At first, I thought he must have pulled a muscle from his elaborate stretching. Honestly, you would have thought he was training for the Olympics, but as I got closer, I realised his pain wasn't muscular.

"What's wrong Dad? Are you crying?" I said quietly.

"Oh, don't worry yerself son. Yer Dad's just gettin,' a bit sentimental and daft. Must 'ave got some dust in me eye… It's just, I were thinkin' on me way back, I'd be by meself… Silly bugger aren't I?" he said, as he dabbed an oily piece of rag below the bridge of his nose.

Nannutarra was actually quite a famous roadhouse, and not just because of its hilarious sign, in fact that was only half its allure; the other sat piled high and steaming in front of me. Baked beans on toast. It's hard to say what, exactly, was so wonderful about Nannutarra beans in particular. It could have been the colour, the smell, or the fact that once you order the beans you get an endless supply of toast. I even read on the wall in the toilet that the beans taste so good because the tins are put in emu's nests for three months and incubated like eggs. Whatever the reason, they were the pot of gold at the end of any trip on the dirt, and by the time Dad came back from ringing Mum, I was about to start on my second delivery of toast.

"Did you get through?" I asked, trying to disguise a mouthful.

"I just let 'er know we made it on to bitumen safely," he said, with eyes smiling at my plate. I gestured toward the kitchen, "Yours are coming, I told them to hold off until you sat down. Did you tell Mum about the bull dust?"

"No, I didn't want to upset 'er. Yer know 'ow she gets." The waitress staggered up under the weight of the biggest plate of beans I had ever seen in my life. No sooner had it touched down on the table than Dad was shovelling it in. We must have sat there for about 20 minutes without saying a word; both content to glow in each other's gorging.

Eventually, after we had forced down as much as we possibly could, and Dad had lit up his customary fag, I felt like it was time to ask some questions. The ones that had been niggling at me for quite some time, well ever since that hair appeared under my armpit.

The road stretched out in front of us like a long grey line, and Dad appeared to be totally fascinated by it, as he changed hands on the wheel and prepared to answer. Finally, after a number of empty sighs, he spoke, "Well… yes… I suppose, sometimes when I were a boy, I would wake up in middle of night with a throbbin' tail. I mean *dick*. But I would 'ave probably been dreamin' 'bout Lana Turner instead of Raquel Welch. I don't quite remember what age I were, when I entered into puberty. I suppose I were 'bout 15."

"Does that mean I'm abnormal for getting arm pit hair when I'm 12? I hope not, cos I don't want to be abnormal," I remarked. "I want to be really normal when I get to boarding school, especially as I won't know anyone." Dad looked at me and shook his head, "Don't worry lad, yer very normal. Me brother, got 'air in 'is pit, when 'e were nine and there were nought strange about 'im. But you will 'ave to be, prepared for some changes. 'Air's only the beginning, yer voice'll probably go down a bit after its jumped all over the place, yer'll start to get whiskers, and, yer'll probably get a face full of spots, before yer done."

I leant over and inspected Dad's cheek, "Is that what happened to you Dad? Did you get a face full of spots?"

"No son, I were one of the lucky ones. I were spot free. I did 'ave, a voice like a kazoo though. Real embarrassing it was."

"Well, that's ok then. If *you* didn't get spots then I'm not going to either. Cos I read somewhere that they're hereditary. And we don't have them in our genes do we?" I clucked proudly.

For some strange reason, when Dad tried to answer, the only sound that came out was a kind of wheeze, and as he turned towards me, I saw despair oozing out of every pore of his body. With tears the size of hailstones teetering on the lids of his eyes, he pulled the car over to the side of the road and began to cry. Not the occasional-silent-tear type of crying that I had seen him do twice before. This was genuine broken-breath sobbing.

"Actually, son, if I'm completely 'onest, I'm not altogether sure," he said, as a thunder storm danced behind his eyes, "Yer Mum and I, love yer, more than life itself… And yer've got to understand… That, is why we 'ave waited this long to tell yer. We 'ad to wait, till we felt yer were old enough, to understand… Stephen yer *our* son, in every conceivable way… but one. Yer not our… flesh and bl… What I mean to say, is yer *our* son but yer not our… biological son. We couldn't 'ave kids yer see and for some reason 12 years ago, a woman gave birth to a child she couldn't keep… And we… We 'ad the incredibly good fortune to adopt yer."

7 SIGNING ONTO THEODORE SHRAPNEL'S SHIP

There was a lot of silence on the remainder of that trip. The only thing you could hear was the bitumen yielding to the Torana's tyres, and the occasional gum tree that was too close to the road slapping its leaves together as we flashed past. Dad had been ever so apologetic for not telling me I was adopted earlier, in fact he was in a real state. If he wasn't cracking jokes, left, right and centre he was staring at the road like an Egyptian mummy. In the end, I had to tell him it was right to tell me. He had done a *very* brave thing and because of this, I had found even more love for him in my already swollen chest. That

seemed to calm him down a bit, and he said if I ever wanted to find my natural mother, he and Mum would do
everything they could to help me. But after a good night's
sleep and contemplation at the Flag motel in Carnarvon,
I assured him that I had no desire to look for her. "If she
didn't want me, she doesn't deserve me," I had announced
over our slap-up continental breakfast.

If I'm honest, I suppose I really only said that to make
Dad feel better. It was going to be a lonely enough drive
back to the Doo as it was. I didn't want to make it any
more torturous. And besides, I really loved my parents.
They were wonderful. 'Why would I want another set?'
I argued to myself, as dad turned into the gates of Perth
Grammar School, and I saw for the first time, what would
be *home* for the next five years. I couldn't help but wonder
if it would prove to be my playground or my compound.

I couldn't get over the place. Every building was double
storey. Nothing was two storey back home on account of
the cyclones. The grounds were so neat and green, and
the buildings were all made of limestone and very new. I
wondered which one would be Jodhpur Boarding House,
and started to scan for possibilities. I must have been
looking around so much that I didn't realise we had come
to rest outside the only non-limestone, non-beautiful,
really old and decrepit building on the grounds. Actually,
I think I *had* noticed it in one of my visual sweeps and
had written it off as a sewage treatment shed. A quick
glimpse through the windshield revealed a rusty old sign
saying JODHPUR HO SE. Suddenly, the Torana's vinyl
seat became the most comfortable place I had ever known.
And I swear as I stepped out the passenger door, after

a little coaxing from Dad, I had a flash of déjà vu and vividly remembered how it felt leaving the womb. As I walked up the lichen-covered cement steps, and whiffed for the first time what a 96 year old building stinks like, my gut started spasming to me in morse code, "Oh shit!" it said, "Shit Shit Shit!"

The corridor was damp, and lined with brass hooks and lockers made of chicken wire. I followed Dad, as he followed a sign that read, "Housemaster Theodore Shrapnel this way."

"It's certainly clean and tidy Stevie," Dad said, as he tapped his hand forcibly on the housemaster's door. "Yer goin' to 'ave a great adventure." After a series of squeaking footsteps, the door swung open and revealed the considerable bulk of Theodore Shrapnel. 'Shit, there's little wonder the floor was yelping,' I thought.

"Hello, hello, hello," said a voice three times the size of the man standing in front of us. "Don't tell me, Gerry and Stephen Briggs. Theodore Shrapnel, at your service. I'm head rooster of the house. Mrs Briggs called last night and said you'd be arriving this morning. Please come into my office." He led us down yet another corridor and into an office that was as large as our lounge room.

"Do have a seat, won't you both," he said directing us into two waiting chairs. I'm sure it must have just been a coincidence, but he really reminded me of the guy who sold Dad the Torana, not to look at but he acted the same way, as if he'd known us all our lives.

"Firstly, allow me to welcome you to the large and exclusive family, that is Perth Grammar School. A family that's based, on 96 years, of tradition. A tradition, of educational excellence. The school makes a firm commitment to its students. It will do, everything it knows how, to ensure that a Perth Grammar boy is not only equipped with a superb scholastic education, but just as importantly, a broad life education as well. Which together, will prepare the boy and indeed give him, an excellent run-up for the game of life. We believe that discipline, is crucial to success, and I don't mind telling you that if a boy is out of line, he will receive six of the best across the buttocks from me..."

Mr Shrapnel kept talking for what seemed like a week. Every time it looked like he was going to take a breath, Dad would try and get a word in, but miraculously the big fella would find some air from somewhere, keep going, and sedate Dad with his rolling rhythm of speech.

I must admit, after that bit about the cane I kind of vagued out. I found the question of his breathing much more interesting than the content of his monologue. The only *possible* answer I could come up with, was circular breathing, like the Aborigines on stations up north do when they play the didgeridoo. I did tune in from time to time and managed to pick up something about pocket money being a maximum of $1.50 a week, socials with girl schools happening once a year, boarders being allowed out three times a term on boarders' weekends, and the fact that most students would be arriving at around five that night, which meant once Dad left, I would have about six hours to kill.

Eventually Dad butted in, right in the middle of Mr Shrapnel's essay on personal hygiene and how a clean ship has a clean captain.

"Look, I don't mean to be rude Theodore, but I'm afraid I 'ave to be 'eadin back. It's an 18 'our drive. Yer will, look after me lad, won't yer?" Dad asked as he rubbed lightly on my shoulder.

"I assure you Mr Briggs — Stephen will be totally looked after, and what's more, I'm certain he'll love every second of his stay in Jodhpur House. Now, if you like, I'll just give you a quick tour before you set off for Pardoo," he said as he led us back down the corridor and into the main part of the boarding house, "Actually, you're *lucky* to have come this year Stephen. Sadly, Jodhpur is condemned by the health department and is going to be pulled down next year to make way for a music school. You only just scraped into history. This is the assembly room. We have roll call down here every morning at 7am after showers. Boys are expected to be totally dressed for the day including ties. After roll call and house business, where anything that needs to be discussed is, we head over to the Brownlow dining hall. Which if you'd like to follow me is across here," he led us down the lichen-covered steps, through a courtyard, round a hedge, and up to the window of a large room with polished wooden floors. "Meals are served hot, three times a day, come with milk or water and usually there's a sweet of some kind," he said with a hint of delight, which was obviously a clue to his mammoth proportions.

Dad's departure found us both leant against the Torana, attempting to digest Mr Shrapnel's sermon and indeed Mr Shrapnel. "Well, 'e's certainly… a *character*," said Dad finally, "Yer'll learn a lot from 'im."

"Yeah, I suppose," I nodded, with a brave face. But, as Dad shifted his weight in the fancy grey slip on shoes he had bought especially for dropping me off, my brave face shattered into a billion terror filled pieces.

While I had often wondered about separation in general, I had never even conceived what it would really feel like to turn my back on my father, walk three steps, turn around and find him gone. Panic lashed through my body. Desperate to grab hold of something, a protracted wheeze signalled that it had decided on my lungs.

"I'm finding it a bit hard to breathe, Dad."

"Yer all right lad, yer just gettin a bit worked up. It's nerves, it's just natural." I couldn't believe that Dad was being so cruel; it was as if he didn't care at all. But as he reached into his pocket to pull out his keys, his broad shoulders started to shake and he held up his big arms for me to run into, like an F 18 landing on an aircraft carrier. I think neither of us ever wanted that hug to end but eventually, after a number of breaks, Dad attempting to leave and subsequent mid-ocean landings, it did.

The Torana must have been doing *the ton* in first gear, or at least it looked like it, as it whisked my dad away and left me with what felt like a middle-ear infection. Every time I moved my head, whatever I looked at seemed to come rushing at me until it was so close I could hardly focus on it. After a number of heavy sighs, I opened my eyes and decided to head back up the hill to Jodhpur House and dormitory number Two.

My new home, with its two facing rows of four single beds, seemed very eerie as I walked in. The afternoon sun sent a blazing column of light through the window, and a pocket of dust was swaying from side to side as it flirted with rising damp. It looked a bit like one of those scenes in which some Mexican lady would say she saw the Virgin Mary. Mr Shrapnel said he would try and look in on me from time to time, in between preparing the ship for its new crew.

Dad thought that I was lucky being in the dorm first cos I would have the pick of the beds. As I had hours to wait for anyone else to show up, I conducted very thorough tests to determine which one would suit me best. All of the beds were identically designed, spaced and covered in fraying blue blankets but for some reason, the one in the far corner on the right as you come in the door, felt the most comfortable. Its mattress seemed to be some three millimetres higher than all the others, and having a wall behind it and alongside it made it a natural fort, with only one side for potential enemies to ensue from, assuming that the neighbour would be a peaceful one.

I must have unpacked and rearranged my things about 17 times, not that I had a lot of gear, but it seemed like heaps when I tried to stuff it into the bedside table that was provided. It was a little wooden cabinet with a drawer, shelf and swinging door. It didn't hold much at all, and felt strangely cold and ancient as I rubbed my thumb back and forth along the length of it. I wondered how many other boys had housed their lives in it over the last 96 years. Funnily enough, it made me crave my brown corduroy beanbag and all the rest of Mum and Dad's furniture. I mean, their stuff wasn't brand new either, most of it was a bit ratty, but at least it was modern; all this old stuff made me feel creepy.

Eventually I decided to put my underpants, which incidentally were a mixture of dependable bullet-proof y-fronts *and* French-style jockettes, my writing set, and my Blue Stratos deodorant in the drawer and all my clothes on the shelf bit. I didn't know what to do with my school blazer, so I just threw it over myself, as completely unpacked, I lay down on my new bed and stared up at the way-off in the distance ceiling.

I don't know why it didn't happen to me until then. Maybe I was too concerned with my immediate surroundings and situation to worry about bigger issues. Whatever the reason, as I lay there entering that strange land that lies before sleep; I had my second out of body experience. And a lucky thing it was too, because just as I nestled into my hammock, and sat watching a little boy trying to relax on a strange bed, a huge black spider, that had actually been next to him all along, suddenly became visible, jumped onto the bed and started crushing him with its big, spiky, hairy, legs…

I was adopted. Adopted? Like one of those puppies that's suckled by a pig and grows up thinking it *is* a pig. Mum and Dad weren't *really* my parents. Which meant somewhere in the world were my real parents, and they gave me away. I wasn't sad that they *did* give me away because if they hadn't, I wouldn't have met Mum and Dad or Kimba. But why did they give me away? Why didn't they want me? What was wrong with me? Maybe Mum and Dad up in the Doo sent me to boarding school cos they didn't want me either. Because there was something really wrong with me. Something so bad they couldn't even tell me what it was.

These thoughts, were looping around in my head so fast, it felt like someone had erected Disneyland in there when I wasn't looking. I had read a story on aneurysms in *Reader's Digest* and was certain I was about to have one, when I felt a slight tapping on my toe.

"Excuse me. Um, I'm sorry to bother you, but I think you might be on my bed," said a voice that sounded like it was being played through a reed. I opened my eyes to find a very large, red-faced boy, standing in front of me, shaking under the weight of four suitcases. On closer inspection I had to rub my eyes and blink; this boy wasn't large, he was *ginormous*. It wasn't so much his height, as that was quite average, but his trunk was the incredible part. He was as wide as he was tall. If it wasn't for his head, he'd almost be a perfect sphere. As it was, he looked like a 'Superball' that had been left out in the sun for six months.

"My name's Winston Knight," he said meekly as he pointed to the foot of the bed, "And I dunno, but it looks like I'm supposed to be here… W i n s t o n K n i g h t," he read slowly, "Yeah, that's me all right." I jumped to my feet and moved down to the end of the bed. Half of the reason I did this so quickly was because I didn't want to annoy him. But I also just had to check him out from the back, and what a back, my God, if you put him in a black suit you would swear he was a bowling ball.

"Yeah, you're right, I'm sorry Winston, I didn't even see that there were name tags," I said, deflated at the prospect of having to set up house all over again.

"Your name's not, Rhys Carlisle is it?" I shook my head. "What about, Harry Lappin?"

"Na my name's Stephen Briggs," I said, trying to gauge just how much intelligence is affected, when it's housed in a coca-cola earth ball.

"Oh, here you are, over here," to my horror, he pointed to the bed that had the worst strategic position in the whole room, slam, bam in the middle. I wandered down to see if there was any possibility of digging in some trenches. As I stood staring at my future residence, I heard my preferred bed squeak in pain, under the weight of the four suitcases Winston had just placed across it. I rushed back over there, desperate for him to see my jockettes before my y-fronts, but as I skidded to a halt beside him, he had already opened my drawer.

"Oh jeez, I feel real bad, you've already unpacked and you done a grouse job." I didn't have a clue what he meant by 'grouse' — at first I thought he said gross but the tone of his voice made it sound like a *good* thing. "Oh, look in here, that's ace that is," he said with nodded respect.

"Look Winston, it's probably because I come from the Doo and we're a bit behind up there, but…"

"The what?" he smiled.

"The Doo. It's what the locals call Paraburdoo. It's a mining town up north. Anyway, we don't use the words 'grouse' and 'ace' and I was wondering if you could tell me what they mean?" I was going to tell him how words were kind of my hobby and if I heard one I didn't know, it could effect my sleep but I didn't want to bamboozle him with too much information.

"Oh, that's right. You'se guys don't talk like that over here. Grouse and ace both mean," he scrunched his face up, as if he were trying to flick through a dictionary by moonlight, "They mean… good."

"Oh, so if I did a *grouse* job, I did it well and if you say my shelf is *ace* then you like it."

"It's a darn shame to move it. I know how much of a hassle moving is, and I can see you put a lot of work into it."

"Well, I did have a fair bit of time to perfect it. Dad dropped me off a couple of hours ago cos he had to start making his way back up north. It's a bloody long drive. Where are your parents? I thought most of the kids weren't coming until later this afternoon," I said, taking a seat on the bed opposite him.

"Mum and Dad had to get back to the farm, they only bought it six months ago. We're originally from Victoria. Anyhow, the mare is about to drop a foal, so they had to drop me." He reached into his pocket and pulled out a bag bursting with licorice.

"But I don't care, cos we dropped in at Ahearns Department store to get my blazer cos they had to make it up special, and anyhows we stopped off at the lolly section on the way out, and I hit the jackpot." He methodically showed me the contents of each of his seven pockets, some of which held four or five different bags of delight.

"I reckon that should certainly *sugar the pill* of being dropped off early," I chimed, trying to enjoy his passion for confectionery.

"Na, I don't take no pills. Me Mum does, but I don't have to yet." That was strike two in the misunderstanding stakes, and I decided to take it as my cue to start moving my stuff. So I pulled my case from under the bed and began opening it, for what seemed like the hundredth time that day.

"Wait a second," Winston twitched, as if going back for another round with the dictionary and the moon, "I've got an idea. I dunno if it will work, but it's worth a try. Why don't we, switch the..." he twitched some more, "the name tags," he spluttered, with a look that suggested he had just seen Jesus *and* the Virgin Mary, in the dust by the window. It was a lovely gesture, and I couldn't help but like him.

"Oh, you don't have to do that Winston. I mean it's wonderful of you to offer, but I can't accept. For a start, this bed is three millimetres higher than the one in the middle. You'd be much more comfortable on this one."

"Comfort doesn't matter. A bed is a bed, and it's only gonna get flattened when I've finished with it." I couldn't argue with that particular piece of logic, and after seeking three more reassurances from him, helped him carry his four very heavy suitcases to the middle bed. Shit were they heavy, but I didn't mind carrying them. It was the least I could do for the keys to the fort in the corner, and I was glad that I had made an ally in Winston. I kinda knew we would never be best friends, but Dad always said it's better to get along with people than not to.

Living in peaceful Paraburdoo, I had never seen firsthand what a bombsite looked like, but here, in dorm two of Jodhpur House, I was standing in the middle of one. Winston Knight had more *stuff* in those four suitcases than I had seen in my life and most of it was perishable. There were jams, biscuits, preserves, pickled onions, biltong, fudge, chocolates, fairy cakes, cheesecakes, fruit loaves, profiteroles, shortbreads, two pairs of jeans, two t-shirts and two pairs of socks. And just about all of it was home made (apart from the socks — they were from Ahearns).

"Your Mum is quite a seamstress, running up those jeans Winston — they look just like real ones from the shop," I said, wriggling the white lie out of my neck.

"Our family used to have so much trouble buying jeans, that we ended up making 'em ourselves. And the best part is, we make 'em for next to nothing. See that?" he held up one of the legs for me to inspect, "See normal jeans are made out of denim but these jeans are made out of a very soft hessian that some special pig feed comes in, but you couldn't tell could ya?" I shook my head in disbelief, which he read as agreement. I mean, I certainly was no expert on fashion, my taste, began and ended with muscle shirts and 'Scoops' shorts, which incidentally Mum had bought me four pairs of, since she saw Kevin's with the sports' stripe. But I knew enough, to know that hessian dacks that looked like they came to Australia on the first fleet, were definitely not in. But regardless, I *could* see how getting a size to fit him would be a problem, and I did everything I could to help him put his stuff away, or under, is probably a more accurate description.

The entire floor space under his bed was taken up with jars and tins of home-made delight and we had just started to tuck into some fudge, when the booming voice of Theodore Shrapnel came bouncing through the door, "Stephen?" followed by the man himself, "Just checking to see how you're… Well, well, well. You must be Winston

Knight? Very pleased to meet you, and where are your parents boy?"

"They had to get back to the farm."

"Sir! They had to get back to the farm, sir." informed Mr Shrapnel pleasantly but firmly.

"Sorry sir." there was an uncomfortable pause while Mr Shrapnel tilted his head from side to side.

"I think, Mr Shrapnel wants you to repeat the sentence correctly Winston," I said trying to diffuse the situation.

"Oh, sorry. They had to get back to the farm, sir."

"Oh well, that's a shame. Do give them my best when you talk to them next. You both settling in ok then?" Mr Shrapnel enquired, as he peered across my chest into Winston's cupboard. I didn't realise that was what he was doing until he was right next to me. With him leaning down on me on one side, and Winston on the other, I thought I was in the land of the giants.

"Quite neat there Stephen," he said, as if making a mental note. I was just about to tell him that it wasn't *my* cupboard, when he did a double take at the floor and thrust his head downward like a snake chasing a rat.

"Stephen Briggs! What on earth have we got here, a tuck shop? This will not do! This will not do at all. You might as well send out an open rodent invitation. How on earth did you get all that up here? Well, I'm waiting boy?" I didn't want to upset Mr Shrapnel but I couldn't drop *Winston* in it, not after he had let me swap beds with him. "I am still, waiting. Stephen Briggs, there are two types of boys in this house. Ones that are addressed by their first names, who are seen as pleasant, courteous, likeable boys, and those who are addressed by their surnames, who are seen as naughty, disreputable scoundrels, and once a boy has been classified as the latter, it is very hard to return to the likeable section. Your Christian name is rapidly disappearing from my memory."

I looked at Winston as if to say sorry, "Please excuse my silence sir, as I have no wish to be classified as a scoundrel, it's just, the tins and jars, aren't mine sir, they're Winston's sir. Sorry Winston."

"I see Stephen, so, they're Winston's are they? Well what are they doing under your bed?" I went to answer but Winston got in first.

"Actually sir, it's my bed."

"Don't be ridiculous Winston, your bed is over there, along side Harry Lappin's. Knight is next to Lappin. Wonderful thing alphabetical order, once you've mastered it." Mr Shrapnel flapped like a humming bird in a calm wind.

"Um, we... swapped beds... um sir," Winston explained matter of factly. The calm wind ignited into a cyclone, "You what? You swapped beds! Oh now, this definitely won't do! We can't have boys swapping beds." He tapped his foot on the floor. "Hear that? That's my cane, saying utilise my services. I'll teach those rascals to rock the boat." He tapped the floor again. "Swapping beds! Now that kind of free thinking is bad for the crew, bad for the ship and ends up in mutiny. Swap them back, immediately and then report to my office in 20 minutes. By then, I'll have decided, exactly what punishment, befits this heinous crime."

I couldn't understand how the day had taken such a terrible turn and all I could think of, was whether or not Mr Shrapnel used circular breathing to assist him in delivering six of the best across the buttocks, when suddenly Winston spoke, "Excuse me sir. I just want you to know, how *real* sorry we are. We didn't know we done something wrong. To show how bad we feel, I'd be honoured if you would accept this jar of my Mum's home-made melting moments, as a way of apologising sir." There was a very strange pause, when they seemed to look into each other's eyes, as if both searching for the same affliction. Then, after a moment of what seemed like spiritual contact, they both shifted their weight simultaneously and adopted the same strange stance.

"Why, thank you Winston, that's very thoughtful of you. But I couldn't take a whole jar, I could only have one." And one was all it took. I swear, as the moment melted across his tongue you could see his scalp ripple, as if a wave of joy had just broken over his skull. After a period of blissful enlightenment, he spoke, "Actually boys, perhaps this was more of a misunderstanding than an act of treason. I mean the nametags could probably have been, bigger. Look, seeing as you're new, I'll let you off lightly this time. After you have moved into the right beds, I would like you to go past the chapel, down to the boatshed and pick up any litter you find, for a period of one hour. And as for the tins and jars, I think that once they're under the corner bed, they should be fine. Rodents, are renowned for never looking in corners. That will be all, Winston and Stephen," and with that, he headed downstairs, with the jar of melting moments clutched firmly in a policeman's hold.

8 THE UNTAPPED MEDICINAL PROPERTIES OF THE SWAN RIVER

As we followed the path down past the chapel, I counted the cracks between the cement slabs to stop my mind dwelling on the dormitory. The move into the middle bed had gone pretty smoothly and I'd taken extra care with the precious cargo under Winston's bed, after seeing the way Mr Shrapnel had buckled under its spell. That's not to say I *wanted* to move though, there was nothing I wanted to do less, but I was rapidly learning that life at Perth Grammar would be full of things I didn't want to do.

I was in the middle of resigning myself to this, when a reeking stench, heavier than air, grabbed me around the neck, flipped me onto my back and started boring into my nostrils. I thought I must have stumbled across a half decomposed whale, but when I tried to look, all I could see was a green haze setting in around me. Then, as suddenly as it hit, it receded. The cloud parted and I was greeted with the largest, bluest, calmest creek I had ever seen. Actually it looked more like an ocean than a creek, "So, have you ever seen the Swan River before?" asked Winston.

"Na, I haven't. It's amazing. Are you sure it's just a river? It looks like a sea. It's so wide!" I gasped.

"Yeah it's a river... Dunno about you Stephen? But I can't see much litter down here."

"No, you're right Winston. Maybe we'll just have to look around a bit and while we're at it, do a spot of exploring," I said trying to tailor my words to suit my new highfaluting surroundings. There was nothing like this in the Doo. I mean I used to think 'Howies Hole' was big but it looked like a puddle compared to this. And how could so many different plants and grasses all grow in the one place?

As we made our way behind the boatshed, the bamboo became so thick we had to use sticks to hack our way through it. Honestly, I felt like Tarzan was going to jump out in front of us at any second. I've got to say, I was pretty impressed with Winston though. After the first few hacks at the tall yellow reeds, he went awfully red in the face, started to dribble a little and looked like he would pass out right in front of me. I was just praying that if he did, he'd land on his back because my understanding of mouth to mouth was pretty ordinary at the best of times, and if he fell on his front, I'd have no chance whatsoever. But my anxiety was for nothing because once Winston got up a head of steam he was unstoppable. Admittedly his dribble did get a little bit frothier, but that was it. I had only been at my new school a few hours and I was already having my first lesson in Darwin's Theory of Natural Selection. Winston had adapted to his jungle surroundings in minutes, and who knows, if he had to stay in that thick jungle for a few hundred years, that frothy dribble may have turned out to have medicinal properties, or been useful in sticking leaves together to make grass huts or skirts.

After what seemed like hours of hacking, we finally made it to the water's edge and the source of the smell. You couldn't tell from a distance, but up close there was no missing it. The water was teeming with millions of big, brown, mushroom-shaped jellyfish and they stunk so bad even my eyebrows were wilting.

"Smells a bit like a fly blown sheep," said Winston, with a stalactite of crystallised dribble hanging off his chin.

"People don't swim in it do they?" I stammered through the stench.

"Not that much. They prefer to *sail* on it," said Winston gesturing behind me. I turned around, to find a fleet of enormous pleasure boats, gently rocking in wooden pens. Winston pointed towards the biggest boat, which kinda looked like a couple of road trains stacked on top of each other, "That one on the end, belongs to Alan Bond." I was about to ask who that was, when a large siren, blaring out from the direction of the boarding house made me look at my watch, "Oh shit! We've been down here for an hour and a half!"

The stairs back to Jodhpur House were so steep, they often resembled a ladder, but that wasn't the reason I took my time getting up them. I did that out of respect for Winston. But I must admit, I really had to hold back the urge to bolt — especially when I took the distant sound of a jack hammer to be the tap, tap, tapping, of Mr Shrapnel's cane.

The house was quiet when we finally puffed up to its lichen covered steps. Deathly quiet, and when my attempts at tip toeing were drowned out by the sparking spurs on Winston's cowboy boots, I made a mental note to think long and hard about any future association. We walked into the recreation room and found 40 boys standing in five perfect lines, with their arms held out so that they resembled a squadron of planes getting ready to take on the Red Baron. I suddenly became aware that another boy, had slunk in behind us.

"Right you are then boys. Now that we have a, full, complement you can all put your hands down. And the rest of you, can see the *faces* of the boys that have made your arms so sore."

Without thinking words started tumbling out of my mouth, "Sir, we are extremely sorry we're late, it's just that there was so much litter down by the river, it took longer than expected to get the area looking, shipshape. Sir."

"We done a grouse job sir," added Winston. Mr Shrapnel didn't look like he enjoyed me speaking up in front of everyone, and as he walked over, I really thought he was going to blast me, but then his eyes caught Winston's and they both adopted that strange stance again. "I see. Picking up litter was it? Running late, because of the litter. Well, let me say to you all, that I can't stand litter… Hate it… Despise it… Can't stand it… Almost as much as I can't stand, lateness. I'll let you off with a warning, this time. Into line both of you, quickly, quickly." Mr Shrapnel pushed us towards the line that contained the smallest amount of boys, before turning his attention to the other boy who was late. "Late comer number three, how say you?" The boy didn't say anything, he just stood with his feet at right angles, chewing bubble gum and running his fingers through his shaggy, black, Duran Duran hair. "What is your name boy?" The boy thought long and hard about this, taking a handfull of chews before answering.

"Carlisle. Rhys Carlisle. I'm a diabetic and I had to unpack and inject myself with insulin." A collective dislike for needles groaned around the room.

"I see," said Mr Shrapnel with a quiver of compassion. "Well, you'd better let Matron know about your condition as soon as possible. Oh and Rhys, in future, address me as sir. In fact that goes for you all."

The rest of the meeting was pretty dull really. We were told that each dorm gets up first on different days and as I was in dorm two, that meant Tuesdays would be no sleep in day. Five minutes after we were woken up we would have to be in the showers, or risk detention. Then we would have morning inspection, roll call, followed by breakfast and finally school. As I followed the rest of my dorm up the stairs, the excitement about being in a new place and doing new things started to wane for the first time and a tiny bubble of home sickness burped out my mouth and roamed around in front of me before gently bursting on my forehead. I didn't want to go into the dorm and meet the other boys. I didn't want to be surrounded by all this sophisticated opulence. All I wanted was to be watching *Countdown* with Mum and Dad, and waiting for the Shepherd's pie to be ready.

As I brought my weary frame to rest on my allocated bed, with its allocated blue bed spread, in the middle of the allocated dormitory, I could almost feel Mum's warm, chunky, gravy trickling down the back of my throat.

"They call me Maurice," said a voice that almost sounded like a girl's, to the right of me. "Maurice, as in Fleece. Not Morris, as in Boris. I'm far too *gregarious* to be Russian." The strategist in me breathed an instant sigh of relief; a peaceful neighbour. I mean, you could hardly see yourself having an all out war with someone called 'Maurice, who described himself as gregarious'.

"I'll have to tell my grandmother that Morris, she grew up in St Petersburg. I can't stand blokes that insist on poxy pronouncing of their names" said a voice to the left of me, that was dripping in freshly taken piss, "and I don't like Bogans much either." I couldn't be sure, but I think that comment was aimed at me. I thought I'd just ignore it and savour some more of Mum's cooking, but out of the corner of my eye I was horrified to find Rhys Carlisle staring right at me, "What's your name, Bogan?"

"Hey, do you reckon I could see ya needles?" bellowed Winston from the other side of the room. As soon as Carlisle heard his voice, he spun around like a tiger snake, desperate for somewhere to strike, which was great, cos it took the heat off me, but it was also really sad because it gave him time to watch Winston walk towards him. In fact, Winston had to walk about 5 metres to make it over to his bed.

I hadn't actually noticed it earlier but now that it was the centre of my attention, I couldn't help but see it. Winston Knight had a very peculiar walk indeed. His arms paused and quivered half way through their swing, while his hips waddled. If it was dark and he was in a cage, you'd swear he was go-go dancing. Unfortunately I wasn't the only one to notice it. Rhys Carlisle let out an enormous high-pitched cackle.

"Man, you're not only the fattest thing I've ever seen, you're also the most uncoordinated. Look at that walk. You look like an elephant that's been drinking too much. Man you are a real Dumbo aren't you?" Winston tried not to let it worry him but the dribbling gave him away. Carlisle moved in for the kill, "Look, Dumbo's drooling. Look at it pouring out of his mouth."

"What did you call me?" muttered Winston, building up speed as he approached.

"I called you Dumbo, lard for brains." That was about all it took to turn Winston's dribble to froth, and to start dorm two's first fight of the year. Mind you, Winston certainly didn't bother laying down a formal declaration or challenge, he simply got within range, charged at Carlisle, and bounced him off his bed with his belly.

Had he opted to keep repeating this strategy, I'm sure he would have been the victor but instead, Winston was keen to wrestle, and while that was fine from a spectator's point of view, there was never really going to be a winner.

Carlisle was just on the heavier side of wiry and definitely had the height advantage, while Winston had three to four times the bulk but lacked the agility of his opponent. So what resulted, was the two of them rolling around on the floor, with Carlisle generally managing to ride Winston like some kind of mechanical barrel. It also gave the dorm its first taste of togetherness; initially as we all yelled, "fight fight fight," and then a little later, as we all yelped, "ouch ouch ouch" after Mr Shrapnel's cane had dealt us our one stroke punishment for aiding and abetting. Poor Winston spent his first night in Jodhpur House nursing three welts on his backside, while Carlisle escaped with none, on account of his diabetes. Winston said that his didn't hurt a bit, cos of all the extra padding he was carrying but I'm pretty sure I heard him whimper at least once in the night.

As we all lay there, in the freshly striped darkness, we decided that as we would be spending the next year together, it might be time for some quiet introductions. In fact, as Mr Shrapnel was on the war path, whispered introductions. A little voice came squeaking out of the corner and got the ball rolling, "My name's Hawwy Lappin. And me olds sent me to Gwamma school, to get me a decent education and some help with me speech, cos I'm not too good with me 'wahs'. We's got a bake-a-wee in Mawgwet Wiver." After a bit of rustling around in the darkness, Harry produced a torch and proceeded to sit up in bed and point the beam at his face so we could all see him. After a few moments, he handed the torch to the guy in the bed next to him, who decided to light himself for his whole introduction.

"I feel like a bit of a goose holding this, this bloody torch up to me face but here goes." I thought that Winston spoke funny, but this guy was incredible, his voice was much deeper than everyone else's, that was until he finally reached the end of his sentence, then his voice would go up an octave and honk like a blast on a mini-moke's horn. "George Monger's the name but don't wear it out. Come from a piggery just south of Geraldton and like to play the jaw harp." Before anyone had a chance to stop him, he was serenading us with 'Thank God I'm a Country Boy' and, though he did have some musical ability, I found the whole concept of a harp, that goes in your mouth, particularly George Monger's, so absurd that I couldn't help myself, and started giggling after the first few twangy bars.

I discovered that night, that I was blessed with one of the most precious gifts a human being can own, something much more valuable than a Mercedes, rarer than depilatory cream in the bathroom cabinets of the Paraburdoo Women's Tug of War Team, and something that was *even* capable of preventing wars. My laughter was totally infectious. As soon as I started to giggle, it swept across the dorm like an outbreak of chicken pox, everyone came down with it, even Rhys Carlisle. Not that it stopped George though. Later on, we would learn that he was completely deaf in one ear, and that was the one facing us, so we were in hysterics and George, still shining Harry's torch in his face, was on stage with John Denver.

Next to receive the torch, was a bloke who was so tall his feet almost poked out the bottom of his bed, "Hi everybody. Um I'm Danny Gethem. You'll have to excuse me, if my voice cracks, it's been doing it a fair bit lately. Um, I don't really know where to start. I come from a wheat/sheep farm and I'm the number two ranked junior tennis player in the southern district." Danny briefly flashed the torch at his face before tossing it on to the bed of the next kid.

For a minute or two the torch just sat there, as the kid rocked back and forth. "I th... th... th... th...thing introducen yoursel is d...d...d...d.dumb," he said, before chucking the torch, at the aforementioned, gregarious Maurice. I think we were all a little stunned by the last guy. It wasn't just that he had a stutter, he also sounded a bit retarded. I'd never had any spastic friends in the Doo. Well, that's not entirely true. I knew a lot of spastics up there, but none of them were actually retarded.

"Maurice Cowper... Sagitaurius... I'm into water sports, ping-pong, suntans, Brazilian culture and the West Indian cricket team. In particular the Big Bird, Joel Garner. I like Dungeons and Dragons, Hot Milos, and anything in maroon velour. Oh and I just *love*, The Village People," he burst into song and Latin shoulder shakes, "Do the Milkshake. The Milkshake. Do the Shake. And oh, this, is my favourite. Young man. There's no need to feel down. I said young man! Pick yourself off the ground." Even though it was dark, I could see that Maurice was performing that particular song in my direction. And then suddenly he stopped mid-note and whispered in a very dramatic voice "Always keep them wanting more." Then, he held the torch up on a strange angle and pulled a face similar to one you'd see on Benny Hill.

The next thing I knew, the torch was placed very delicately, in front of me and it was my turn to lift up my fur and expose my soft underbelly. I must say, as I picked up the torch, there was no way I was going to illuminate myself for the whole speech, after all, I was from the Doo and drawing any undue attention to yourself just wasn't done up there. And besides, I was no sissy, you just had to pull back my blue bedspread and have a look; my pyjama shorts were at precisely the right height. Anyway, I think it must have been all those thoughts about who I was and where I came from that were my downfall, cos when I went to speak, I found I couldn't, all that consumed me was my longing to taste the warm Pilbara breeze. And it knew I had strayed because it was whistling through the ghost gums and screaming through the creek beds, begging me to come home. Even though I wasn't an Aborigine, the land had still taken care of me since I was a nipper and as Billingarra, Dad's Aboriginal stockman friend always said, the land was the only thing up there that *was* colour-blind. Which was kinda lucky for him because he was an albino.

I wasn't the toughest kid in the Doo, but ordinarily I was no fairy either. That's not what my dorm would have thought of me though, because instead of sprouting a few chosen words, to give an insight into who I was, I sprung a leak and dumped a deluge of cyclonic tears. And, as the rest of the room looked on, I couldn't help but think that they all knew precisely what it was that was so wrong with me. They knew why my parents had left me so far from home, and worse still could understand why they had done it. After a few goes at speaking and only managing to string Ste.. and Stephen across a gorge of sobs, Maurice announced to everyone, that I was just homesick and might have another go later.

I had just hopped up, into my warm impenetrable hammock, when Rhys Carlisle's face lit up next to me. "I guess you all got to see me downstairs. Just in case you've forgotten, it's Rhys. I come from Augusta, where my Dad's got the biggest building company on the south coast. My family owns a bunch of racehorses, my passion, is girls and my hobby, the five Fs." There was long silence while every one racked their brains.

"Well, someone's got to ask," honked George, "What the heck… are the five Fs?"

"Oh, you got to be joshing. You *can't* tell me you don't know about the five Fs? The rest of you guys know about 'em don't ya?" A few honest "nos" and bluffed "yeses" followed. "How old are you George?"

"I'm 14."

"14 and you don't know about the Fs. That's criminal. Look mate, I'm gonna do for you, what your father should have done years ago. The Five Fs, are the only things you need to remember, in order to lead you, to a constant supply of quality pussy. When used correctly, they will make you the envy of your friends and the talk of the girls' school next door. The first F." Rhys obviously had a bit of experience with story telling, cos he chose this point to clear his throat and in doing so, string out the drama. "The first F. Find them. Pretty obvious but you'd be surprised how many guys luck out, cos they don't look. Second F. Follow them. Persistence my friends. She may just be playing hard to get. Third F. Finger them. There's *nothing* more satisfying, than slipping your finger, and that's middle finger, in and out of a wet pussy. And of course afterwards, you can give your mates, a bit of a sniff. Fourth F. Fuck em. Oh my Lord. Now I don't know how many of you guys are virgins but I lost my virginity when I was 10, and fucking a tight pussy is like, nothing else, in God's glorious Kingdom. And finally, the fifth F. And this is my favourite. Forget them. Once you've had your way, time to find new challenges, with new pussies, cos the *last* thing you want, is them hanging around trying to get all *emotional* with you. And that my friend, is the five Fs, otherwise known as the Handbook for Plentiful Pussy."

"Well, thanks for filling me in," said a tad excited George, whose bedspread suddenly resembled a Teepee.

As I lay there, in my homesick coma, I couldn't help but have a few doubts about Rhys. I could understand that girls were his hobby, but when he spoke about them, he didn't seem to get excited at all; if anything, his words had seemed tinged with distain, rather than respect. I've got to admit though, I was pretty relieved when he caught my giggling bug. It was pretty obvious he didn't like me initially but maybe now he'd give me another chance.

9 REGIMENTED HYGIENE

It's true to say that I heard every breath, moan, snore, belch, creak, rustle and fart that occurred that night, and even though I was safely tucked into my floating hammock, I couldn't sleep. Mum said that as a toddler, I had often cried myself to sleep, but that hadn't worked either. In fact, I had just managed to empty my entire tear reservoir, when Mr Shrapnel bounded into the dorm like a two tonne butterfly.

"Ok everybody, time to get up and face the day. Come on, out of bed and into the showers please and remember, once in the shower, a maximum of only three minutes," he shouted, as he bounced down the hall and into the next dormitory.

Honestly, you would have thought a bomb was about to go off. Everyone was on their feet, out of their pyjamas and into their towels, in the time it would take Mr Shrapnel to give three of the best. The bloke in the corner who wouldn't give his name, was actually walking around completely nude. It gave me the shock of my life, and not just because I hadn't seen a naked boy before, there was something really weird going on with his tail. I mean dick... No... Actually... I mean tail. It had this bizarre piece of skin on the end of it, that looked kinda like the end of a balloon — you know — the part you blow into. I had never really seen anyone, except Mum and Dad, first thing in the morning, and it felt really yucky to be sharing such a private time with so many strangers. I slipped my towel over my pyjamas to ensure no one else would see my privates, and was a little surprised and relieved to spy Rhys Carlisle, out of the corner of my eye, doing the same.

With my towel done up nice and tight, I followed the rest of the dorm down the hallway and stairwell toward the almost mechanical sound, of Theodore Shrapnel's regimented hygiene. As my feet fell into the rhythm of the line, it struck me for the first time, that a shower would be bloody wonderful. A shower, would give me one of the things I was really craving. Some *privacy*. That screen sliding shut would mark three minutes to myself, and I would say, if last night was anything to go by, that would be about all the privacy I would be seeing in Jodhpur House.

Well, at least that's what I thought. Even as I was herded across the cold, damp, cement floor, and made to stand in front of the source of the steam, I didn't think twice. I must have written the room off as an area where livestock were drenched. Well, all I had heard about, before everyone dropped off, was lupins, feed and how many combine harvesters would fit end to end from Narrogin to the Wheat Silos and back. The general consensus being; 1600, if you went on the sealed road, and 1150 if you took the short cut through Old man Johnson's abattoir. But no one would be stupid enough to do that, because it's haunted. I even stood there thinking, 'Yeah this is a great place for drenching, one large room garnished with 12 showerheads. One large room, garnished with 12 showerheads, and 12 naked boys washing! But *where's* the shower screens with the frosted glass you can't see through? Where's my *only* moment to be alone, in the whole day?' Totally overwhelmed, I ran out of the shower block, into the confines of a toilet cubicle and slammed the door shut behind me.

Mind you, it wasn't a sanctuary for long. Because, just as I was in the process of sitting down, my sense of smell kicked back in, after being temporarily shut down to help with the war effort in the tear ducts and with my towelled backside, centimetres from the seat, I registered the unmistakable odour of human excrement. Shit! The entire cubicle reeked of shit. I immediately aborted my landing and spun around, expecting to see a three-week-old Grogan floating in the bowl. Strange thing was, there wasn't *anything* in the bowl. Nothing. But the stench was undeniable. I decided to enlarge the search area and that's when I made one of the most grisly discoveries of my life. The turd, wasn't *in* the toilet, it was *on* it. Some depraved individual, had laid an enormous black log, almost all the way around the seat and in doing so set a very macabre trap, which of course you couldn't see, cos the colours blended in. And I had almost *sat* in it.

As I hurried back into the shower block, that was now minus the steam, my tears suddenly found the reserve tank, and set about washing my extremely exposed toes. Fortunately, not too many people saw me, well crying at least. They certainly saw me. Every minute inch of me, even the strip of skin that lies in the valley of my buttocks got a showing. Trust me to drop the soap. "Oh, you betta not *drop the soap* at an all boys school," everyone up at the Doo had said. I must admit, I just picked it up instinctively and didn't even realise its significance until after I had done it.

They say *people* come in different shapes and sizes. Well, people are identical, compared to tails. Not that I was actually looking, it's just while I was bent over, I found myself face to face with a forest of tails. Not that there was anything 'Homo' going on. It was nothing like that. In fact, it was quite funny. There were long thin ones, short fat ones, hairy ones, shiny ones, itsy bitsy ones and there was even one that seemed to bend up to one side. And one thing was for sure, everybody seemed pretty embarrassed about having to show their's off. Everyone except Maurice; he seemed curiously unperturbed, as he whipped himself into a lather with his fluorescent flannel.

Homesickness, fanned by a Northerly wind, came in strong and regular gusts for the rest of the day. And as I walked into the Brownlow dining hall, which incidentally was bigger than our supermarket, I felt like I was going to throw up. And indeed, my stomach muscles had just about gone into that irreversible spasm, when a smell, so familiar and friendly, came dancing over my shoulder and tumbling across my tongue. Beans! They served beans! Bloody ripper. Hunger, until now completely banished, suddenly possessed me and sat fidgeting in my mouth as we progressed up the line.

The small lady serving the food seemed surprised when I spoke, "Hello, my name's Stephen. I'm new and I love beans! Mountains and mountains of beans!"

"Well you won't get that round here. You'll get one scoop, like the rest of 'em." My eyes must have given me away. "All right! One big scoop. The name's Joan. And that's Joan, that's Joan, that's Pete, and that's Joan as well. You can never have too much of a good thing. Ain't that right Joans?" The other ladies all agreed loudly. I thought they seemed very nice, and would have stayed and talked to them longer, but I had *one* thing on my mind; securing the other half of my breakfast equation. Toast.

I could see people milling around the two opposite ends of the hall and I assumed, from the odd billow of smoke, that must be where the toasters were. But where was the bread to toast? A shrill voice jabbed me in the back and interrupted my concentration. "You hoo! Over here Stephen! Feeling any better? Oh, well you've certainly got some colour back. Didn't you give us a scare. You were paler than a Revlon number six. Now, put your plate down here," Maurice guided me to a vacant table, "And there's some bread for you, there. Now, let's go for a little stroll over to the toasters."

When we got to the toasters, there was quite a large group of kids from Jodhpur House standing back from them, as two older boys towered over the big silver machines. Maurice, too engrossed, in detailing the personal likes and dislikes of *The Village People's* 'Construction Worker' to notice, walked straight up and dropped the bread into one of the many vacant slots. The response was swift and brutal. The bigger boy spun 'round. His top lip creased back in anger, which revealed his sizeable teeth, that were so crooked they resembled fangs, "What the fuck do you think you're doing?"

Maurice glanced behind him to see who the guy was talking to, "Oh me! You're talking to me. Well, I was hoping, to do a bit of toasting. If that's, not *too* much to ask?"

"I was hoping to do a bit of toasting," repeated the other older boy.

"You talk like a poofter. And who's this? Your boyfriend. Couple of little poofters! Aren't ya? I bet you suck each other's cocks don't ya?" With no warning whatsoever, the bigger one grabbed me by the shirt, punched the ejector handle, which sent my toast flying and slapped me across the face.

The other guy grabbed Maurice, intending to do the same but to everybody's surprise Maurice dodged the arm coming at him, stuck his shoulder into his attacker's chest, elbowed him in the stomach and proceeded to fling him onto his back. Then he went after the bigger bloke that had slapped me; who was now, rather understandably, backing towards the door. Which he ended up making but not under his own steam. Maurice leapt into the air, his hips whizzing past my head, his foot landing right in the middle of the big guy's chest, sending him rocketing back into the door. Ordinarily, a thud that loud would have been deafening, but this was a room full of starving boarders and hardly a soul lifted their gaze from their plate, as the *only* thing they heard, was the voice in their head chanting '*eat*'.

My beans were still sloshing around in my stomach as I followed the rest of the boys up the tar-laid hill to the chapel. I thought it was pretty stupid that I had just had to walk all the way down to the school from the boarding house, only to get there and come back again. At first, I tried to stay with the rest of the dorm, but with each step they seemed to disperse further away into the swirling tangle of blue and grey uniforms. I must admit, I sure felt stupid in the school get up. The only other time I had ever seen a tie was when Charlie Crabbe used one as a tourniquet, after a King Brown snuck up on him and his missus getting a bit fresh, in their veggie patch. All I can say, is it's lucky it bit him on the *end* of his tail, if it had got any higher, there would have been nothing to tie the tourniquet to. Even though I felt stupid, I sure wasn't going to show it. I'd only been at Perth Grammar a day and a night, and already it was like living in a *National Geographic* nature documentary. Any sign of weakness at all, the pack gets a sniff and you're on the menu as Joan's surprise. Just keep watching those shoes and socks in front I told myself. Watching those shoes and socks. After a while, I went a bit giddy and as we streamed into the imposing shadow of the chapel, I was sure I could see dingos jumping across the calf muscles that engulfed me.

Filing into the enormous building, that looked more like an entertainment centre than a humble house of the Lord, I got my second glimpse of the Swan River. Perched high on a cliff as it was, the chapel was the perfect place to view the majestic waterway, as it playfully twisted and splashed in front of me. For what seemed like an eternity, I completely forgot about my new surroundings and how alien they made me feel. I was totally consumed with appreciating this new section of landscape that sat puckering up in front of me. To the innocent bystander, I probably looked like I was blowing kisses back and maybe even thinking about going in for a tit off. It wasn't my fault the view was so breathtaking and that I didn't have any experience with chapel protocol.

However, when I did manage a sideways glance from the Swan River's irresistible stare, I found that the thousand boys surrounding me had sat down in their pews, while I, stood and gushed out the window. Which, in itself, probably wouldn't have been too bad. But the fact that the priest had asked me to sit down three times, then went on to compare me to a mullet he'd caught on the weekend, and finally to add insult to injury, chose to ease into his welcome sermon by referring to the *wonder* in a young boy's eyes and its somewhat dubious relationship with the wonder of Perth Grammar, kind of obliterated my plan, of simply *blending* into the woodwork. In fact a Martian, with a three metre boob in the middle of its forehead, would probably have been less conspicuous than me. Because, every few minutes, the priest would repeatedly point at me and refer to the wonder in my eyes. All I could do was smile, while my adrenal glands tried everything in their power, to jump through my chest and throttle the hell out of His Holiness.

Eventually, he sat down but not before finishing with the wonder *point point*, the wonder *point point*, the wonder *point* is yours. The headmaster was much less theatrical looking but equally charismatic. Well, as charismatic, as someone who is leaning on 90 and a walking frame *can* be. Instead of starting his speech with a spontaneous invention, he opened with what seemed to be a rehearsed pause. I couldn't be sure but I thought I heard someone whispering at him, from off behind the altar. I'd never actually seen a live ventriloquist act, but the headmaster looked just like a ventriloquist's dummy I had seen in *Reader's Digest*. The funny thing was, he was not only the dummy but the ventriloquist as well, because when he spoke, his mouth didn't move a bit.

"Good morning boys… For those of you who don't know me my name is… Peter Halfhide and this, is my last year, as headmaster, of Perth Grammar. May I say, it is a pleasure, to see you all here, resplendent, in your blue and grey. For some of you, this will be your first impression of your new school. If you *are* new… then, good for you. I was new once. Not any more… but once I was. New… everything was new back then. Nothing like waking up new… You know, it might surprise you to know, that I remember my first day at this school like it was yesterday. Never forget it because I was… new… and, someone tried to give me a wedgie. I say 'tried' but I should say 'did'. For those of you who don't know what a wedgie is, it's when two or more boys, lift another boy, off the ground by pulling his pants up his nether regions. Wedgied me really well they did. I mean, there were a few of them and only five and half stone of me. So needless to say, they had me at shoulder level and the pain hurt almost as much, as the humiliation. And there was a lot of humiliation, for young Halfhide. So much so, that I begged my parents to transfer me to some other school. But they refused and I had to keep turning up for my regular morning wedgie. Which I hated. But in retrospect, it was good for me. It taught me things about life. Because eventually the wedgies stopped. I don't know if I got too heavy, or the other boys just lost interest. But I learnt *two* things, from my regular wedgieing; the first is, that persistence under adveristy, is the mark of a truly great man... and the second is, you're only new once. For God's sake enjoy it!"

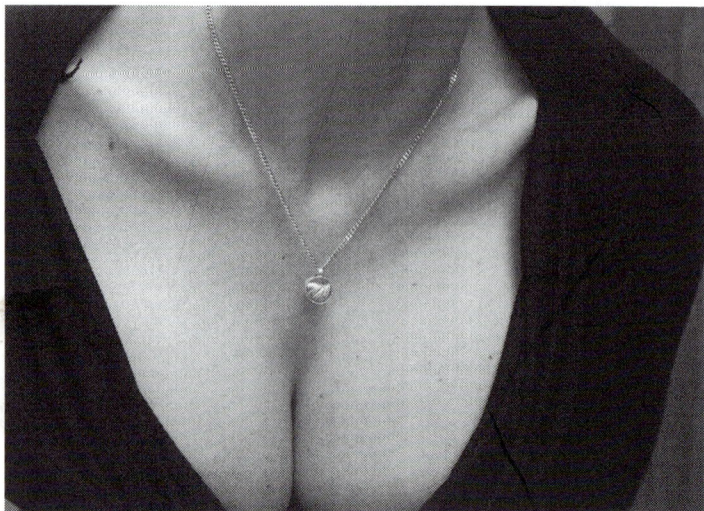

10 tHE SIXtH F

I really wanted to *help* Maurice, but I just couldn't move. I was so scared, that my subconscious had pulled my pyjama pants up to my armpits. The rest of the day after chapel, had gone ok. Strangely enough, I found it easier to hide in a class of 30, than I did in an assembly of 1000. But nothing could have prepared me for this.

We had done our homework, which Mr Shrapnel called prep, and had a bit of an after lights-out chat about what we thought of the day, and the assembly, and Halfhide's story about being wedgied. I think we must have all been in that place that lies between being awake and being asleep, because none of us heard them come in, and there were six of them.

The first I knew, was when I heard a scuffle coming from the bed next to me. I looked over to see six big older boys holding Maurice down on his bed. The poor bugger wouldn't have stood a chance. One of the boys spat a whisper across the room; "Now the rest of you little shits, shut the fuck up, and you won't get hurt."

The unmistakable voice of George came honking out of the darkness, "What are you doing to him?"

"We're just teaching this little faggot, some respect," said the older boy gleefully. I don't know if squeezing an entire tube of Dencorub up someone's bum, would teach them much respect, but they sure seemed to think it would. It wasn't until my eyes began to focus, that I could see *how* ugly this really was. One guy was pulling Maurice's bum cheeks apart as far they would go, while another guy was inserting the Dencorub. Three others were holding him down, and the last guy had slipped a plastic bag over Maurice's head. I don't think he was actually *trying* to kill him, I'm sure in their minds, they were just doing the 1980's version of the wedgie that appeared in Halfhide's story. But as I lay there listening to Maurice being suffocated, I couldn't help but wonder if that's what Kimba sounded like, while he was being gutted.

It's funny but the whole time I had been at boarding school, I hadn't thought of Kimba once, but suddenly I was gripped with the most vivid image of him. It was almost as if *he* was the one, that reached under my armpits and regained my dignity by adjusting the height of my pyjama pants. And it was *his* paw, that stretched under

119

my bed and grabbed the ceramic biscuit barrel Winston had left there for safekeeping. Mind you, it was certainly *my* voice that bellowed louder than a Kimberley thunder storm, "They're killing him! They're *suffocating* him! Let's get 'em!" By the time I had actually made the call for reinforcements, two of them had already felt the sting of Winston's biscuit barrel. And it was almost poetic that the third one felt the full force of Winston's belly, as he was the first to arrive, followed by George. And a few minutes after the intruders had retreated via the fire escape (which incidentally was a tow rope tied to Harry Lappin's bed) in came a smoking jacketed Mr Shrapnel.

It wasn't until the following morning, after breakfast, that the dorm had its first real chance to discuss what had happened. Of course, the night before, we had told Mr Shrapnel that it was too dark to see the faces of the older boys. And Maurice had been taken to sick bay, where he had been diagnosed as suffering from a minor case of shock, and sent back to the dorm for a good night's sleep.

It was clear, as we all sat around on our beds discussing what had happened and how I got the guts to fight them off, that Rhys Carlisle wasn't happy. I think one of the reasons for his discontentment, was that I had been the one who had led the rest of the cavalry. Of course, he wasn't able to actually express that one, but it didn't take him long to get the other one off his chest. "What worries me about all this shit, is we have a suspected *poofter*, living right under our noses. I mean, those guys must have thought Maurice was a poofter, for a reason…"

Harry Lappin squeaked up from the corner, "Yeah you're wight… Those guys wouldn't wisk coming in here, without a weally good weason." Winston, always keen to support the underdog, came to Maurice's aid, "Come on guys, what proof have you got that he is a poof?"

"What proof have we got that he isn't?" barked Rhys, "Well, what have you got to say for yourself, Maurice?" Maurice jumped off his bed, and began to pace, like a cross between a Willie Wagtail and Rumpole of the Bailey, "I can't believe I'm *hearing* this. You guys... really think... that I could be homo... homosexual? I'm as heterosexual, as the next, red-blooded, Aussie, red-blooded, bloke. In fact, I've been living by the *six* Fs for donkeys' years."

Carlisle broke Maurice's stride, "Six Fs! Now we know you're lying, there's only five!"

"Well for some," Maurice countered, "But those in the know, know there's six, and I can prove it to you!" Maurice said dramatically, as he pointed his finger and stared at every one of us. You see the proof's in the pudding, or is that, the mattress?" He strode purposefully over to his bed, lifted up the mattress, and returned with an inch thick red file, which he opened in the middle of us. "The sixth F gentlemen... FWOR... look at *the norks* on that." The dorm FWORED in agreement, as they flicked through the considerable collection of centrefolds and it was obvious, everyone was convinced that Maurice was no poofter. The only guy, that didn't join the chorus of FWORS, was Rhys Carlisle; he had something else going on in his eyes.

The house bell told us it was time to head down to school, and as we all trundled down the stairs, Maurice leant over and whispered, "Have you got a fire extinguisher?"

I said, "No, why?"

"Liar Liar. My pants are on fire," he smiled.

When I finally got to form class, everyone was sitting up completely straight, with their hands on their elbows. Mr Milton, a short, rotund man with an angry sea of white hair, sat with his back to the class in a swivel chair at the front. I was just about to walk in when he spoke very loudly, yet effortlessly, "Simple Simon says, hands on, shoulders." No sooner had he spoken, he was spinning around, to see who he could catch moving. I opened the door and walked in. "Don't they knock in your house, boy?" I stood motionless, dumbstruck that a guy trying so hard to avoid attention, was receiving so much. "Come from a family of mutes, do you?" I didn't know what to say. I certainly couldn't tell him that I'd just found out the guy who sleeps in the bed next to me, was a poof. So I decided to play along, and did some very swift and deliberate flicks of my hands and wrists. For a while there, I think I had everyone believing me, but of course I soon ran out of credible gestures, and had to resort to the old bird flapping its wings and the dog opening it's mouth to bark.

Everyone found this pretty funny, especially as the bird was dragging me all over the class as the dog chased. Everyone, except the teacher, *he* thought it was excruciatingly hilarious, he was slapping his hand on his desk, as his rosy cheeks roared with applause. "Very good, boy. Very good. What's your name?"

"It's Stephen sir," I said, feeling relieved that he seemed to like me.

"No, not your Christian name, your surname. No-one's interested in Christian names here."

"Oh, sorry sir. It's Briggs," I smiled.

"Briggs. Briggs. Oh yes, Briggs. Here we are. Right, well you have a detention Briggs, for being late. I will not stand, for lateness. You will meet me here today at the end of school, for a period of one hour. Sit down young man." He directed me to a seat, just in front of him.

"Now, you all no doubt, heard the chaplain and headmaster's addresses yesterday; allow me to reiterate their welcome, with one qualification. You boys, are *very* lucky, to have come to a school, as glorious as this. A school with a magnificent tradition. A tradition of excellence and discipline. *Discipline.* It's a bit of a dirty word these days. Modern thinking, believes, that it isn't too important. Well I'm here to tell you that it is. And my classroom's success, depends almost entirely upon it. Now, a disciplined mind, is a mind you can trust in any situation and one of the best ways of disciplining a mind, is by the use of the exquisite words and meter, of Gilbert and Sullivan. I am passing around a section of 'The Pirates of Penzantz'. You will be required to learn it, know it, and breathe it. Is that clear?"

The world was getting stranger and stranger. I mean, what on earth, does, "I am the very model of a modern major general," mean any way? And how is it relevant to anything? Nevertheless, once a week, at every form class, we would spend an entire hour pounding through it, until it sounded like it was coming from the one singular oracle of heaven, or so Mr Milton said. I spent that afternoon in detention, stumbling through Mr Milton's vocal orienteering course. That is to say, my tongue did. My mind was grappling over something far more difficult. I was trying to work out what I thought about Maurice's admission. I suppose I felt a little privileged that Maurice had felt comfortable enough to confide in me. But, I just couldn't get my head around actually *knowing* a poofter. See, poofters weren't allowed in the Pilbara, some of Dad's work mates had t-shirts with 'Poofter free zone' written on them. Everyone I had ever known had harboured an indefinable hatred for poofs, and yet, Maurice was the most sensitive and caring person I had met at Perth Grammar. He was intelligent, funny, and by all accounts, decent. Did it really matter, that his favourite part of the day was working himself into a fluorescent lather in the shower block?

Back up in the Doo, Science had always been one of my favourite subjects, and, as I filed into my first class, I was really looking forward to it. But, I was a little surprised to only see dayboy faces and none of the rough and ready boarders from dorm two that I was slowly becoming accustomed to. It wasn't just the day boy's rather angelic faces that threw me, it was also their hair. Every single one of them had their hair cut quite short on top, and very short on the back and sides, whilst mine was just long all over. And as the teacher let his Bunsen burner rip, by way of introduction, I was starting to feel like I was the star of the *Sesame Street* song, 'One of These things is not like the others'.

"My name is Dr Oxley," said the gentleman behind the flame, "Welcome to set one science. Where, as well as being the most advanced class in your year, you're also the luckiest. Because, you get to do very exciting experiments, like this!" He put his hands under the desk and produced a large bubble, that seemed to be filled with a shimmering blue gas. "Observe!" He guided the bubble closer to the flame and just as it was about to touch, he moved his body away to the full length of his arms and ka-boom! The bubble exploded, in a huge yellow flash, right in front of us. "Welcome to set one," he smiled.

I think, in his eagerness to impress, Dr Oxley, could have possibly got a bit carried away with the size of his bubble. It wasn't that his shirt had actually caught fire, it had just had its buttons completely blasted off. Once he became aware of this, he signalled to one of the boys to take the class, while he changed. I couldn't believe that he would have actually brought a change of shirt to school with him. Back in the Doo, we were lucky if the teachers changed their shirts once a fortnight.

The boy who took over seemed to know Dr Oxley already, and by the looks of things, he was no stranger to everyone else. In fact, the majority of the class burst into applause as he strode to the front.

"You showed them Ruskies, didn't you Charles?" shouted one boy.

"Five nothing is not a rout; it's an annihilation!" beamed another.

The boy stood at the front and soaked up the clean-cut adulation. When he did speak, I couldn't get over how little his voice was. Not that it seemed to bother anyone. "I guess advanced calculus isn't all that popular on the other side of the Iron Curtain," he said matter of factly. Later on, the boy next to me explained that Charles was the captain of the Australian Mathematics Olympiad team, and he had literally just got off the plane, after defeating the Russian team in Helsinki.

Even though it sounded a bit nerdy, I couldn't help but be impressed. I was bursting to get up to the boarding house after school and dial 0176, the reverse the charges number, on the red phone. Mum and Dad would be over the moon, to know *I* was in the same class, as the Australian Maths captain, especially as the class was graded on our scholarship examinations. I thought that the school was just being nice, when they said I narrowly missed out on a full scholarship, but it seems like they were telling the truth. Mind you, it didn't actually make the class any easier. I was trying to absorb as much as I could, but shit I was a long way behind.

Funny thing was, when I did call Mum and Dad to tell them about Charles, and the explosion, and Dr Oxley having three shirts in his office, I completely forgot. All I remembered was how much I missed them, and my desert home. I just stood, emptying my eyes on the red phone's battered mouthpiece, as steam from the shower block tumbled into the damp corridor. We must have been on the phone for at least an hour, and just before the receiver at the other end did finally click, I was sure I got a whiff of the eucalyptus that used to fill the back yard, as white cockatoos sat in the gum trees, biting off leaves and getting high on the smell.

11 LIGHTNING DOES STRIKE TWICE

The mood in the line for the mini bus was weird. Really weird. Everyone should have been overjoyed. At worst, we were getting out of the depressing dormitories of Jodhpur House for three and a half hours, and at best, we were about to be surrounded by a room full of St Henrietta's girls, and they were supposed to be hot. Yet, everyone boarded that bus with a solemn purposefulness, almost as if they had been drafted off to a war. This was in stark contrast to the shenanagins that went on while we were getting ready.

The collective expectation, of possibly 'cracking on,' was electric. The dorm was buzzing with descriptions of what each of us was looking for in a chick, what our plan of attack would be, and where we would try and take them, if we got a bite. Which, considering none of us had even been to a girl's school, let alone St Henrietta's, was pretty optimistic. George, was attempting to memorise the five Fs out loud but he only ever got as far as 'Find them' and 'Fwor,' which strictly speaking, meant he was trying to remember Maurice's six Fs.

I couldn't help but feel a little sorry for Maurice. This would probably be the first, of many, empty journeys for him. Not that he could let anyone know though. In fact, I think it was his decision to place one of his centrefolds on his bed, and attempt to kiss it on the mouth while humping his pillow, that raised the hormonal fervour from eight boys ready to mate with a goat, to eight boys who would seriously consider going the tonk with a chunk of Sky-Lab's burnt out hull. Harry Lappin *claimed* that his tiny piece of astronomical history was genuine but I thought Sky-Lab went down over Meekatharra, which was about a thousand ks from Harry's place. Danny Gethem got so excited, he didn't know whether to lie down or get up, so he just did sit-ups for 40 minutes.

Optimism was rife that Saturday afternoon. Even Winston had taken the precaution of blowing his whole weeks worth of pocket money on a canister of breath freshener — and it sure was in hot demand. Bloody thing was empty by four o'clock, and the social didn't start till seven. Mind you, if anyone did have bad breath, you sure wouldn't have been able to smell it, cos every one in the entire house, bar Maurice and I, had been given Brut 33 for Christmas, and for most of them, that meant the special Talc, Splash On and Soap on a Rope commemorative pack, and shit didn't it show. Honestly, by the time we left to get on the mini-bus, the walls in the dorm had been stripped back to the undercoat.

As the bus pulled up on the grassy oval next to the hall the social was in, we were boarded by the girl school's equivalent of Mr Shrapnel. Her posh English accent seemed a little out of place, in the painting smock of a brown robe, she was wearing.

"Now boys. I won't bore you with a long sermon. I know you're all as eager to meet the girls as they are to meet you. I just ask you, to keep one or two rules in mind, please. Swearing or vulgarities, will not, be tolerated. Dancing, of a lewd nature, will, not, be tolerated and lastly we insist that you keep your hands and your lips, to yourself. Remember boys. Petting — no matter how trivial — is the work of the devil."

Suddenly, a large thunder clap ripped through the bus. Everyone thought it was hilarious, but I wasn't *trying* to be funny, I just couldn't help it. The Joans had given us Chico Rolls for lunch again. Thankfully by the time we actually got into the hall, the DJ had already cranked up *The Eagle Rock,* and I could empty my bagpipes without anyone knowing, well, so long as I kept moving around. I tell ya, it's lucky there wasn't a smoke machine, because if there was, I reckon I would have been leaving a vapour trail all over the place.

I must have been well into the last phase of deflation, when I went to get a plastic cup for the punch, and almost grabbed a hand, that was attached to the most sophisticated and foxy looking girl I had ever seen. It wasn't just her amazing dress, that was made out of four different colours and textures of denim, nor her earings that were perspex triangles with lightning bolts painted on them. It was her face. She looked like a cross between Veronica Chrystal and Raquel Welch.

I certainly wasn't going to wait for a roo shooter in a Monaro to whisk this one away from me. "Where did you get them grose, I mean grouse earings from?" I inquired. The girl kept staring at the dance-floor. "Are you waiting for someone special?" I asked a little louder. She didn't respond at all, so I thought I better go around to other ear and ask in that one. "Gee the music's loud isn't it? I mean don't get me wrong, I love 'The Eagle Rock,' but that DJ sure has a *loud* sound system…" I think I would have rabbited on forever, getting closer and closer to her ear, until eventually I was shouting into the side of her head. But she walked off before I had a chance.

I felt very alone in that crowded room, and for a moment, I thought about taking refuge on a plastic chair, and watching the room swirl around me, but my Dad always said 'people who give up, might as well dig a hole and jump into the ground now.' I never really understood exactly what he meant by that, but I knew the gist of it was to keep fighting on. And then I had a brainwave. I estimated that as my drink of punch was almost empty and we had both filled up at around the same time, hers must almost be empty as well. So I made a beeline for the punch bowl and moments later buzzed around looking for my queen, with two full pots of honey. I found her, almost directly opposite where we had been standing.

"Excuse me," I said trying to sound suave, "I, took the liberty, of getting you, a punch."

The girl turned and looked right at me, well, at my shoulder, "Can't you take a hint?" she said, before turning back to her intense study of *The Hucklebuck*.

"Yeah of course I can but... can *you*?" I smiled.

"What?" she said, looking at my eyes for the first time. I could hear Dad's voice saying, 'Well played son, well played.'

"I think you're the most attractive girl I've ever seen. Admittedly, I haven't seen that many, cos I grew up in the desert, but you sure are the most gorgeous girl at this social." I think I even shocked myself with that little outburst. I must have taken the Veronica Chrystal thing harder than I had realised. Anyway, she looked at me as if to say 'Der Fred,' and I was about to launch into my last ditch effort to get her on the dance-floor, when the laughing breath of Rhys Carlisle started prodding me in the back of the neck.

"So *you* reckon she's pretty spunky, do you Bogan?" I spun 'round, to find a jeering Carlisle pressing into my face. "What a pity that (a) she thinks you're a disgusting, ugly, puny, oily, zitty, smelly, little bog and (b) she's my girlfriend." Normally, I had something funny to say in *any* situation, but I kinda realized, that there are occasionally times in life when jokes are powerless. In the end, I think I said, "It couldn't have happened to two nicer people." Well, five minutes *after* they had moved onto the dance floor.

The morning after the social, I was a little hesitant to leave the safety of my slumber. Not counting Dencorub raids by older boys, sleep was the one time when you could retreat into a place that wasn't Jodhpur House. The small slot between the wake up bell, and a house master actually appearing in person to say, "Wake up," was spent savouring every square centimetre, of sleep's blanket. Mind you, that particular morning was a little different, because my nose was the size of my elbow.

After Carlisle's humiliation, I had decided to sit the rest of the evening out, in the plastic- chaired hinterland. And it was from there, that I saw Maurice, surrounded by a flock of chubby girls with imperfect faces hidden under tonnes of make-up, who squawked uncontrollably at his impressive collection of dance steps and various different claps. You know, the high soft clap, the low loud clap and the behind the head continental double clap. The way these girls were treating Maurice, you'd think he was Gene Simmons. Honestly, every time he shimmied, they'd wet themselves. But credit where credit's due; his mimed rendition of Madonna's *Holiday,* was superb. If you squinted, you really would have thought it was her, especially when Maurice lifted up his jumper to show off his belly button. I didn't really fancy any of the girls he was dancing with, in truth they were probably the girls at the social I fancied the least. But when Maurice waved me over to join them during the YMCA, I thought, 'Why not?' after all, the plastic chair was making my back sweaty and it *was* Maurice's favourite song.

I don't know *what* I thought I was going to do, if Carlisle's girlfriend had said "yes" to dancing. I didn't have any cool steps. I just kind of shifted my weight from one foot to the other, occasionally shook my shoulders vigorously, and tried to blend in with everybody else. Which wasn't all that difficult, especially as Maurice's groupies were much better screamers than strutters. They didn't dance any better than they applied make-up. It's odd that I say 'strut,' because up until that moment, I had never really bothered to think about dancing, and its particular bits and pieces.

But as each new song accompanied by its beat, found its way onto the dance-floor, I discovered that I really had *quite a few opinions* about dancing and what's more, the *moves* to back them up. Little did I know, all that time watching stupid disco film clips on *Countdown* while I waited for news about Kiss and ACDC, would actually come in so handy. By the time the Boney M Medley was on, I *was* Rasputin, the dance-floor was my *Rivers of Babylon* and everyone down our end of the room knew it. Especially Maurice, he was loving my new-found funkiness and making loud whooping noises, as he mirrored my steps and bopped around me.

For the first five or six songs, I was really hoping Carlisle's girlfriend would notice me and reconsider being my dancing partner, but after about 40 minutes, I wasn't even looking for her. All I was concerned about, was dancing myself into a frenzy, and it felt great. It was just as this had occurred to me, that the strobe light came on, and I became aware of two lightning bolts, swaying in space next to me. I'd know those lightning bolts anywhere; they had been seared into my very being. It was her. She was dancing next to me. I couldn't help myself and started to shake my booty in her direction. I mean, I know she was Carlisle's girlfriend, and he would kill me; but she was gorgeous. And just as the male Red Back Spider knows he will be eaten by his mate and still goes in for a peck, I too was driven by nature, albeit, painted on perspex triangles.

The incredible bit, was the longer she danced next to me, the closer her steps came to mine. In fact, at one stage we were about 30 centimetres apart, but then the strobe's flickering *bleach* ended, her eyes adjusted, she screeched, "Oh SHIT! It's the Bogan!" and ran off dry retching.

I tried not to let her latest dose of rejection bother me, but it did. My steps started to miss beats, my wrist twists became less frequent, and just as that enormous spider from the dormitory started ripping open my chest to lay eggs in my lungs, Rhys Carlisle, mid-way through doing the worm, came sliding across the dance-floor and collected me like a bowling pin. I attempted to incorporate my brief spell in the air into my routine, but unfortunately my useless bogan brain wasn't able to come up with anything, in the quarter of a second or so before I landed nose first on the ripple sole of Carlisle's brown desert boot.

The St Henrietta's housemistress was quite sure I had broken it, "It can't have swelled up that much and not broken something," she kept saying, as she clamped the bridge of my nose shut, with plastic salad tongs. By the time I got back to Perth Grammar, the Matron had been notified, and she had taken the precaution of calling out Dr Castleton — the school's official GP and board member. Dr Castleton obviously wasn't too thrilled about being dragged away from his black tie dinner, and it took him a matter of seconds to grunt, prod and disappear.

The Matron, was without a doubt, the kindest person I had met at boarding school. When she asked me questions, I felt like she honestly wanted to know the answers, and wasn't just saying things to uphold silly school traditions. She said I must have been enjoying the dancing so much, that my body had manufactured something called endorphins and they were the reason I wasn't really feeling any pain. I was going to tell her I had read all about endorphins, but I never like to butt in when people are talking about their work stuff, and I didn't want to seem like a know-it-all. She also told me that the doctor had said, that although it probably should have been, my nose *wasn't* broken, just badly bruised. Then, she gave me a chocolate and sent me back to the boarding house. I couldn't help but feel better after seeing her. She reminded me of my Mum, except Mum was twice her age and size.

As I stood in line at the pre-breakfast roll call, I was doing everything in my power to attract as little attention as I could. I didn't say a word, or look at anything other than the floor and the pulsating red beacon that lay between it and me. But despite my best efforts, everyone wanted to know whether it was broken, how much it hurt, and where on earth I learnt to dance like that. Everyone was fascinated, except Mr Shrapnel. He was uncharacteristically late. Something that Carlisle was keen to capitalise on, "Well if you think his dancing was good, you should have heard the lines the Bogan, was using on my girlfriend. They were about as smooth, as his zitty face." The room fell silent, apart from the odd nervous chuckle, while I deliberated if I should reply or not.

"You can't blame a bloke for trying... But... But I sure wouldn't have, if I'd known she was *your* girlfriend," I said finally, knowing that even the meanest bulldog, will relent, when offered its opponents neck. But Carlisle was no bulldog.

"Briggs, if I were as ugly as you, the only thing I'd try it on with would be a fly-blown sheep. I mean look at you. You've got oily hair down past your shoulders. Your chin's covered in bum fluff. And you wear *scoops*. You're a freak."

"Yeah, you're probably right." I said, half believing him.

As I stared at my plate of beans, I felt like a tiny, insignificant, worthless, ant with a huge honker, peering over the edge of an enormous orange dam. Everywhere I looked, I saw things that were foreign to me; the uniforms, the cooks, the cooks hats, the huge toasters, the polished jarrah floors. I didn't belong in all this. I belonged in a creek bed, with nothing more than my wits, my scoops and my thongs. Maurice's soothing voice patted me on the shoulder, "I hope you know, *everyone*, thinks he's a fucking prick."

"It doesn't really matter what they think. He's right. I *am* a freak. I don't belong here." I managed to stammer, before leaving the steaming bean banquet and heading out into the cold morning air. Even the bloody air was against me. The thought of trundling down to form class, for a solid hour's recital of Gilbert and Sullivan, made me go limp. So I quietly snuck down to the stairs, that were really a ladder, and within 10 minutes I was sitting next to the beautiful Swan River.

Even with a million jellyfish rushing around inside it, its surface was as smooth as my bedroom window at home. Home. How wonderful it would be to be back in the Doo. I could almost picture Mum and Dad sitting either side of me, as we tucked into a plate of Mum's home made chips. But of course, I wouldn't actually be seeing them in the foreseeable future, and even if I did, it wouldn't be like it was. Everything would have changed. Three relatively simple words. Flesh and Blood. That's what Dad said, "You're not our, flesh and blood."

I thought it extremely cruel that the river could lay there that still, while my entire body, shook out each tear. Bill's Billabong would never do that to me. But Bill's Billabong wasn't here. Only *I* was. A little boy with a big red nose and nothing to hold onto. I was starting to get *hysterical,* when I saw a bright light, shining from beneath the water a couple of metres from where I was standing. "Kimba!" I screamed. "Kimba, you've come to save me!" I yelped with delight, as I ran faster than a big red kangaroo into the water. I was so ecstatic I didn't even think about my school uniform and new leather shoes. Kimba had come to rescue me, and I was so eager to see him that by the time I reached down to pick him up, I was completely drenched. Which is why, it was kinda good that it *wasn't* Kimba, but in fact an old chrome VW hubcap; Kimba probably wouldn't have recognised me. Looking into the dull reflection, I hardly recognised myself. I had always worn my hair as it grew, sort of forwards over my face. But my journey through the jellyfish had pushed my hair back and flattened it down, and the scratchy image I saw looking back at me didn't have any of the stagnant bum fluff that grew on my chin.

By the time I reached the top of the stairs, I was convinced that I *had* seen Kimba, and he had left the hubcap to help me, and it did. Cos *after* I snuck back into the house, and borrowed Danny Gethem's shaving cream and bic disposable razor, I had an idea.

12 tHE FIRSt CUt IS tHE DEEPESt

The first time she brushed past my knee, I thought she just must have made an honest miscalculation. I mean, she was on her feet all day and constantly sniffing the fumes from the shampoo and conditioner. But after the second brush, third rub, and fourth slide, I kinda realized she was deliberately placing her fanny on my knee, as often as she could. She wasn't an ugly lady — a little bit fat — but she wasn't a bush pig, and she was a good five or so years older than me.

Maybe she was itchy? I thought. Or, maybe she didn't *like* having to finish off her boss's work, while he went and got some afternoon tea, and she was taking it out on my leg. At least she wasn't taking it out on my haircut, I thought.

I must admit, I was quite surprised how easily I had been talked into a short back and sides. Every time Mum had ever *suggested* I have any length cut off, I told her the story of Samson and Delilah, and she would let me just get a trim. So the hairdresser, Giovanni, wasn't too shocked when I said it had been three years since I'd had any *length* taken off. He was nice, and listened very intently to my plight. I told him, that I didn't want to feel like a dingo at a pedigree dog show anymore. He had six enormous cabinets full of trophies to prove what he could do with a pair of scissors. So when he said, "Listen my friend, your hair, I fixa for you, and you looka a million bucks." I had no reason to doubt him, and Dad had always told me to consult experts, whenever I could.

Mind you, I got a *little* worried, when he handed me over to his young assistant to finish off the back and side bits. Maybe I was just being hyper-sensitive, but I swear, she spent about two seconds on the back, and two hours grinding my knee, as she perfected the fringe to within a micrometre. I guess she must have been really proud of that fringe, because as she did the final snip, the muscles in her face appeared to break dance and her eyes rolled back in her head.

By the time she did, finally lift herself off and unveil her handywork, my leg had gone to sleep. And so had my brain. I mean, I'd been watching *during* the haircut, but I don't think I had actually taken it all in. It was only now, with my new do staring me in the face, and the old *Doo do* scattered all over the floor, that I suddenly realised what I had done. I had changed tribes and committed to Perth Grammar. I looked like a *totally* different person. For a start, you could see my forehead, and no one had seen that in years. And with all the length taken away from the front, my jaw and cheekbones really stood out. In fact they were so symmetrical and defined, I almost looked like a girl. There's no way any one in the Doo would be seen dead with me looking like this.

I don't know if it was this scary realization, or the blood flowing back to my worn out leg, or a combination of both, but I started to feel very claustrophobic, and quickly paid my five bucks before heading out into the shopping mall's fresh air. I thought I should probably get back to school pretty quickly. Especially, as I didn't actually have permission to leave the grounds. But as I slid down the modest banister outside Lenny's surf store, I came across a smell so *viscous* you could lick it, a wave of deliciously scented ecstasy engulfed me, tossed me around, and playfully lowered me to the ground. It didn't take long to discover where this airborne ambrosia was coming from, because a group of about eight JLC day girls, enchanted in each other's gossip, came trickling around the corner.

I tried not to stare, but I was as powerless as an Aborigine who's had the bone pointed at them. Each girl had skin that was as mesmerising as ochre at sunset, and their own irresistible scent that could *only* have come from that now distant luxury; *individual bathing*. When they did look up at me, it took all my strength to avert my eyes, well my face at least. The curious thing, was they must have known I had just had my haircut, cos each one of them was staring at me. And not just staring but *gawking,* like no one had ever gawked at me before. It really made me feel self-conscious, like they were all thinking, 'Oh, look at that boy, who does he think he is, trying to look like one of us.' Mind you, it wasn't like they were staring in a stern way, in fact, the only part of their face they were moving, was their lips and they were kind of pushing them forwards and outwards. After our paths had actually crossed, I stood still, swaying in their collective perfume. If I could, I would have stayed until the morning wake up bell, swimming in their smell, like a spinifex bush washing in a cyclone.

I *had* intended heading straight back to Jodhpur House. But Claremont was full of all sorts of different shops, with all manner of shop windows, and after my experience with the day girls, I felt like a cockatoo that had sniffed too much eucalyptus and was flying around with a bunch of twenty-eight parrots, trying not to get busted as an imposter. I must have stood in front of every one of those shop windows, taking in every aspect of my new reflection that I could.

Eventually, one of the girls from the group walked past me again, and asked me if I'd like to go and have a milkshake with her. I decided that I must have just been feeling paranoid, and did actually look like a local. And though it was nice to feel like I fitted into my new environment, I couldn't help but feel like a traitor who had betrayed his own kind.

I'm not sure *who* exactly it was that told me, it could have actually been our next door neighbour Charlie Crabbe. Anyway, someone told me just before I left, that if I wanted to impress women, I had to be like Steve McQueen and not *say* much, not *do* much, and most of all, always pull an expression that suggested a cattle tick *might* be biting me on the shoulder blade. Well, it may just have been me, but this piece of advice seemed a little out of place as we sat in the pristine surroundings of Bar Ferrari.

The girl looked up from her straw and did that thing with her lips again, "My name is Samantha Carrington-Browne but everyone calls me Sammi," she said, in an accent I hadn't actually heard before. It was *Australian* but only just. She looked at me, her lips jutting out so far they looked like they would burst. I knew I wasn't supposed to *talk,* but I had to, otherwise she might think I was a mute.

"My name's... Stephen Briggs and my friends call me..." what did they call me? Lately, the nicest thing anyone had said was, 'Zit Faced Bogan.' God, this was turning into an awfully long pause, it would have to be good, think, think, Charlie Crabbe, do much, say much, "Ticks..." I looked like a kangaroo in a shooter's spotlight, "Ticks........y, everyone calls me, Ticksy". I studied her face, as my words washed across it. "Steve McQueen was bitten by a tick, when he was young... I mean I was... bitten by a sponge... I mean a tick. Hence Ticksy."

"Oh, Ticksy, that sort of rhymes with Sammi, I like that. I like that very much Ticksy. I can tell you and I, are going to get on famously," she said as she touched the sleeve of my jumper. Even though I was wearing a layer of wool and a layer of cotton, that touch sent so much electricity through my body, I didn't dare sip on my milkshake, for fear of it electrocuting me.

"So Ticksy" she said, leaning in towards me. "Where do you live?"

"Oh, about 1537 kilometres away," I said matter of factly.

"You're funny," she said, as she roared with laughter.

"No, it's not a joke, I come from a place called Paraburdoo. It's *way* up north," I beamed, hoping if I were enthusiastic enough, the Doo would sound *exotic*. Sammi gave just the hint of a frown, which was almost reassuring; I was starting to think everything except her lips, was made out of wax.

"So where do you stay down here?"

"Oh at Perth Grammar, in the boarding house."

Her entire face burst into movement, "You're a boarder!!! I... I... didn't realise that! Look, I don't want to appear rude... but... but I'm late for my cello lesson... Mum's picking me up. See you...Tacky er... Ticksy."

I actually ended up missing dinner, and getting back to the house just in time for evening prep. Luckily no one seemed to have noticed that I'd been gone. I should have got back way before dinner, but I wanted to try and wear my new hair do in and get used to it, before anyone I knew saw it. As I sat down in my chair, a tubby little hand tugged on my sleeve, "Excuse me mate, you can't sit there it's saved for Stephen Briggs," said a stern faced Winston.

"Yeah, I know," I replied, expecting to see recognition ignite in his smile.

"Well, you're going to have to move, aren't ya?" he stated a little more emphatically. I tilted my head, so any shadow that could have been blotting his view would be eliminated, but he still stared through me blankly.

"Winston, I appreciate your loyalty, but it's me. Stephen. I've had a haircut." Winston pushed his face into a squint, hovered for a moment, and burst out with a laugh that sounded like an adolescent deer with whooping cough.

"Oh, ya got me a gooden then, didn't ya. Shit a brick! You look... like a totally different bloke! I mean, I never would have said anything *before,* but now you've had a trim, I s'pose I can. Ya used to look like *Cousin It* off the *Addam's Family,* but now, now you look like John Bloody Travolta."

That was one of the few times I could remember someone neutral, ie, not Mum or Dad, paying me a compliment, and for the first time in my life, I found myself fishing for another one, "Oh steady on Winston, it's only a haircut. I mean, I hardly look like a film star."

"Oh yes you do. You're the bloody spitting image of him," Winston bleated. "Hey, look at bloody, John Travolta over here!"

I thought it was kind of ironic that the theme song from Travolta's big film, *Saturday Night Fever,* was called *Stayin Alive.* Cos, I was just growing accustomed to this supposed new resemblance, when a spit ball, fired from the pen of Rhys Carlisle, slammed into my top lip with enough force to make me sneeze. This was followed by a high-pitched, puckered-lips kissing sound and though that didn't have all that much to do with Staying Alive, what followed certainly did.

I had just got off the red phone to Mum and Dad, and was wiping away the regulation tears that came with every call to them, when I was grabbed from behind, by at least three sets of hands. Some kind of sack, which I think was a pillowcase, was pulled over my head and I was dragged down the hall, through the deserted shower block, and into the far cubicle that didn't flush properly, and consequently always had small reminders of its last client bobbing in it like fishing floats. I suppose I could have tried to scream, but somehow, I realised that screaming would have been against the rules, and so I just kicked and tried to punch as much as I could.

Unfortunately, they had a very good grip and my struggling didn't really bear any fruit, but I did get a couple of foot stomps in. It didn't take long for my suspicions about who was behind this kidnapping to be proven. The unmistakable high-pitched pucker that Carlisle was doing earlier in prep, came ripping through my execution-style hood, like a bronze cast of a fingerprint tearing through tissue paper. In fact, the puckered kiss noise was so loud that it even drowned out the sound of the toilet flushing. Mind you, it did become more distant as the flushing came closer.

At the point where the smell was so overpowering, it was actually starting spot fires on the little hairs in my nostrils, I knew what was coming, so I began hyperventilating, just like this guy from India I read about in *Reader's Digest*. Somehow, he could hold his breath underwater for 13 minutes. I had problems with 40 seconds. It probably would have been easier if they'd taken the hood off, but they didn't. In fact, it was pulled even tighter as the cold stinky water raced firstly across my nose, then lips, then cheeks and finally the back of my neck. After the first few plunges, they lifted the hood just a little, so they could expose my lips and take turns lining them up with what they referred to, as the floating cigars. "Get the cigar. Get the cigar," they enthused. There wasn't really much I could do, I just had to keep my mouth closed and take dunk after dunk, while Carlisle whispered, "Who's a pretty boy? Bogans, don't like pretty boys. Can't go home now, cos everyone will hate you. Just like they do here. Don't they pretty boy?"

I thought that I would die in that toilet, and Mr Shrapnel would find my head floating in the bowl with a human cigar smudged all over it, in the morning. But a strange thing happened that night. Well, firstly I was amazed that I didn't scream. Up until that point in my life, I would do anything to avoid a confrontation, and the obvious thing to do would have been to scream. Especially as my freshly washed, conditioned and cut hair, was taking a bath in a spot where every boy in the house had emptied their bowels at least once. But somewhere deep inside me I heard a voice saying, almost in Gilbert and Sullivan style, 'Don't give the fucker the satisfaction of hearing you scream. Don't give the fucker the satisfaction of hearing you scream.' And you know what? It worked. Well, at least it appeared to. After my 16th dunny bowl baptism, I was dragged out of the water, turned around, and my hood removed. As you could imagine, I sucked in, enough air, to fill an entire party's worth of balloons. I think the water must have affected my sense of smell, it certainly affected my sight, cos there's no way I would have inhaled at all, if I'd known Carlisle's bare arse was a couple of millimetres from my face. I did stop however, when I felt his rectal sphincter starting to open and close on my nose.

I say it was Carlisle's, but I suppose I will never be certain, but he was the only one who hated me enough to do something as low as that. After a couple of humiliating minutes of nasal anus kissing, the hood was pulled down over my head again and I was thrown back in, for one last flushing. As the toilet's waterfall slowed to a trickle, I became aware that there were no longer any arms holding me, other than my own. I gently eased myself out of the ceramic helmet, pulled the pillowcase off, put the toilet lid down, turned the latch to engaged and curled up into a ball.

For a little while, I actually seriously contemplated committing suicide by taking a run up, and diving into the s bend. But then I remembered my new do, and reasoned that no one at home would recognise me when they came to pay their respects as I lay in my coffin. Which made me regret getting my hair cut even more. I mean, I would have to wait at least six months before I could top myself. But after a little while, I couldn't help but crack a small smile; partly because I was imagining my grave stone and an epitaph saying 'Tragically taken by an S bend at the tender age of 12' but mostly because I had not buckled and given Carlisle what he wanted.

It sure felt bloody weird, tiptoeing back into the dorm though. I mean, I'm pretty sure none of the other guys would have been Carlisle's accomplices, cos they all seemed to like me well enough, but there wasn't any way to be sure. I couldn't help but sleep with one eye scanning for any would be Brutuses.

By the morning, I had made up my mind that my days at Perth Grammar were numbered. I'd taken everything into account, and could see no other possible option than to go home. So after school, I was going to ring Mum and Dad and tell them that I appreciated they were trying to do what was best for me by sending me to boarding school, but either they pulled me out or I was going to do something so bad I would be expelled. I knew that they would require examples, so I ended up settling for setting fire to the chapel's pipe organ and chopping down the goal posts on the oval. So that was that. At the end of school that day, I would make the call and deliver the ultimatum.

It's funny how one decision can change your whole outlook. Not even being the last dorm into the Arctic showers could wipe the smile off my face that morning. I found myself singing and shaking disco style, as I leapt into an extra sudsy soaping of Imperial Leather. I was feeling so elated, that I actually took the shower *next* to Rhys Carlisle, to stick it up him that I hadn't screamed.

You know, it's absolutely amazing, but Carlisle honestly seemed afraid of me that morning. Every time I looked in his direction, he turned, almost cowered away into the corner. In fact, the same corner he always showered in. Come to think of it, I couldn't remember Carlisle ever showering in another shower. He always went to the one in the far corner, and he always leant up against the wall with his back to everyone. I guess I'd just put it down to part of being cool, or him not being a morning person, like my Mum. But as I stood there in the frozen jet stream next to him, I sniffed something, and it wasn't his arse. I smelt fear. I smelt vulnerability. And I smelt an opportunity to get something back. After all, I was going to be on the first plane back to Paraburdoo that afternoon.

As Carlisle had his back to everyone, he didn't see me casually lean over and knock his shampoo and conditioner off the shelf, a metre or so, towards the middle of the room. He definitely heard them bounce and spun his head around, to find me smiling right at him, "I see your shampoo and conditioner have fallen onto the floor," I beamed, in a voice that came from the balls of my feet, "I wonder how they got down there? I guess they must have been, *flushed* there, by the power of the water."

Carlisle creased his lips, like a Taipan does before milking, "Pick them up, pretty boy," he said menacingly.

"Sorry, no can do, dunny brush. Has anyone ever told you, your hair looks just like a dunny brush?" I stated simply, shocking myself in the process.

"Well, you'd know all about dunny brushes, wouldn't you? Now if you know what's good for you, pick the fucking things up. Now!"

I looked right into his eyes, hummed a few bars of *Leaving on a jet plane,* and whispered, "I know that you and your mates were wanking each other off while you were watching me drown. And I know that the reason you call everyone else a poof, is because secretly you're one yourself." My whisper, suddenly transforming into a hate fuelled funnel, "So go and fuck your mother's armpit, you pathetic, little, fucking cunt!!!" I really stunned myself with that one, but didn't it feel good? I didn't even know I knew the c word; I guess I must have heard it while I was sleeping, and soaked it up subconsciously.

However I managed to know it, it sure got the message across. Carlisle was dumbstruck, and I could sense that he was terrified again. But why? I mean he was still bigger than me, and a better fighter and he was more popular. What could he possibly be scared of? And *then,* I saw it. Only for a split second, cos he had taken the precaution of having an emergency plan, for just such an occasion, that consisted of a strategically placed flannel, that covered his genitals and made him look like one of those Amazonian Indians. He had planned it so well that it should have worked perfectly. But he wasn't counting on the first piece of luck I had received since leaving the Doo, arriving precisely as he took his first step towards the bottles. Because, just as he took that step, Mr Shrapnel opened the door to tell us to hurry up, and in doing so, let a sufficiently large enough gust of wind in, to blow Carlisle's cover, literally. For a moment in time, Carlisle's penis sat for the world to see. Well, what there was of it. In fact, the whole lock, stock and barrel including scrotum, was nothing more than a tiny, protruding flap of skin. A Proboscis.

My grin was stuck on with super glue that morning. I had Carlisle stuck between a corner and a damp flannel. And now I had discovered his secret, I had the pleasure of exhausting the millions of possible ways in which I could exploit it. I found myself constantly scrunching up my face with delight. All of a sudden, Perth Grammar wasn't such a bad place. I was still leaving, but I thought maybe I should delay my departure in order to reclaim my ounce, I mean, *gram,* of flesh.

13 SURVIVAL OF THE FASTEST

I had no idea that athletics trials were on that morning. I thought it would just be a normal phys ed class, which usually consisted of a lecture about hygiene, some push-ups, chin-ups and a 1500 metre run. I hated the run cos I always came last and felt like a real loser. No matter how angry I got with them, my lungs just wouldn't work over long distances. So when Mr Trembath, our moustached teacher from the east end, said year eight would be joining year nine for sprint trials, I breathed a huge sigh of relief. I wouldn't say I was relaxed though. Vomiting up my breakfast behind the cricket nets proved beyond reasonable doubt, that definitely wasn't the case. In fact, as the race came closer, I felt that familiar winch in my stomach winding my guts in. Mind you, it didn't take the smile off my face.

I suppose when Mr Trembath said that the two years would be trialed together, I thought that we would race in our form classes. I was secretly thinking, well at least in a class of 20, I should be able to finish in the first eight. But when every boy in year eight was instructed to stand across the width of the bottom oval, and get on their marks, my plans were dashed, and frankly I was totally overwhelmed.

I mean, I know I was the fastest in the Doo, but this was like running against three whole Doos. I was still adjusting to this as Mr Trembath fired the starting pistol and the line leapt off without me, "Run Briggs, you bloomin slow coach," yelled an unimpressed Mr Trembath. I looked down at my frozen legs and then up, at what appeared to be an army of yellow soldier ants sprinting away from me. I tried to move, but it was no good. It was like that recurring dream I had been having since I was three, where I was marooned in Wittenoom Gorge, had lost my voice, and a blue asbestos cloud was rolling in around me. Maybe I was having a delayed reaction to the multiple dunny flush, I thought consolingly, and then it struck me. What if *Carlisle* beat me? I mean, I didn't mind the fact that he was bigger than me, or more popular in the dorm, but the thought of him being faster than me made my toes grip so hard, huge chunks of grass and earth flew behind me, as my legs catapulted me after him. The group had already moved through about 35 of the 100 metres and even though I was really flying, it wasn't enough to catch the first three boys. If I'd had another 20 metres I may have got close, but I didn't.

Mind you, it was certainly enough to have been able to catch my breath, and be waiting patiently for Carlisle to cross the line. As his languidly loping legs came dawdling across the finish line, I couldn't help but enquire, "What happened…Proboscis?"

He looked at me, with hardened white spit coating his lips, "What did you call me?"

I smiled at him, offering my brow in a polite informative arch, "Why… Proboscis of course. That's what everyone calls you, or will."

In truth, I never really meant that. I was just trying to intimidate him. I had no more intention of spreading around that name, than I had belief that anyone would start using it. But it sure was satisfying watching Carlisle try and work out (a) what it meant and (b) how damaging it could be to him, as he tried to get his breath back.

Mr Trembath came rushing over, "Briggs! You've been holding out on me, Briggs! That was bloomin' unbelievable! You gave them almost half the bloomin' course, and you reeled them in, like they were toddlers on leashes. Marvellous stuff! You're a credit to your house!" A credit to my house? I thought that was going a bit far.

The year nines raced next, and they sure looked fast, especially the guy with the buzz cut who won by about five metres.

"Ok Briggs, let's see what you can do against some real competition," challenged Mr Trembath. "Right, listen up everyone, I want the first 30 place getters from both races up on the line."

I know these guys were only a year older, but just looking at the differences between their bodies and mine, sure made the concepts of puberty and the next 12 months, seem very daunting indeed. I mean that much physical growth would have to hurt.

Anyway, I'm not really sure why, but as we got into the set position I was engulfed by the desire to win, the need to win. I was totally consumed, like a praying mantis stalking a ladybird. So much so, that my right leg jerked forward involuntarily and Mr Trembath had to fire the gun twice, for a false start. My jerky leg must have been quite conspicuous, cos the guy with the buzz cut, who won the year nine race, moved right along the line to come and start next to me. His bulging calf muscle rubbed against mine as Mr Trembath yelled, "On your marks... Set..." The sound of the pistol shot grabbed me by the neck, flinging me out onto the grass and into the race. It was quite honestly the fastest start I had ever had, which I was quite pleased about, until I realised the year nine guy was right next to me. Then something *really* weird happened. I became aware that the other kids in my year were crowding along the sidelines chanting, "Go Briggsy! Go Briggsy! Go Briggsy!" The lump in my throat told me I couldn't let them down, and in my mind, I pictured myself riding a fully customised Drag-Star bicycle along a desolate stretch of Pilbara bitumen. We were halfway and still neck and neck, when I pushed the gear lever forward into top, and left the year nine guy almost running on the spot. I was so *convinced* I was a Drag-Star, that after I screamed across the line I went into a sideways power skid in order to stop. The year nine boy was the first to rush up and congratulate me, closely followed by the rest of my year and Mr Trembath, "That! Was something else Briggs! Something else! Can't wait to see you at the Inters! You're a natural, a bleeding natural!"

After all the cheering and singlet patting had died down, everyone headed back towards the change rooms. Not feeling too comfortable being in the centre of the mass of yellow singlets, I started edging toward the periphery. And it was *as* I made my way to the safety of the edge, that Rhys Carlisle made the biggest tactical blunder of his life. He took a swipe at me, in front of everyone. Well, verbally at least. "You're still a fucking smelly bog but, aren't ya, pretty boy?" The entire group pricked up their ears, and were visibly agitated as they turned to hear my reply.

And it was brutal, "Oh get fucked, Proboscis. You're not exactly a vase of roses yourself. In case you haven't noticed, your eyes are too close together, you've got an underbite and your nose is bigger than your penis and scrotum put together. Which wouldn't be hard, because all you've got down there is a teeny Proboscis." And then I did it. I simply held up my index finger, curled it up into itself and said "Proboscis, Proboscis, Bosci, Bosci, Bosci!" And just like a gospel congregation picks up on the words of the preacher, the year eight boys surrounding me launched into a series of giggles and loud choruses of "Proboscis, Proboscis, Bosci, Bosci, Bosci!"I actually felt sorry for him after that... well... for about a second.

The combination of being the year eight/year nine sprinting champion, and the creator of the Proboscis craze, which swept through the entire school faster, and more virulently, than that year's outbreak of Bejing Flu, gained me a kind of celebrity status. Everyone wanted to say hello, share a joke, or just hang out. Which, I suppose was better than being hated, but only just. The anxiety was horrendous. Every day was like a survival course in mental orienteering-*slash*-name remembering. It was like walking into an elevator of strangers, and everyone knowing who you were and wanting to talk to you. Only this was a thousand times worse, because the elevator was five acres wide, and only ended at the school gates.

Mind you, this sensation did die down pretty quickly, which was probably due to a combination of me getting used to it, and people losing interest after they were distracted, firstly by the Coca Cola yo-yo craze, and then the subsequent Donkey-Kong delirium. It's funny, but once I got over the initial anxiety about people liking me and accepted that it looked like it was here to stay, my time at Perth Grammar actually became more bearable. I still asked Mum and Dad if I could come home — to which they replied, "Of course you can son... For the term break."

14 EXCUSE ME WHILE I JIF THE SKY

As the Mac Robertson Miller Airlines Fokker F27 swung into its final little turn, before the pilot completely opened up and made the plane want to fly so much it shook, I couldn't help but smile so hard I thought my lips would split. There's nothing I love better in the world, than take off. Sometimes, I imagine jumping out of my seat and sprinting up the aisle screaming, "Up baby up!" just as the big metal wings turn into feathers. I guess I was also smiling because my first term at Perth Grammar was over, and I had survived it. But I suppose the major reason for my elation was I had escaped, well for the next two weeks at least. Two whole weeks in Paraburdoo — what a treat! No stupid bells. No stupid uniform. No stupid food, and best of all, no stupid group chats after lights out about wanking. Honestly, it had got to the point where not a night went by without someone crapping on about their new technique for flogging the log, as everyone called it.

I'm sure half the time they were making it up. Harry Lappin actually tried to tell us that the best way to have, what he referred to as an organism, was to do away with your hand completely and rely instead on two pillows, some glad wrap, a liberal dose of baby oil and a handful of beach sand for some added, 'fwiction.' I mean really, what a huge effort. And for what? From the couple of tries I'd had at the conventional method, I just couldn't see what everyone was so fascinated about. Actually the night before school broke up, I decided as everyone had gone to sleep, to give it a good go and see what all this orgasm business was about. But to no avail. No matter how much I squeezed it nothing happened, except a fair bit of discomfort and a nasty cramp in the palm of my hand.

Normally I'm not too worried by turbulence; in fact, I quite like it, cos it's natures way of letting us know that we don't belong in the sky. We're just guests. Anyway, apart from the old lady sitting next to me kissing these funny beads, what seemed like a million times, I didn't realise it was bumpy until the hostess asked me if I wanted lunch. She really took me by surprise, cos I was daydreaming about swimming in Bill's Billabong. I looked up, and there she was, and gee was she pretty. In fact, she was one of the prettiest girls I had ever seen. And try as I might,

I couldn't help but stare at her and her bosoms, as they pushed against her low cut uniform like the dinghys down at the yacht club tug at their moorings on the incoming tide.

I knew that it was rude to stare, and so did she, but it didn't seem to bother her, cos when she caught me doing it, she just smiled. Maybe I was getting a bit carried away with myself, but she seemed to take an extra long time to place the tray down on my little table. Well, that is to say she *was* taking an extra long time, until Mother Nature hurried her up with an air pocket. I guess if I'm honest, I had actually been wondering what it would feel like to have her pressed up against me, but I sure hadn't counted on having her on my lap, and her boozies in my face, that instant.

To her credit, she was very professional and managed to save most of the meal. Everything except the jelly desert. That ended up all over my uniform. Mind you, I can't say I didn't like being escorted up to the galley by her, and wiped softly clean with a sponge. I liked it so much, that as she handed me a fresh jelly and gestured towards my seat, I couldn't help myself and blurted out, "I hope one day, I marry someone as beautiful and caring as you are." She delicately showed me her perfect teeth and replied, "I think a boy like you will have his pick of hundreds of beautiful, caring girls. You'd better get back to your seat, there's more turbulence forecast." And then as I turned to go, she stroked my head and said, "Lot's of girls… If you were five years older, I'd go for you myself." Well, that was all it took, to give me the biggest stiffy of my life, and my first, in an aeroplane. Luckily, I had the tray holding the

161

jelly to place in front of my, '*Roll up Roll up have a look in the big Top*' shorts.

But, what was my biggest ally on the way back to the seat, turned into my archenemy once I was in it. She was right about the turbulence; it was pretty bumpy and pretty constant. Which would have been fine, if I didn't have a red jelly shaped like a boob giggling about all over the place every time I went to slice it with a spoon. The thing is, I couldn't have scooped it even if it wasn't bumpy, I was totally transfixed by it, and silly as the idea was, I couldn't help but think that's what the gorgeous hostie's would look like. I couldn't get it out of my mind, and when she came around offering a pot of tea, it looked like either her boozies would bounce out of her blouse, or my stiffy would spear straight through my shorts, so I had to do something. Despite the turbulence, and recent after lights-out failures, something, possibly the same thing that tells coral that it's time to spawn, led me to that incredibly sexy and spacious place that is, the aeroplane toilet.

Once inside, and spurred on by the security of the 'occupied' *ding*, I was relentless with myself. My shorts were off in seconds. My tail stuck out like an air traffic control tower, and I grabbed it with all my might, squeezing and kneading it, like it was play dough that I was squashing into the shape of a sausage. All the time, gripped by the *hope* of leaving the toilet five years older, so I could marry the hostie.

I reckon I could have stayed in there until way after landing and probably right into the next sector. Cos no matter how much I squeezed, squashed and almost mangled it, nothing was happening. It was getting to the point where I would be spending two weeks in the Doo with a hamburger patty for a tail. That was, until my old friend turbulence gave me a little nudge, well quite a big nudge actually, big enough to make the old lady with the beads scream loud enough for me to hear her, and big enough to make the plane bounce up and down quite dramatically. In fact, the bounce was so big that I momentarily lost my grasp, and by the time I'd managed a decent grip again, my hand had travelled almost to the top where the traffic controllers sit.

And that was all it took. One clenched move *forwards,* did what 10 000 *stationary* clenches never could. I felt like God had wrapped my soul in a 'Wet One,' grabbed it from both sides and given it a good buff, before he took the life energy he would normally put into 1000 elephants and slammed it into my tingling teeth. I didn't just climb the mountain and shake hands with Jehovah, I redesigned his kitchen as well.

But strangely enough, even though this was the most intense experience I'd ever had, I still managed to jump up onto the bench, and watch myself spurt the white stuff onto the mirror, "All this fuss over some high pressure Jif," I thought. For a moment, I actually considered not cleaning it up. You know, spraying my territory like a tiger, but then I realised the person who would probably have to clean it up would be my hostie. As I walked back to my seat I felt every inch a man, in a pair of size 14 boy's shorts, and couldn't help but wonder if 'The Mile High Club,' handed out Associate Memberships.

When I stepped off the plane's staircase and onto the sticky asphalt of the Paraburdoo Airport, the Pilbara wind came rushing up to me with so much zeal, it almost knocked me over. I wondered if it would be able to tell that I was now a man, as it giggled and gurgled around me, chasing itself across my skin. Mum and Dad weren't far behind it, as they wrapped me up in their arms and carried me over the airstrip's edge, and placed me down onto the gravel. "There yer go lad. Get that genuine Paraburdoo gravel under yer. Don't get nought of that at boarding school do yer?"

Mum couldn't keep her hands off my head; "Will you look at his face. He looks so, different, without that mane of hair. He's right handsome, i'nt he?" I was kind of surprised to find myself almost ducking and weaving around Mum's complimenting hands, which struck me as pretty odd, cos I had spent many a night in Jodhpur House yearning for just that.

The nine kilometre car trip back to town was the most peaceful thing I'd done in the last three months. I mean, I did a hell of a lot of talking, telling Mum and Dad all about Mr Shrapnel and Proboscis, and me getting him a gooden. I left out the bit about him giving me a royal flush. And even though I hardly drew breath for the entire journey, as I sat nestled in the Torana's glorious back seat, I didn't feel anything but the serenity of the Pilbara, stroking my belly and playfully blowing air onto it, like grown ups do with a baby.

As we mounted the driveway and got out of the car, I was delighted to find Charlie Crabbe and his Mrs waiting for me, with a wrapped present, well at least I thought it was a present. I couldn't be *totally* sure, because it was wrapped in newspaper. Don't get me wrong, I was extremely pleased to see them. It's just, I never really realized, how much of them there was, and indeed how rich they were on the nose, and lastly, what an uncanny resemblance they bore to Homo erectus, the early hominid we had just been studying in biology. Charlie's wife said something to me that I didn't catch a word of.

Anyway, fortunately I could understand her gestures, and took the box wrapped in newspaper from her hand, thanking her very much as I did so. I think that the land must have known that they were on the nose, cos suddenly a gorgeous cloud of ochre dust came skipping through the ghost gums, and ushered their stink away. I always loved smells, and this would have to be one of my favourites, and I guess I must have been totally distracted by it, because apparently I just stood there gazing off, as Charlie and Mrs Erectus stood staring at me. Dad's hand on my shoulder snapped me out of it, "Well, go on lad. Open it up then."

I smiled, with dust coating my tongue, "Oh, I'm so sorry Charlie, I must be suffering from a little jet lag," I said politely, well at least the words came out of my mouth, the accent sounded like it came out of the House of Lords. Not that I was trying to sound posh, it's just compared to their voices, mine sounded like it was wrapped in velvet rice paper.

Within seconds, the delicate *Paraburdoo Times* wrapping surrendered to my fingers, and left me holding a three pack of Mars Bars.

"Oh wow," I said, "Mars Bars. Three of them. Thank you so much. I doubt they'll... they'll make it till dinner time."

"Damn right they won't," said Charlie, as he grabbed them from my hands, proceeded to rip them open, drool like a deranged dingo, and divvy them up between himself, his Mrs and me. After two gulps, their's had completely disappeared, followed by Charlie and his Mrs straight after.

I'm not, totally sure how the subject of my adoption came up so quickly. I think we had just had a beautiful Shepherd's Pie and were waiting for the custard to set so we could have it with the apple crumble, when Dad said, "Bet yer missed yer Mum's cookin'?"

"Oh yes," I replied, with love spread all over my face, "No one cooks like Mum. The Joans at school try, but they don't come close."

"That's right love, they can try but yer've only got one Mum," Mum added, as she carried the steaming pudding in with mittened hands.

I wanted to agree, but technically speaking that would be lying, so I just smiled and said, "Yeah, I suppose."

"Yer 'aven't found another Mum down there 'ave yer?" Dad said jokingly through his motley collection of teeth. I had never noticed how many were missing before.

"Have one of those cooks taken my place?" Mum chimed, keen to play along.

"No, of course not." I said emphatically, eager to stop talking and start eating. But then I spoke without really bothering to think, "It's just, I suppose, as Mum didn't *actually* give birth to me. There must be someone that did, and that would mean I have two mothers."

I really didn't mean to hurt anyone's feelings, especially not Mum's. But I did more than that. She literally went green, staggered out of the room and spewed up in the sink. Dad looked up from his still steaming pudding, "Thank you. I 'adn't actually told 'er I told yer yet, 'ad I?"

Mum was inconsolable. I tried to reassure her, and told her how much I loved her, and that she would always be my Mum, but she actually seemed to get worse rather than better. Normally if Mum was upset about something, she would start off *really* upset and via a number of jokes and tissues, would be better about half an hour later. But not this time. She actually appeared to lose weight, right in front of my eyes. She just kept saying over and over, "I can't believe yer told him, and now he thinks I'm not 'is mother... Not 'is mother." After about an hour of trying to patch things up, Dad suggested, while Mum was in the loo, that I should leave them alone to discuss it. Which kind of upset me, but also excited me just a little as well, cos it meant that it was time for a night ride.

I half expected my Drag-Star to be covered in red-back cobwebs, but I should have known my Dad better than that. Even under the beer shed's flickering, fluorescent light, it looked like it had just come off the production line. Dad hadn't only oiled it, he'd polished it as well, the sissy bar looked like it was made of left over solid silver from Prince Charles and Lady Di's commemorative goblets. And the best thing, was sitting on it. Even though I'd grown a reasonable amount while I was away, and had twice the amount of underarm hair to prove it, the groove my bum had worn in the seat still fitted so well, that as soon as I slotted into it, I became an extension of the bike.

I'm not sure if those 1500 metre runs had anything to do with it or not, but shit my legs had some pedal power in them. As I rolled down to the bottom of the drive, I suddenly realised, *this* was where Darren Bignell had called me a choker. Me, a choker. The year 8 and 9 Perth Grammar Sprint champion, a choker. The thought of him still living here made me see red. I felt like a cowboy that had a score to settle; the small matter of pissing up my nose. My legs dug into the pedals so hard, that I left a large amount of my nobbly back wheel splayed along the bitumen, asking why? I wasn't *really* expecting to bump into him, but it sure felt good to know there was a possibility and to have a purpose, as I cruised around the vague empty streets.

Night brought a whole new palate of smells to the Doo. The strongest of which was the eucalypts. They had spent the entire day holding in every minute droplet of sweat as they fried under the Pilbara sunlamp, terrified in the knowledge that if one drop fell, an osmotic gradient would form and every particle of H_2O they contained would be ripped out of them in seconds. Leaving nothing but a dead wood target for God to throw lightning bolts at. The thing was, by the night-time they were so exhausted they had to drink. And in order to drink, they had to make room for the water and so they would allow tiny beads of concentrated sweat to escape through their leaves, and that would paint the night sky with amazing colours of scent.

By the end of that particular thought, I had to pull over and catch my breath. Other than the smell, I had never known any of that. So I must have learnt it while I was away. Maybe Perth Grammar wasn't such a bad place after all?

Shit I loved my Drag-Star. I reckoned that if I added all the journeys I had taken on it, end to end, I would have travelled to the Saucepan and back, maybe even the Big Dipper. The guys at school reckon *Close Encounters of the Third Kind* was good, but they *should* have seen this. The sky was like an enormous cobweb, that stretched from one horizon to the next, which was teeming with zillions of spiders, sporting luminous abdomens. Wow! It was incredible and enormous. So enormous, that you couldn't help but feel a little insignificant. Insignificant like a tiny ant. A tiny ant that doesn't know where it came from, and a tiny ant that has hurt its Mummy. I slipped the gear lever forward into third, in the hope that if I went fast enough, the tears would dry before they had a chance make it onto my cheeks.

I don't know what Dad said, but by the time he brought me my cup of coffee in the morning before he went off to work, he had managed to smooth things over with Mum. He didn't make her totally better, in truth, I don't know if she ever recovered totally, but she was all smiles when I got up — lured out of my bed, by the smell of the bacon sandwich she was making for me.

I always seem to borrow mannerisms and that morning was no different because as I tucked into the sandwich, I pulled the face of Kimba devouring a malteser.

169

"Mum, I'm truly wuly sorry," I whimpered, fresh tears blanketing the runs of my last ones, "Of course you're my Mummy. And I love you, more than anything in the whole world." She pulled me up onto her knee, placed her hand, in that spot behind my head that only she knows, and stroked my tears away. I looked up at her, my smile cracking the dried up tear beds on my top lip, "Well, next to your bacon sandwiches…" We just sat there laughing and sobbing until our bodies fell into each other's rhythms and calmed us both down.

Mum was *surprisingly* calm, as she reached up into the top cupboard where Dad kept his important papers. She actually seemed to have a glow about her, that I had only ever seen on the faces of Born Again Christians, on one of their sidewalk crusades.

"I thought, yer adoption papers, were somewhere up here, but I can't seem to find 'em. I think, maybe, we might have lost 'em, when we came out on the ship." It was weird to hear Mum say adoption so matter of factly. Now that the subject had been raised, I wanted to jump right into it, but I could see that the flood waters in Mum's eyes had only recently receded.

"Was it fun, coming out on the ship Mum?" I asked genuinely.

"Yer father and I loved it, but *you* hated it. Yer bum, was red from the moment we left dock in Portsmouth, till we tied up in Melbourne and for some time after. Yer had terrible nappy rash and nothing would fix it. Give yer yer due though. Only complained, for first few days and then yer just got on with it."

"Did it take very long to get here?"

"Oh, about six weeks. Went pretty quick though, once we made it 'round tip of Africa." Mum stared into the bedspread. "Funnily enough, that's how old yer were, when we got yer. Just six weeks. Yer were, so tiny."

"Well, I'm not that big now. Certainly not big enough to not need my Mum."

"Son, I'm sorry I b'aved like I did last night. Yer father and I had been meaning to tell yer for years, but the time never seemed right. And I guess when I found out he'd told you, I went into shock. Don't take this the wrong way. I'm glad you know now, but it does hurt me to think, that yer have another mother and it hurts me to think that she didn't want yer."

"But why didn't she want me, Mum? I mean I'm glad she didn't, cos if she did, I wouldn't have met you but why didn't she want me?"

"All we were told, was yer Mum was very young when she had you. I think she might have been about 16 and she couldn't keep yer, because she was still at school and unmarried."

"Did they say anything else?"

"No love, that's all they told uz."

"What about my biological father?"

"I'm sorry son, I can't help yer."

Normally the Torana's front seat is a place where I feel nurtured and content, but as we rolled back down the drive and headed up to the shops, it struck me as a very sterile place, in which I felt very little. As a matter of fact, the shops were the last place I felt like going. I really wanted to be heading out to Bill's Billabong, where

I could be alone with my thoughts, and the only thing I would be able to hear would be dragonflies beating their wings as they skimmed along the water looking for bugs. I was glad that Mum had decided to talk to me but I guessed that this was, what my form master referred to, as a hollow victory. Because really, all Mum's words had done, was whet my appetite. Almost as if she had prepared an exquisite bacon sandwich in front of me and then fed it to Charlie Crabbe's dog, Scamp.

There were so many things I wanted to know… and it seemed, I wasn't the only one. We hadn't even made it *into* the shops, before friends of Mums were mobbing us and firing off millions of questions about boarding school, and what living in the big city was really like. I'm sure to anyone watching on, it must have looked like a scene from The Elephant Man. There I was, reluctantly cast in the spotlight, whilst wide-eyed middle-aged women with varying degrees of facial hair, clambered around me soaking it all up. I shouldn't be too mean cos they were all *genuinely* interested. It's just, having a bunch of women, that looked uncannily like the entire cast of The Wombles, peering into my life and telling me how much I had *changed* and was different to their kids, didn't really make me feel any better. And in fact, when one of them said, "Oh, but your Stephen was always different," I couldn't help myself and burst into tears. I told them it was homesickness and that I missed them all, which in turn, made *them* all burst into tears, but the truth was, I was crying because I didn't miss them at all. I didn't miss anyone, cos I didn't feel like I belonged anywhere. I certainly didn't belong at boarding school with Gilbert and bloody Sullivan. I didn't belong in the Doo, where the men looked like pregnant women and the women seemed to be racing to see who could plait their beard first, and I didn't even belong at home, because Mum and Dad weren't my real parents.

For the slipperiest of moments, I honestly believed that I actually belonged in the roots of the gum tree with Kimba. I imagined myself with a withered tap root tangled around my heart and my decaying body laid out just as I had planned it, in undulating folds, that gave Kimba a special dirt track to scamper on and nuzzle up to.

When the two weeks were up, and it was time to take the Torana up to the airport so I could catch the big silver bird back to boarding school, I found myself feeling less anxious about the adoption business. In fact, I had almost forgotten all about it. It wasn't really that I'd accepted it, more that I just wasn't thinking about it. I had spent a lot of time with Mum and Dad and their friends, and was actually quite liking the fact that I was different. Mind you, I did have to pre-empt any discussion about the big smoke with, "Well, you know I'd much rather be here, where I belong with the people I know and grew up with. You know, real people." This would usually diffuse any possibility of tension, and allow me to regain, unrestricted access, into the Passion and Hobby sections, of Mum and Dad's friend's minds. I did find my pronunciation of words became quite sloppy though, I showered less often and the occasional bit of knuckle-walking came in quite handy.

But overall my holiday was quite revitalising. I accepted the fact that your average Doo resident was a little backward when it came to tolerance, hygiene, knowledge of the outside world and dental floss. But they had done me just fine for 12 years, and I knew there was a good chance each subsequent visit would nurture me less and less, so I jumped into their mud pool and rubbed up against them, like a hippo occasionally does with a herd of elephants.

15 EMBRACING THE TRIBE

When it was finally my turn to take off my towel and enter the jet stream, the water was still lukewarm, but it didn't take long to turn Arctic and leach out all the positivity the Doo had allowed me to muster. I just *didn't* want to be back at Perth Grammar. I had only been away for two weeks, but 14 days walking, eating and sleeping in the *same jacket* I had worn for my most of my life was a pretty long time, and though it may not have been a particularly fashionable one, it sure was comfortable.

Coming back to Jodhpur House was certainly different this time though, compared to when I first arrived there. I suppose I just put it down to knowing what I was in for, but it was more than that. I guess what I'm saying is, I was popular. It's amazing how you can forget something like that after two weeks in the desert. It certainly took me by surprise when Harry Lappin and Danny Gethem stopped me in the corridor to tell me about their holidays, in a way which suggested they wanted me to approve of what they had got up to.

In fact, it was just after their blow-by-blow description of two weeks worth of mulesing and tailing that Maurice came bounding along the carpet, with a grin so big, it didn't seem to have a beginning or end.

"Have I got some news for you guys!" He beamed, eager for a response that didn't come, "Well, aren't you going to ask me what it is?" Danny, Harry and I looked at each other. At first I thought that they weren't really interested, but then it suddenly struck me; they were waiting to see if I was.

"What is it Maurice?" I said eventually, followed by a chorus of agreeing mmms.

"Oh come on, this is *huge* news, you're going to have to be more excited than that. You'll never guess what it is. Never!" he shrieked as he played ping-pong with our eyes. "Well, come on, take a guess," he implored.

"The Village People have released an album called Fluorescent Purple Flannel, and on it they do a cover of the song, *The only man who could ever reach me was the son of a preacher man*?" I offered teasingly.

"I wish. No it's huge news, but it's *not* about The Village People."

"They've caught the bloke who keeps shitting on the toilet seat," barked Danny, with the conviction of someone who had just filled in the blank, on Blankety Blanks.

"Well if they have, they've got the wrong man... No that's not it."

"The weather buweau is fow... fow... say there'll be heavy wains on the wheat belt this year?" Harry muttered, in a monotone.

"I don't know, but I know someone who'll be able to tell us, first hand."

"Yeah, who's that?" the most animated Harry that I'd ever seen, gushed at the prospect of suggesting the clue that provided the answer.

"Oh, just, Rhys Carlisle. His parents have decided that they need him to help out with the building company, so they've taken him out of school. Isn't it *fabulous*? I can't wait to choreograph a new dance routine to celebrate his departure. I think I'll call it, You're wrong. You're gone. Fuck off Carlisle!"

My initial response to the news about Carlisle, was absolute delight. I couldn't believe my luck. Half of my dread about returning to Perth Grammar lay squarely at Carlisle's feet, and the thought of not having to see him, let alone interact with him, made me want to hug everyone in sight. But later that day, when I overheard a group of boys saying that the real reason Carlisle wasn't coming back was because he couldn't hack the nickname Proboscis, I couldn't help but feel a little guilty.

I mean, I know he was really nasty to me, and if anyone was allowed to hate him, it would be me but I couldn't help but feel like I had squashed his only chance of getting a decent education. After all, that was the reason our parents paid the school all that money, so we'd have a better chance in life. What chance was Carlisle going to have in a tiny country town? I was really starting to take this to heart, and it must have shown, because that night Winston actually went without seconds, so he could follow me out of the dining hall and walk with me back to the house.

"Hey! Wait up Stephen," he bleated. I slowed up, so he wouldn't have to run too far to catch up. He was self-conscious enough about his walk as it was, and running exaggerated it heaps.

"I just wanted, to make sure you're ok," he puffed as he finally caught up.

"Me? Oh I'm fine," I bluffed.

"It's just, you've, been acting kinda strange, since you got back from your holiday. I hope you had a good time at home?"

"Good time? It was great. They're a little backward up there, but gee they're good people. None of the falseness you sometimes see down here," I claimed, with about as much sincerity as someone has, when they're trying to pass off a glossy block mounted poster of a dolphin, as art.

"Oh great," nodded an unconvinced Winston, "So, everything's ok then. I mean, I'm sure it is, but you know sometimes, if things aren't, it's good to talk... to somebody."

For a split second, I actually contemplated telling Winston the whole sorry tale that was my existence, but something — possibly the memory of his spurs clinking into our first house roll call — stopped me. Instead, I wrinkled up my mouth and gave the other issue a go, "It's just… Well, I've… Well I've kind of, been feeling bad, about Carlisle not coming back. I know that must sound pretty stupid, especially after all that shit he did to me, but I kind of feel, responsible, for stuffing up his education."

"Oh Stephen, don't go worrying yourself about that fucking wanker. The *only* person he can blame for not being here is himself, and he can do that twice. First, for being such a prick in the first place, and second for being so fucking gutless that he didn't come back, in the second place."

I could certainly fault Winston's grammar, but I couldn't fault his logic, nor the heart-felt passion, with which he delivered it. But it wasn't until later that week, when I was watching a wildlife documentary in Biology about 'The Serengeti' in Africa, that Winston's words really made sense. Admittedly, they had to come out of David Attenborough's mouth. The film was basically about the survival of the fittest and how in the Serengeti, if you're not fit, you get eaten. It sounds strange but I actually felt comforted, by the sight of lions pigging out on gazelles and zebras. Cos that's what happened with Carlisle. We were both living on the same savannah and he tried to kill me, so I had to fight back. Nothing could be more natural.

Rhys Carlisle leaving Jodhpur House was probably the best thing that could have ever happened to me. Well, for my confidence at least. Without him in the dorm to undermine me, the rest of the term went pretty quickly. In first term, a single day would take an eternity to pass, but in second term, a whole week would fly faster than a stroke from Mr Shrapnel's cane. Not that I felt totally content. I still felt like a gecko trying to pass as a poodle. But at some time during that term, I decided to stop fighting Perth Grammar, and just go with it.

As much as it distressed me to acknowledge it, the Doo was now something from my past. Admittedly I could still visit, but that was all. The majority of my life was happening in Perth and it was pointless resisting. Don't get me wrong, I still loved talking to Mum and Dad on the phone, and I still missed them, it's just that I suppose in my heart of hearts, I knew that I would never really *be* like them, or *think* like them again. They lived in one world and I lived in another, and the longer I stayed away from them, the stranger their world would appear. You know, I don't even remember where I was, when I realised that. I think it may have been during one of Halfhide's sermons that never went anywhere. Anyway, the weird thing was, once I had realised I *was* on my own, and Mum and Dad *wouldn't* understand, I felt the calmest I had in ages.

The other amazing thing about that revelation was how quickly its calming nature disappeared. Admittedly, for a couple of days I walked around in a cloak made from the finest serenity. But I still had four and two third years ahead of me, pretending that I was from a tribe where the norm was German cars, classical music and conversation during dinner. When actually, I came from a tribe of savages, that were happiest getting around in thongs, listening to beer cans open and whose only form of noise during eating was open-mouthed chewing and the occasional burp.

I guess I just learnt to blend in. In fact, I must have got quite good at it, because somewhere along the line, I started hanging out with dayboys, and not just *any* dayboys; the cool ones. I think they liked me because I made them laugh. I had never realised I could be funny at school in the Doo, but ever since coming up with the concept of Bosci, I had become obsessed with ideas and concepts. Concepts that did things within the rules, but were so stupid they made fun of them.

I guess the clincher with the dayboys, was when I turned up to Human Biology with a four litre Yalumba wine cask filled with urine. I was going to bring a two litre Coke bottle, but I thought a cask was much more civilised.

Our teacher, Dr Oxley, had been telling us for ages, that on Wednesday the 17th, we would be required to provide at least 10 millilitres of 'ureen', as he pronounced it, for some, "complicated and conclusive experimentation." From the amount of times he mentioned it, I gathered that it was quite important. But I couldn't work out if his constant references were just to remind us, or if he was worried that actually donating 'ureen' was going to be too much for some of the suck-hole students to cope with. Cos after all, it *was* set one and these constant reminders might somehow desensitise and prepare them for the big day. The big day incidentally, that I labelled 'Big Wee Wednesday.'

So anyway, I decided that rather than have the sucks embarrassed when they have to wee in a jar, I'd just bring four litres along and give everyone a squirt, like Mum does with the Fruity Lexia at a barbie. Maybe whistling tea for two, as I poured, was possibly taking it a little bit too far. Dr Oxley certainly thought so, and gave me a severe verbal reprimand to prove it.

"An attempt at humour on that level, is insulting to your own intelligence," he chastised. "There is nothing funny, about wee wee."

I know *he* didn't think so, but shit I sure did. I had to squeeze my testicles between my thighs, to stop myself laughing in his face. I mean, in all the time leading up to this, 'complicated and conclusive experimentation,' he had always referred to the liquid as 'ureen' but now, I had managed to get him to say 'wee wee,' and it was bloody hilarious. Somehow, I did manage to control myself, while I was close enough to smell the Earl Grey on his breath at least. But as soon as I returned to my seat up the back, and saw how the other back seat badarses were biting their tongues, I completely lost it and decided to go in for the kill.

"Excuse me sir," I said piously, "I'm terribly sorry for disrupting your experiment, it's just that a moment ago you used a term to describe 'ureen' I had never heard before. I believe it was a double barrelled name."

Dr Oxley looked up over the top of his glasses. "Are you taking the piss, Briggs?"

"No sir, I *brought* it," I said innocently, "It's growing up in the desert sir. I've never heard that term to describe the yellow stuff. We only ever used 'pee,' 'wiss' and 'piss' when referring to the amber nectar. Sorry sir, it doesn't matter. I'm stealing valuable time from the complicated and conclusive experimentation," I conceded.

A righteous Dr Oxley strode up to me, like a noble outlaw does to the hangman.

"Wee wee, Briggs. Wee wee. Wee…Wee." If he hadn't gone for the melodramatic ending, I think he would have just about escaped being humiliated, but that rather bold choice, had catastrophic repercussions. You see, there was a Flu going around at the time, and just about the whole year had it. And as Dr Oxley stiffened up to drag out the second 'Wee', I laughed so *hard,* that a large green goober vaulted out of my nose and tumbled through the air with a twist, before landing safely on Dr Oxley's chin.

I didn't *usually* sit down the back; it was just on that day. I was one of the last ones into class, and the only seat left was on the last bench, right in the middle of the dayboys with the yellowy hair. Come to think of it, those three guys always sat down the back and didn't look like your average set one mathematics Olympiad types at all. They were much cooler than that. I'm not sure if their hair colour came out of a bottle or the sea, but it would be pretty safe to say that they were from the tribe, 'Surfy' which, under ordinary circumstances, would have been a real worry because I, albeit unintentionally, belonged to the tribe 'Bogan,' and generally speaking, either tribe only liked the other one stuffed on their mantelpiece.

Thank God for the Perth Grammar uniform; it enabled me to move around all the different groups, like the Mods, Punks, Goths, Rockabillys, Bogans and anyone else who managed to find at least one other like-minded kid to form a cause with. It's a bit sad really, but the major way these groups separated themselves from the others was with their clothes. Obviously not during school time, but in their own time, they would don elaborate costumes and trinkets that shouted to the world in glaring neon, that they were attached, tribally speaking. I suppose it was all about rebelling against the way everything at school and indeed in society, was so structured. But what they didn't realise, was by getting together with a bunch of people and all looking and behaving the same, they were just making another structure or mini-society, with just as many strict and silly rules.

The Punks used their Mohawks to say they didn't believe in conventional stuff like hairstyles. The Mods had a very traditional English haircut, but prided themselves on their anti-establishment red socks. The Rockabillys used to walk around dressed like extras from an Elvis film, while the Goths were lucky to walk at all; half of them looked too frail to blink their eyes, let alone carry a school bag. Honestly, every time I saw one, I had to fight back the urge to force-feed them with a cheese stick. Lastly, there were the Bogans, who were just plain ugly. In truth there were only two of them (excluding me because I wasn't really practicing) and basically their day consisted of trying to be as uncooperative, rude and mean to as many people as they could possibly bump into. And I do mean bump. So you can see why I didn't want to be associated with them. And anyway, I *liked* to roam from one group to the next, and observe the intricate bits and pieces of each set, just like David Attenborough does with leopards and lions. And that's why I used to say a prayer at chapel each week, thanking the Lord Jesus Christ, for the wonder of the school uniform. Mind you, Jesus never mentioned anything about casuals day.

I didn't even know what one was, until Mr Shrapnel called an extraordinary pocket money hand out on a Tuesday night.

"Right everybody, lets have you in an ordered line, that starts with dorm one and ends with dorm five, and, just to make it interesting, lets have you smallest to tallest. The little guys, can get to go first for a change."

We all milled around in our dressing gowns, glancing at each other's foreheads, as we shuffled into line.

"Now, you will all be receiving, a whopping, three dollars. That's twice as much as your weekly ration, but don't go getting any ideas about spending up big on confectionary. The three dollars, is for charity. You will give it to your form master, first thing tomorrow morning, and in return you will be allowed to wear your casual clothing to school, instead of your uniform."

A cheer went up, unlike any other I had ever heard at Jodhpur House. Who'd have ever thought a bunch of farmers' kids, could get *this* passionate about anything, let alone wearing something different to class. For a second, I almost got carried away with the sheer joy of it all myself, that was of course, until I suddenly realised that I didn't have a thing to wear. Don't get me wrong — my little bedside table wasn't exactly empty, in fact it was overflowing — over flowing — with scoops and muscle shirts. Which was just fine for around the boarding house, but I wouldn't want my new surfie dayboy friends to see me looking like a Bogan. This is what KISS must have felt like, when fans tried to see them without their make-up, I thought to myself consolingly.

Unfortunately, I couldn't come up with any way of getting out of it, and in the half an hour after prep, before lights out, when everyone usually watches tv, I found myself lying on my bed staring up at the ceiling humming 'Beth.' As I lay there, cradled in the arms of my plight, I half expected the big spider to come and try to lay eggs in my chest again. Suddenly, I was surrounded by what sounded like a barber shop quartet. But when I opened my eyes, it was only Maurice.

"*Beth I hear you calling,*" he squeaked in a high pitch opera style, "*But I can't come home right now,*" he continued in a big deep Alabama voice, before slipping into an in-between French approach, "*Me and the boys are playing....*" I wish! What's up Stephen? Why are you humming KISS's saddest song, when you could be watching *The A Team* like everyone else?"

"Because, I'm in a fucked mood, because, I'm fucked." I replied, "Look, I feel pretty stupid saying this but I think if anyone could understand, it would probably be you. And of course I know I can trust you, because you trusted me with your *secret.* "

"What? That I love the nightlife and I've got to boogie?" Maurice interjected light heartedly.

"Mmm," I nodded, "You see, the problem is Maurice, I'm a Bogan. Maybe not on the inside. Well at least, not now that I've been here for a while. But in Paraburdoo everyone's a Bogan, because there's no other option. And so tomorrow, everyone at school is going to see me in my muscle shirt and my scoops, and (a) know my shameful secret, and (b) not want to know me at all. All because, my clothes, were bought in the fucking Doo."

Maurice's bleak expression, mirrored the growing expanse in my gut. It was hopeless.

"If only they'd taken it a step further and made it fancy dress," I moaned, as the pillow came rushing up, to catch my slumping head, "Then going as a Bogan would be funny."

"That's it!" barked Maurice.

"That's what?" I said, without moving.

"Fancy dress! Dressing Fancy! Oh don't worry Cinderella, you shall go to the ball."

Maurice waited until everyone had fallen asleep before giving me the signal. Three quick flashes from his fibre optic lamp told me that operation 'Glass Slipper' was in full swing. Of course, it was his idea to call it that, I didn't even know what it meant. The only thing he would tell me, was that upon the signal, I was to meet him in the housemother's room with my entire wardrobe. To be honest, I was amazed that no one saw us sneaking off, but as luck would have it, we had been served a very gluggy rice pudding that night and everyone was so knackered from trying to digest it, they were almost comatose.

It felt pretty weird hiding in the linen alcove by torchlight, while Maurice fussed over my various items of clothing, not that there were that many, in fact there were only three muscle shirts, two pairs of scoops, a pair of jeans and a formal shirt. But you wouldn't have known that. Maurice had them on the bench, held up to me and then the light, so often and so quickly that it looked like we were surrounded by hundreds of garments. It was quite mesmerising and after about 20 minutes, I was sure that if I'd looked in a mirror, I would have seen a moth in a fluorescent daze, staring back at me.

Not that it wasn't pleasant; in fact, I felt curiously reassured and relaxed, watching Maurice actually working. I suppose that aspect of the Doo would never leave me. He did have me a little worried when he decided to open the housemother's locker with a safety pin, and remove her prized dressmaking scissors. But as he picked them up in his hand, his whole stance visibly changed in front of me. He actually became transformed into a kind of Musketeer. And when I witnessed the confident way in which he sliced them through air and cloth alike, I kind of wished I had more clothes that he could cut up. I'm not sure how long he stayed there tinkering. All I know is, it was pretty close to dawn when he told me to go and get some sleep, while he added the finishing touches.

When I woke up that morning, I found Maurice's creations neatly folded on my bedside table. I looked over to thank him but he had already headed down to the shower block, with his fluorescent flannel. Some of the blokes in the dorm called him the Iceberg, cos he was always the last one out of the water, even when it had been freezing for ages.

"There's nothing more invigorating, than standing under a stream of ice," he'd always lecture. So much so, that kids would always take off the way he said it. Somehow, I don't think they'd have been so eager to take off anything, if they'd known the *real* reason Maurice loved the shower block so much. Not that it bothered me. I mean don't get me wrong, I couldn't really understand why Maurice would want to be a poof, but he wasn't hurting anyone. He was the kindest and funniest kid I had met at Perth Grammar, and he'd just saved my Bogan arse.

As my eyes adjusted to the morning light, I couldn't believe what they were showing me. Honestly, my recently renovated clothes looked like they had come straight out of the window of Barney's Clothing Barn. Maurice's dressmaking genius had transformed my whole wardrobe. Somehow, he had managed to turn my ugly, acid wash, baggy jeans into tight stove-pipe black ones. He'd removed the tiny sleeves from a muscle shirt and replaced them with long ones from my white formal shirt and then used left over acid wash denim as a ruffle down the front. The shirt was straight out of the, *Gold. Always believe in your soul,* Spandau Ballet, film clip. And by removing the money pockets and GT stripes from my Scoops and making the legs flat, instead of curved, he had created swimming trunks that looked like they had once been worn by Tarzan. I felt about as Bogan as Adam Ant.

I couldn't help but be a little self-conscious, as I stood in line for morning roll call. I was sure *someone* would say something. But that's the great thing about boarders; they don't have any eye for *detail*, well, not of a fashion nature. Not one single resident of Jodphur House even batted an eyelid, which was in stark contrast to the sick bay Matron.

I'd been feeling a bit scratchy in the throat during the late night fitting, but didn't mention anything for fear of disturbing the Maestro's flow. But by the end of breakfast, I had what felt like a mature spinifex bush lodged in my throat. As Matron pulled the thermometer out of my mouth, I could almost see it throbbing in her hand.

"No school for you today I'm afraid Stephen," she said softly, as she dabbed at my brow with the yellow, school issue blotting paper. She must have been able to tell that my skin wasn't enjoying it, cos half way through dabbing, she disappeared into her quarters and returned with a box of her own tissues. "That's better isn't it? I keep asking the bursar for softer paper," she uttered almost absent mindedly, as she stared at my forehead, "You know Stephen, you have the longest eye lashes, I've ever seen. They must drive the girls crazy. Have you got a girlfriend yet?" she inquired, in a way that made me feel like, she was someone I'd known half of my life.

"No, not really... Well, not at all," I smirked.

"Well don't worry, it won't be long and you'll have them flocking to you. With eyes like yours..." she giggled, as she led me into the room furthest down the hall.

My temperature was 40 and half that day, and I can't be sure that all of it was because of my throat. I don't know when, or where, it had occurred in the last nine months, but somewhere along the line I had realised that Matron was absolutely gorgeous — what blokes in the Doo call, 'a real root'. Mind you I'd never say that about her; she was far too pretty and nice to talk about like that. I think it could have had something to do with my associate membership of the Mile High Club, or possibly Rhys Carlisle not coming back, or my new clothes and haircut, or maybe a combination of all these. But one thing was for sure, I was alone in sickbay with a big spunk who thought I had gorgeous eyes. What a shame that for the seven days I spent in her care, I was so full of fever I couldn't even string my dressing gown together, let alone a sentence.

When I did *finally* make it out of sickbay, it was Tuesday morning, which meant my first class would be Science with Dr Oxley. He seemed to have forgotten all about Wee Wee Wednesday, which was more than I can say for me and my dayboy friends. We were in real danger of pissing ourselves, every time we entered the Science block.

I guess it wasn't Dr Oxley's fault that he was bald; or at least would be if he didn't comb all of his hair from the back and sides up and over his shiny pate. Our favourite game was coming up with ways to actually measure the length of the greasy pushed over bit. I tried everything, from dropping exam papers next to him and pretending to have a slipped disc so that he would have to pick them up for me, to complex scale models that utilised trigonometry, pipe cleaners and upside down test tubes, to come up with the magic measurement. But to no avail. He was always one step ahead of me, or at least his brylcream was. He must have had a good tub and a half of the stuff on at any one time, and after about six months of trying, I decided to scale down my efforts and concentrate on my studies. Which I must admit, had suffered a little since I started hanging out with the dayboys.

The dry Northerly wind must have approved of my new approach to my books, because no sooner had I had a talk to myself regarding pulling my academic finger out, than the wind came rushing down to reward me.

It started out as a usual September morning. Cold, wet and as far as Dr Oxley was concerned, a day when half a tub of brylcream would be fine. However by first period, an unseasonal northerly, as Dr Oxley put it, had blown everything away, including his usually bullet proof attempt at Do It Yourself stick on hair transplantation. I felt like a hunter that had cornered a blind, paralysed, elephant bull in a paddling pool. Honestly, the Samaritan in me wanted to sit on the bench next to him and constantly spray him with a fine mist of water for the entire lesson. No one could have come close to estimating the *actual* size of the pushed over bit — I mean it was enormous. There was little wonder there was no fire escape in the room — it was obvious that the School Council had appointed Dr Oxley's pushed over bit, to be the escape rope.

I know I said I felt sorry for him, but it didn't stop me from moving in for the kill. I mean, you can't go through life, with a longer length of hair on your head than most people have hose in their garden, and expect to get away with it. Every time Dr Oxley would turn around to write on the white board, I'd delicately whisper, in the voice of an angel, "Rapunzel, Rapunzel, beware the northerly wind." And each time he'd spin around to see who it was, his hair would follow him, in slow motion, as it unfurled all the way down to his belt.

Actually, I could pinpoint my academic slide to one particular weekend. The second designated Boarders Leave Weekend. I expected to spend it, as I spent most of them, lazing in the palatial confines of Jodhpur House, while every dick and their dog went back to the farm, but my day boy friend Matt Rodgerson had other ideas.

"Hey Briggsy, are you going home to see your oldies this weekend?" he asked, as we endured the back leg of the first lap of the 1500 metre PE run.

"I was going to…" I started, as we ducked behind the big ghost gum tree and watched every one else stream past, "But it's too far to go for one weekend."

Rodgo smiled, "Great! Then you're coming to the Irvy with me. It's cool; I already sussed it with my old lady."

16 SWIMMING WITH CARP

As Mrs Rodgerson's Mercedes pulled out of the drive and we cleared the school gates, I was consumed with simultaneous fear and delight. I couldn't believe I was actually *in* a Mercedes, fleeing Jodphur House for the weekend, and going to an Irvy (whatever that was). But just as I started to revel in my new adventure, I remembered that in a few minutes I'd have to step out of the sanctuary of my school uniform, and present Maurice's creations to the world for the first time. Not that I was doubting his abilities, I just hoped that his designs weren't too *extravagant*; all I wanted was to blend in.

I must admit, that car sure did smell good — kinda like a cricket bat that's just been oiled — and it was very smooth on the road. But secretly I suspected that it didn't have as much poke as the Torana. It's weird that I should think of the Doo at that point, cos as we sped up Stirling Highway to Peppermint Grove, it may as well have been in another universe. It and everything in it was completely foreign to this brave new world. Speaking of foreign, the gates at the front of Rodgo's place looked like they once belonged to the Tower of London, but they were nothing compared to the front door. As we approached it, I genuinely thought it was a drawbridge. There's no way something that size, and encrusted with that much metal could be a front door, I thought, and I was kinda right, cos there was a door about the size of four normal doors, cut out of the bottom of it.

It was only as Mrs Rodgerson, who insisted that I should call her Erika, fossicked in her bag for her keys, that I became aware of the waterfalls, on either side of us. They were cascading into two ponds, that were more like lakes and filled with the biggest fish I'd ever seen.

"That's *some* gold fish, Mrs Rodgerson," I said, with an open mouth.

"Oh they're a little *more* interesting than *gold fish,* Stephen. Those are my Two Tone Ikarashi Kohaku Koi; picked them up just outside Niigata in '78. Had to import a hundred of the buggers because half of them died in quarantine. See that one there... with the bulbous orange head? Nursed that one back to health myself; amazing what you can do with a bit of Margaret River Brie. Yes, they're quite captivating, I suppose... the first few times."

195

The first few times? I couldn't understand how anyone could possibly think that, until we stepped inside, then I could see precisely what she was on about. When Rodgo hung his school blazer on the suit of armour that greeted us just inside the door, I knew this house was going to be a bit special, but *nothing* could have prepared me for what lay behind the entrance hall's wall of mirrors. As Mrs Rodgerson gestured me in, I think I was so shocked that I farted. I'd been holding it in, for the entire car journey, as it didn't seem right somehow, to let one go in a Mercedes. But the sight of the rainforest atrium was so beautiful, that my entire body went limp and it slipped out. The room, if you could call it that, had trees right around its perimeter that stretched all the way up to the glass ceiling. Inside the trees, were secluded areas that seemed to be almost carved out of the greenery. Each area contained a different thing, like a swimming pool with spa bath, a library, an enormous chess board, a gymnasium, a Persian rug covered with huge cushions, a hammock and a modest sized amphitheatre. All of these *rooms*, were linked by a pathway of tiny broken tiles, that sat either side of a glass tube filled with fluorescent fish. You literally, walked on water, to get from one room to the next.

I could tell from Mrs Rodgerson's previous tone, that being *too* impressed wasn't exactly the done thing, so I tried not to be too bowled over. Actually my mouth started without me even thinking, "Oh Mrs Rodgerson, it really is beautiful. It must be wonderful to come home, after a busy day, to your own Secret Garden," I said trying to not bite my tongue as it hung out of my head.

"My God! Stephen you're the only person who has ever got it," she gasped, "It *is* my Secret Garden. That was my favourite book when I was a child, and that's what I set out to achieve."

"Well I think you've definitely achieved it," I said, a little chuffed.

"I can't believe someone has finally unravelled my secret. How incredibly perceptive. I must have a Chardonnay to celebrate." With that she swung her hair around, like a silent film star and swanned off, while Rodgo showed me to his room. The rest of the house, which kind of came off the garden bit, was relatively normal, well as normal as an English castle *can* be.

Picking Erika's house theme turned out to be one of the highlights of the weekend, because she was so interested in talking to me about her plans for renovations, that I managed to spend the first couple of hours at Rodgo's Castle in my uniform. Of course, Erika kept insisting that I should go and get changed but whenever she did, I would just ask her to expand on her master plan of incorporating, 'The Lord of the Flies,' her *second* favourite book, into the overall *scheme* of things.

"I really want the kitchen to scream of primal conflict, with just a smattering of puce archaic meltdown," she confided, before making a start on her second glass of white wine. We could have sat there chatting all night, and to be honest I wished we had, but to my genuine surprise, after she had reached the bottom of her fourth glass, Erika jumped to her feet, "Shit! I'm late for Lizzie Carrington-Browne's dinner party. She's unveiling her *new nose* at 7.30 sharp! We will have to reconvene… our think tank… tomorrow."

As her Mercedes snaked up the pebbled drive, she bellowed out the window, "I'm seeing a shit load of rammed earth and a mural of dung beetles wearing crowns!"

"Fuck! I thought we'd never get rid of her," said Rodgo fresh from a catnap. "She fuckin' better not have drunk all the booze," he barked, as he wandered through to the kitchen to check, "Fuckin' bitch… Oh no… false alarm. I found a carton in the spare fridge."

I must admit, I was kinda surprised and a little disappointed, to hear Rodgo talking like that about his Mum. I mean, I could see she was a little eccentric, but she was kind.

"Don't you… like your Mum Rodgo?" I said plainly.

"Oh, she's all right. Drinks too much. Talks too much shit. But she's all right I s'pose."

"So when does your dad get home?"

"He doesn't." My chest deflated, "Oh mate, I'm sorry I didn't realise…"

"No! He's not *dead*. Sometimes I wish he was. He's just banging his secretary. I mean wife. I think he's married her. Or was that the previous one? Fuck, I lose count to be honest. Anyway, enough depressing family shit. We've got people coming around in 10 minutes and then, my friend, we have got an Irvey to go to. Oh and Briggsy, did I mention the quality of girls that go to the Irvey?"

"What, are they all right looking?" I asked with suddenly dry lips.

"All right? All right? Mate, it is *full*, of the best looking girls in town."

"You haven't seen one with lightning bolt earings, have you?" I asked, a little *too* eagerly.

"Stephen, there's lightning bolts, thunder clouds, and fucking tornados if you want them. Better hurry up and get changed." With that, he threw me a beer and I went off to have a shower and make sure I put 'the chapters of Maurice's story,' on in the right order. Apparently, that was absolutely crucial.

The longer I stayed in the shower, the worse my nerves got, and the warmer the can of VB became. I never really thought of myself as a suck-hole but I was trying to work out if Mum and Dad, would *mind* me drinking. I mean, it was ok for Rodgo, because he was a year older than me due to the fact that he started school in France. I certainly didn't want to offend him. I was *almost* 14, and Dad had been giving me shandies since I could remember. In the end, I decided that Mum would have said "no" and Dad would have said "yes". So I skulled half and poured half down the sink. 'Can't be fairer than that,' I thought, as I rushed down the stairs to see Rodgo. I'd decided that the best thing to do, was just walk on in and act as if everything was normal. You know, like I'd spent *everyday* in the Doo, wearing a formal shirt with a denim ruffle.

This plan probably would have come off a little better if I hadn't spent the better part of 40 minutes coming up with it. Cos when I strode purposefully into the kitchen, I was only expecting to see Rodgo, not 15 guys I'd never met. Actually that's not entirely true, I think some of them went to Perth Grammar. But they weren't from our year. A couple were from year nine, and one was from year 10. Rodgo staggered up to greet me.

"Here he is. All right everyone," he enthused, as he picked up a glass and tapped it with his ring. "I'd like you all to meet my new mate … Captain Blackbeard. I mean Stephen Briggs. Just jokes Briggsy… Stephen is a boarder, who's *walked the plank* and escaped from the boarding house. He's a good bloke and if you see him with an empty drink, top him up."

For the first time in my life, my brain stalled. Literally stopped. Maurice, had turned me into a *pirate* on the high seas. Maybe, if I looked in my overnight bag, I'd find that he'd crocheted me a parrot to sit on my shoulder and chirp, "Pieces of eight… Pieces of eight…" I think my subconscious was just doing a check of arteries in my brain, to see if an aneurysm was *any* kind of a possibility, when the kitchen door swung open behind me. Rodgo jumped to his feet.

"Piers! How the fuck are you, man? How was Paris?" The room was suddenly buzzing, with people acknowledging the arrival of Piers (whoever that was).

I turned around, to see a confident smiling bloke, who didn't look too dissimilar to me, especially when he took off his jacket.

"Oh no, not another one!" Rodgo bleated, "What is it with you guys? Is there a fucking pirate convention on or something?" Piers shook his head,

"Just because every shirt you own is a La Coste, Rodgo. This is the hottest new look. Everyone in France is wearing them. Everyone."

"AARRGH You Landlubbers wouldn't understand," I barked in a pirate accent that was so authentic, it took *me* by surprise. I actually had no say in what I was saying — the words just kept buccaneering out.

"See the problem, with people like you is, ya get too many greens. Out on the high seas, the only greens we get, are the scabs off our sores. AARRGH AARRGH. And we got our sores, from the bearded clams, in the snatch atoll, AARRGH AARRGH." As I stood there listening to myself, I couldn't help but find the story a little bit funny and I certainly wasn't the only one. It started with sniggers, but by the time I had drawn my cutlass and started a fight with an imaginary Barney, from Barney's Clothing Barn, to "liberate the good people of Claremont, from the tyranny of La Coste bondage," the room was in hysterics.

Before we left to go to the Irvy, I popped into the entrance hall to use the loo. It could have been the alcohol, the surreal decorator chat, or just a bad case of land legs, but as I stood, surrounded by such unthinkable opulence, peering into the massive wall of mirrors, I had absolutely no idea *who* the guy looking back at me was.

The Irvine Street Yacht club's imposing façade, stood up to greet us, like a limestone cliff. Which is kind of handy, because most of us needed something to hold on to. After my outburst about sores and scurvy, the party erupted into an enormous drinking game, in which everyone had to name something you would find on a pirate ship and if you couldn't, you had to skull a glass of beer. It turns out Dad's shandies had been quite a good call after all, because the beer seemed to effect me less than just about everybody else, so much so, that Rodgo had insisted I skull a glass of Scotch before we left. To which I replied, "Bugger that. AARRGH AARRGH. Gimme two AARRGH." And for the first 20 minutes or so, it looked like my Doo drinking gut was going to handle that as well.

In fact, I had completely forgotten about it, as I stood near the window looking out at the night, as the boats tapped against their pens on the river, and I took large but discreet wafts of Samantha Carrington-Browne's gorgeous scent. At first, I didn't even know it was her; Rodgo just lent down to talk to the back of a long, blonde haired head, "Did Mum make it to yours ok? She was fucking plastered when she left."

"Was she? You couldn't tell at all. She was absolutely... Ticksy! What are you doing here?" said a puzzled face, as it chased the hair over her shoulders.

"Ticksy? Said Rodgo, with a look almost like indigestion, "Who the fuck is Ticksy?" Charlie Crabbe jumped into my head, 'Steve McQueen! Steve McQueen!'

"Fucked if I know," I said binding on to Rodgo's tone. Samantha looked visibly hurt.

"Don't you remember? We had a milkshake."

"A milkshake? ... Oh yeah... The milkshake... Was that you?" I asked with just the hint of a raised eyebrow. Sammi's pout suddenly deflated on the sides.

"Oh, there's Emma Sorrenson." She blustered, "Excuse me."

"How do you know Sammi?" said a slightly bemused Rodgo.

"AARRGH, that would be telling,' Rodgo, and a good pirate never reveals his sources, particularly when they are as, saucy as her. But suffice to say that she asked me to share a milkshake with her one day when I had shore leave."

"Stephen, I've known her all my life. She would *never*, ask *anyone*, to have a milkshake with her. *I* couldn't do it. It'd be like getting with my sister, but she's pretty hot."

It was while Rodgo went to the loo, that I went to make my move. I was in the middle of scouring the room for her, when a hand, jolted me on the shoulder. I turned around, to find her pouting her lips so hard, they were quivering.

"I can't believe… you don't… remember me. You *must* remember me?" she insisted. I looked up, as if mentally searching for the refresher towel at the bottom of a Red Rooster bag.

"I do have a vague recollection, of someone, running away from me when they realised I was a boarder." Where was this coming from? I mean, I hadn't realised that she was running away from me at the time, but now, I was absolutely certain of it. And what was with this *cool guy* thing? It was unbelievable, and yet from her point of view, *totally* believable. My God, this was a Darwinian adaptation *and* an epiphany, rolled into one. Sammi blinked first.

"I don't know why I did it, Stephen. I suppose, because *boarders* have a terrible reputation for being dumb and smelly. Ordinarily, it's, just not done. But… thing is… Stephen, seeing you here now, I realise that you're different. There's something *really* special about you."

It was around about then, that Sammi's hair started trying to attack me. I started to go green and the ground seemed like a really sensible place to be, so long as I spread my whole body out, as far as it would go, in every direction. That way, there was no bit that could fall over.

"Are you all right?" she inquired as she eagerly guided my head into her lap, and stroked her hand across my brow. Even in my alcoholic stupor, her skin felt like liquid velvet trickling across my face. "Not, really," finally came my reply.

I wanted to tell her about how helpless and abandoned I felt, and how the soccer team used to call me useless, and maybe they had been right. But it didn't come out like that at all. Instead of telling her about it in a box labelled despair, I told it like it was a series of jokes, in which *I* was the punch line. And she laughed so much her funny pout disappeared all together. All I could see, were her perfect white teeth and smooth olive skin, jostling for supremacy. At least, that's what I saw *before* the scotch grabbed hold so hard, it put me to sleep. Well, semi-sleep. I remember that Sammi told me stuff about her horses Zeus and Apollo, and that she wanted to quit the cello, but her Mum wouldn't let her, but that's about it. The rest was a complete and utter black out, and that scared the shit out of me. I could have *said* anything, or *done* anything. Maybe I chased after people calling them all chokers for having their pants too high. And what did I say to Sammi? And why was I smiling, every time I even thought of her name?

"Stephen. Stephen."

God, Sammi sounds a little rough this morning; she must have the flu, I thought, as I pulled the sheet up under my chin. Now my legs were cold.

"Stephen Stephen."

"They're not really chokers," I mumbled, "Well, technically speaking they are, but we're not in the Doo now."

"Stephen." A hand gently rocked me into consciousness, "I've brought you wheat grass." I opened my eyes, and found Mrs Rodgerson decked out in a ripe lemon kimono, peering over at me. The room slowly shuffled into focus. I was lying in the hammock with my school blazer draped over me. How did I get there, and why had the Great Sandy Desert moved into my throat?

"Stephen! I'm so sorry to wake you, but I couldn't contain my excitement. I've just had a brain wave." She opened her mouth to speak, but exhaled to calm herself, before doing so, "Ok...Ok... Now it's only embryonic... But here goes... Boomerang, knives... and forks?" She looked at me, as if she was seven and had just done her first duck dive.

"Sounds great Mrs," she titled her head and furrowed her brow, "Erika." She still looked disappointed. "In fact *Erika,*" I said, before clearing my throat and adopting a theatrical tone. "I think it's *genius*, and I'll tell you why ... One word... A short word, but a good word and I'll tell you what that word is... Ancient... An *Ancient* ritual performed with ancient tools. It's sheer genius." She was delighted, and handed me the juice.

"Well, I can't take all the credit, your performance last night was the inspiration," I had *absolutely* no idea what she was talking about, and hoped taking a large gulp of the green liquid didn't give me away. "What did you say your name was again?" she asked, I feigned modesty, with a tight-lipped grin. "That's right, Mookamunda, the

Aboriginal custodian of the Ashburton River, and you wanted to know if (a) I had any chocolate cake and (b) whether the Carrington-Browne's knew any kangaroo shooters, and if they did, their shooter friends better look out. Because *nothing*, was going to come, between you and their Samantha."

Unfortunately quite a bit *did* come between Sammi and I. Usually in the form of Mr Shrapnel or her parents. We did manage to see each other, about three times, before we decided that maybe it wasn't going to work out between us.

The events of that week turned out to be an almost perfect blueprint of how the rest of my time at Perth Grammar would be. It's funny how you can spend so much time and effort climbing a cliff face that seems totally insurmountable, and then one day, you happen to look down, and suddenly realise you've made it onto a plateau that stretches as far as the eye can see, behind you.

Each week would involve going to class and walking an electric tight rope between doing enough work to get a decent pass, and cracking enough gags to keep my friends laughing. All the time consumed with longing for the weekends, where I would be allowed out of the boarding house and into my dayboy friends' playground. Of course as I got older, and moved into the bigger boys boarding house, the restrictions were eased somewhat. Basically what every other weekend boiled down to, was staying at a different friend's house, heading off to whatever party we had on that weekend, and getting with girls. Lots of them. I guess nothing eased the pain I still felt about who

I was, and made me feel more wanted, than when I was getting lucky.

My dayboy friends sure were kind. Each week we would sit around and come up with new reasons to break me out. Then their Mums would ring the house master and tell them that, "Sadly, Bartholomew the Dalmatian had surrendered to diabetes, and I was required to be a pall bearer *and* match striker at his cremation," or "the local parish lamington drive was on this weekend and nobody cubes a sponge cake, like Stephen Briggs." More often than not, it was Mrs Rodgerson calling, and the sad part was most of her outlandish reasons were true.

17 ADULtS ARE JUSt CHILDREN IN BIG BODIES

As the years went by at Perth Grammar, my prediction about feeling less and less a part of the Doo rang completely true. I loved Mum and Dad more than anything, and I loved seeing them. But my big city affectations and desires used to get the better of me, and Mum and Dad found me returning to the Doo less often, for shorter periods of time, with more and more clothes, and an ever-growing list of people to make long distance phone calls to.

I was 17 years old, when my father was diagnosed with leukemia. Ironically enough, it was the same week that

I lost my virginity. A day after Dad told me, I couldn't help but donne the cap of the fundamentalist Christian, and wonder if my passage into manhood hadn't somehow *caused* his illness. It's weird how much blame you can attribute to yourself, at a time like that.

When Dad told me of the diagnosis, I could see how scared he was, despite his bravado, "Don't go worryin' yerself lad. I've 'ad worse. Member that time wasp stung me on 'ead? And I 'ad ingrown toenail. Life's all about battles son, and this one, ain't goin' to beat me." It was surprising how he had aged, without me really noticing it. I wondered, how many of those lines had developed while I was at Rottnest Island on rich dayboy's boats. How many times he had wanted to tell me things but couldn't, cos I was on the phone to a girl I'd known for a week and how many times he had patiently counted down the days until I'd return home. Only to find, that I didn't actually *want* to go home, that particular holiday.

I s'pose the best thing about Dad getting sick, was it forced him to retire, leave the Doo and move down to Perth, where he could be closer to treatment and where I could see a lot more of him. It was a really bizarre time for all of us. I was in the middle of my Tertiary Admission Exams and was working out what do to do at Uni. Mum and Dad had to leave the place they had been living in for the last 11 years, and start a new life in the city. All the while waiting to hear from Dad's specialist, to see how long they thought he had to go.

We weren't really big fans of fate at that time, but as fate would have it, the day Dad found the house he wanted to live in was the day the specialist opened the envelope. Of all the leukemia's you could get, Dad's was the best one to have. It was chronic lymphatic leukemia, and that responded very well to treatment. In fact, it was possible to live for 10 or 15 years, and rarely was it the leukemia that killed you; usually, it was some sort of other infection or complication. After Dad had told us the good news, we all burst into tears. At first, we cried with relief, that Dad's life wasn't about to end. But then we cried cos we realised Dad's retirement wasn't going to be the Pride of Erin through Tunbridge Wells that he had always wanted. Instead, it would be a constant and often gruelling battle, against the very liquid that gave him life. His own blood.

The first few weeks were probably the hardest. Every time I woke up, my first thought was, "Fuck! Dad's got leukemia." And then I'd jump out of bed and run through the house looking for him, to make sure he was all right. Often I'd find *him* in the garden and *Mum* sobbing into her teapot, as she watched him from the balcony.

"The gods were lookin down on us when we found this place," Dad always used to say, and he was absolutely right. It was a beautiful old block on the side of a hill, with black boys the size of men, a family of blue tongued lizards, the occasional peacock from the nearby wildlife sanctuary, and an enormous ghost gum, that grew right through the balcony. It needed a bit of work, but so did Dad. In fact, that's precisely what he needed. So long as he was busy and his time was occupied, he was happy, and when he was happy we were happy.

Of course, the first 12 months were hardly a walk in the park. There were the night sweats. The daily chemotherapy.

The mood changes from the steroids that he was given to combat the effects of the chemo. Every cold was a potential flu that could then become pneumonia, and did on one — almost two — occasions. And worst of all, was that most unwanted passenger — the reality that if we weren't really careful and alert, he could die.

Needless to say, we were all quite anal when it came to hygiene. Particularly Mum. I'd sit and watch her each day as she disinfected everything, from the floors, walls and doorknobs to the Christmas place mats and sun visors in the car. At first I tried to help her, but then I realised that this was her way of feeling like she had some sort of control, over the uncontrollable. I'm sure it was no coincidence that she would sing Vera Lynn war songs like, '*Bless em All*' as she went about her scrubbing. Actually, it was one early evening as I sat in front of *Home and Away*, and she took to the fire grate with a left right combination of Glenn 20 and Mr Sheen, that we touched upon that other simmering geyser.

I don't know what made me think of it at that point, it could have been the lady who processed my Uni Card insisting that I must be Italian, that did it. I'm not sure, but for some reason I decided to wade into the stagnant swamp once more.

"Mum. Did I have a name before you adopted me?" I asked, in a concocted yet believable, off-the-cuff manner. I guessed that Mum didn't hear me because she made no response whatsoever. She just kept cleaning the grate with a diligent and evenly measured stroke. After a couple of minutes, I decided it wasn't the right time to be asking such sensitive questions, and returned to the serene sedative that was 'Summer Bay'. Actually, I was waiting for the spunk of the show to appear, because I had it on good information that in real life she was addicted to anal sex, and apparently you could tell when she walked. I was very skeptical, but it created an interesting diversion. It was just after the spunk had appeared in three consecutive *seated* scenes, and I was starting to give the rumour some credence, that Mum spoke; in a voice that lacked any trace of intonation, "What was the name of that boy you went to kindergarten with? The Lonagen boy."

"What, Richard Lonagen?" I offered innocently. Her hand kept its perfect stroke and rhythm, as she looked directly at me "Yes, Richard." She nodded, before turning back to her scrubbing, "Richard... that was your name... Richard...Limb, I think it was." She didn't say it in a loud voice, and yet it was more deafening than a cathedral's bell. Each word sat so squarely in the middle of its truth-note, that it felt like someone had stuck an industrial strength hoover up my arse, and was sucking everything right out of me.

"Oh," I said, "I think I better make us a cup of tea," before sprinting, as slowly as I could, out through the kitchen and onto the balcony.

My chest was hurting. My heart was palpitating. My head was about to explode, and I honestly thought I was going to drop dead on the spot. It wasn't the first time I had had one of these attacks, I'd been having them on and off since Dad got sick, but I hadn't told Mum or Dad because I didn't want to concern them. I sure thought about it that time though. But, as they had before, after five or so minutes it subsided, and I went back inside to talk to Mum.

"Richard? God, I'm lucky you guys came along and changed it. Stephen is a much better name than Richard," I insisted. Which was totally true, I just thought it might help Mum to hear it. Which it probably would have, had she been there.

"Mum?" I boomed down in the direction of the driveway. "There's no need to shout," she lectured, as she snuck up behind me.

"I thought you must have gone down to disinfect the post box," I joked, a little embarrassed at just how high I had jumped into the air. She sat on the couch and gestured that I join her, "I found these when we moved down from the Doo."

It was just as Mum said, my original or birth name was Richard Limb with b. For a moment there, I thought I might have been Asian, which would have been quite cool but rather unlikely, with my olive skin and big camel eyes. As well as a letter confirming that I was *available*, should Mum and Dad want me, was a copy of my original birth certificate. I tried so hard to be casual, as I held it for the first time and my curiosity scampered amongst its old-fashioned type. I know it was only a piece of paper and it had nothing to do with my upbringing, well day to day at least. But it was tangible proof that I did come from somewhere else, and at one time, I had had another identity. Richard Limb.

Actually, I must have done quite a good job of being casual about it, because it wasn't until about my fourth pass over its contents, that I saw it. I guess I was only looking at the longer bits, not the shorter ones like… mother's name. Claire Limb. That was her name. Claire. It seemed so surreal. Somewhere in England, was a woman called Claire Limb, and 18 years earlier she had pushed me out into the world.

I didn't let on to Mum or Dad, but finding out *my* name and *her* name absolutely gutted me. I would stand in front of the mirror brushing my teeth, thinking, 'Who the fuck am I? Am I Stephen Briggs or am I Richard Limb? Do I know who I am? I mean *really* know.' And then I'd get that feeling in my chest, with the shooting pain in my arm, and the sensation that my head was about to splatter.

18 PATTING A DOG CALLED INDULGENCE

It was bloody lucky that Mum told me my *other* name on a Wednesday, cos Wednesday was Black Market Funk night at Limbo nightclub. Which meant two things; Free entry, and free shots of vodka between nine and eleven. And by the time the big hand had made it around to the 18, in 18 past nine, I was absolutely shit-faced, running around the dance-floor, dousing as many Acid House Groovers with disco petroleum as I could.

As far as dancing went, I guess I had never really moved on from that first social, where I discovered I was a time capsule from Studio 54. Of course, I had refined and developed my repertoire, but essentially it was disco in its purest form, and there was no better place in town to take it out and shake it, than Limbo. Limbo was in essence, a dark, sweaty box with bad airconditioning, over zealous bouncers, two toilets and a stench of misspent youth so thick, it would collect on your upper lip like the froth from a beer.

On paper, the place should never have worked. But when Clarence Carter was *"Strokin his woman,"* and the line to get in stretched down to James Street, no one could deny the vibe was more exciting than unprotected casual sex in an alleyway under a full moon. Its tiny dance-floor stood about five metres by three, and was flanked by steep towering tiers, that more than one punter had fallen from and required stitches. The hand written sign above the cigarette machine said Limbo was licensed to hold 96 patrons, but on any given night there were well over 400, and tonight a huge chunk of those were devotees of the latest craze to hit clubbing; the Acid House Phenomenon.

To be honest, I fucking hated the whole ACEEEEEEEEEEEEEEEEEEED thing. As far I was concerned, it was the silliest thing to happen to music since *Black Lace*, 'drunk pineapple and shook the tree.' Apart from the pathetic smiley face t-shirts, and those fucking deafening whistles, which made it sound like you were at an umpire's academy, rather than a nightclub, there was *that* ludicrous formation dance. Honestly it made the YMCA look like ballet and the Hucklebuck, kabuki.

Over the last few months, what started as small isolated splinter groups, had turned into a full blown cause. In fact, I had just completed a rather deft step ball change, lifted straight from a print of *Saturday Night Fever*, when a chance upwards glance at the mirror ball revealed the magnitude of how bad things had got, and how ugly pack stupidity could really be. I know I was totally off my face, but for a second there, I really *knew* what a Hitler Youth Rally must have been like.

The DJ was standing on his mixing desk, which you had to get to with a ladder, shaking his arms as if he was the robot from *Lost In Space* trying to flick off dishwater. Meanwhile, the entire club gazed up at him like he was a prophet and followed his movements to the letter. Of course, this could have had some artistic merit if there had been anything more to it, but that was it. Grind your teeth, so everyone can see that you've taken your ecstasy and your leap of faith. Shift your weight from side to side. Shake off the dishwater, and get higher than you already are (which for the DJ was pretty bloody high), on the fact that you're all united in a common cause that's greater than yourself. The cult of the Smiley Face winking with an X. Of course to anyone else, they looked like extras from *One Flew over the Cuckoo's Nest*, that had had a little too much red cordial. But they weren't concerned about anyone else, unless they were wearing the team's ridiculous jumper.

I guess in a way, I actually liked the fact that they were offending me. In truth, I loved it. What better place to park my anger and twisted bitterness about Dad and being adopted, than in those pathetic lost fucks. In some sort of strange way, I think I even envied them. Imagine how simple life must be, if you can just embrace every hollow-wombat-dildo-fuck-face-idea that happens to stray in front of you, I thought, as the delicious amber venom bit into my tongue and slithered down my throat. I mean, it's fucking hard work being vigilant, and holding up the shit sieve to every, single, everything.

I was at that dangerous point, where any second I could find myself patting a dog that I thought was called insight, and rolling it over to find the name indulgence, branded onto its stomach. Fortunately, a gormless looking girl with a skirt so short you could see her gingham gusset, threw me a rope.

"You're a great dancer. What's ya name?" she squeaked, in a vain attempt to cut through the thick fog of bass. Luckily, I could read lips.

"Engleburt. What's yours?" Sadly, she couldn't.

"What?" she screeched, with a look that suggested she thought I had just said...*Engleburt*.

I tried again. "Engleburt, as in Humperdink. My parents were huge fans." Her eyes suddenly lit up with recognition as she lowered her voice and belted out,

"Please Release Me... Let me go..." she laughed at her own gag, and I joined her. Not that it was that funny. Really, it was pretty obvious. The thing was. Just before she said it, the most sublime lime-washed duck-down innocence leapt across her eyes and back again, almost as if, the right side of her brain had conferred with the left side and sent a messenger back, agreeing that the gag was worth giving a go.

It could have just been my vodka goggles, but there was something about that pure, childlike, nothingness that I needed. Not in a, come here and let me take care of you, little girl, would you like a boiled sweet and a bare back ride on the horsey, kind of way. It wasn't like that all.

Don't get me wrong, she was attractive, but what I was feeling had nothing to do with sex. It was about a place. Somewhere I used to know, but hadn't been for many many years. Somewhere I would love to visit, but would never be able to. A back yard that had a fence, a guinea pig, a mum and dad that were healthy and *were* my Mum and Dad, and no reason to leave.

"You know it's funny, that of *all* the guys I could have spoken to, I picked you," she barked in a louder more confident tone, "because my parents had a thing about names as well. They're Danish, and when they came to Australia, they really wanted us to fit in and not feel like second class citizens, so they gave us good 'Australian' names. Well what they *thought* were. My name's, Corolla. Corolla Pajonk."

When I woke up, I was convinced that my head was an artificial vagina, that zookeepers were using to take sperm samples from a large herd of rhinoceroses. Its entire contents had been bored right out, and what little remained had been coated in a jelly that was so viscous, it was like tiger balm that had been left out in the sun. As hangovers go, *this* was a big one. A tsunami. In fact, my faculties, were making the 10 or so kilometre walk back to the beach, post ocean-surge, when I suddenly realised something rather drastic had happened to my bed. It was full of water. And it wasn't in my bedroom, or the bedroom of anyone I knew, for that matter. And my wrists and ankles weren't hurting because of disco RSI. They were tied, quite tightly, to the bed.

'Well, who's been a naughty boy?' I thought, nonchalantly gazing up at my hands, expecting to see them locked in an embrace with a pair of silk stockings. My oesophagus spasmed. Since when have stockings been made out of black electrical tape? The seriousness of the situation had just grabbed me by the side burns and started to shake me, when the door opened.

My eyes blinked. My buttocks clenched and my eyes blinked again. I could not believe what stood before me. *He,* was about six foot four, an Islander, covered in tats, wearing dick poker speedos, with a neck the width of a power pole, holding a half mauled leg of lamb in one hand and a cigarette in the other.

"Hanging out for a fag, hey." He said, with an informative nod and a casual glance at my bound hands and feet. What the *fuck* did he mean by that? Was he asking a question, or describing my situation. I felt like a pig on a rotisserie. He took a couple of steps closer. I swear, I could taste death's, singeing vapour. "Need a…" He rubbed his thumb against his fingers, "hey." What the fuck was that? Was it a lighter, or some kind of code for a hand job? Fuck! My brain flicked through the file entitled, 'Great lines to get you out of a jam with a giant in swimming togs'

"Whatever gets you through the night." I beamed, in a, if that's what *you* think, then how could it possibly be wrong, kind of way.

He stared at me for what seemed like 137 days.

"Look bro, are you gonna help me out or not?" he said finally. I tried to calculate which was worse, losing my dignity and back-door-hymen, after being split in half by

Jonah Lomu's big brother, or, losing my life. Suddenly, my lungs were filled with helium, "Mate I'd love to but…."

"Don't tell me…. You don't fuck…" His eyes, violently writhed in their sockets, "kin smoke." Smoke! He said smoke. He didn't want me to be his sex slave, he wanted me to aid and abet, his long drawn out suicide. Well at least, I thought he did. His face was now so close, I could feel, little burning globules of lamb-fat, slamming into my neck.

"Fuckin Jesus Cuntin Fuck!" The grinding of his teeth was deafening, "The world is full of fucking soft cocks."

'If you say so', I thought, as an agitated ripple surged through his arm, and the leg of lamb he was holding came so close to cracking, it began to bleat for its Mummy.

"No one, fuckin' smokes any more, hey." His tone almost sounded, as if he was looking for reassurance. I didn't disappoint, putting my best tugboat skipper's voice on, and trying to turn the enormous bulk carrier around.

"Yeah, it's *fucked* mate… …HEY… …You know the ridic… fuckin stupid thing is, up until re… recently I was a three pack a day man. Some days *four*."

"Fuck me, hey." he nodded, like a man who had just be shown that the world wasn't flat.

"Yeah. Terrible fuckin timin',"

"Fuck me, hey," he said again.

"Two weeks. Fourteen days. Fourteen, fuckin days too late."

"Hey. FUCK ME!" he snarled. Puffing his chest up so much, it caused an eclipse. Mind you, it was light enough for me to see him make a circle out of his left hand and ram the leg of lamb in and out of it as he groaned, "Cum

A Tae Cum A Tae Ooooh Yeah. Cum A Tae Cum A Tae Ooooh Yeah."

I pissed my pants. Literally, squirted wee all over myself. One of those sprinklers, that pulls itself along on a wire, couldn't have done a better job. Not that he noticed. Thankfully, I was covered with the doona and he was too busy doing the business with the leg of lamb, poking his tongue out at me and cocking his head from side to side. His head, that was coming nearer and nearer, until suddenly, it stopped. His lips rolled back, and his teeth burst forth, like militia onto a parade ground.

"Got Ya a good one. Hey! You should have seen your face. Fuckin funny. Real funny. Don't worry bro, the Claw will be back in a minute. Had to go and get some gear, hey." This was going from bad, to fucking, absolutely, appallingly, *terrible*. For *fucks* sake! It was bad enough, that I was lying there swimming in my own piss, having just been psychologically sodomised by someone who looked like *the reason why* death row was invented, and now, I had to bide my time and wait for the next exciting instalment; with the fucking *Claw*. Whoever that was. I bit into my shoulder, hard enough to draw blood, just to make sure that this *wasn't* some sort of drug-induced hallucination.

If only it was. If only I could blame those Acid House fuck heads. But I couldn't. I just had to lie there and lie there and lie there and lie there and lie there. It was while I was trying to bounce the excess urine off the bed, that someone started banging on the neighbour's security screen. I was convinced the police were doing a door knock, "I'm in here! I'm in here!!!" I yelled.

"I know you are brother." Came a voice, that was now etched onto my eardrums for eternity.

I shut up, and despite my best efforts, couldn't help but go over and over in my mind, what sort of *gear* the Claw was getting, and what he intended doing to me with it. I had just been impaled on a totem tennis pole, while 'Death Row' and the 'Claw' whacked my testicles back and forth for their own amusement, when Jinx, the door bitch from Limbo, came bounding into the room as if she owned it... A bell that once belonged to Big Ben, started clanging behind my forehead. She *did* own it.

"The Claw," I presume.

"You been talking to *Roderick*?" she laughed, as she shook her head, "You been giving my friend a hard time?" she yelled down the hall. "He calls me the Claw, because he reckons I'm the toughest door bitch he's ever met. Bouncer humour."

His name was *Roderick*? I wish I had known *that,* while he was putting me through the wringer. Fuck. Wringer. The sheets. My faculties, finally got their breath back after their hike through the marsh and it dawned on me, that I was lying in the most powerful door bitch in Perth's bed. A bed, that she had been telling me about all the way home in the taxi. Because not only was it brand spanking new, custom made, and the apple of her universe. She bought it, with the proceeds of the settlement she received, from the car crash that gave her whiplash, and her best friend a one way ticket to the after life. And I, had just christened it. My night clubbing life was over.

"Oh Baby, I must have forgotten to untie you," she said, as she took a penknife from her top drawer and started to cut me free. "Don't move, I don't want to slice you. Fucking tapes, much easier to get on, than off."

I didn't even look to see if she had cut me. I was too busy reading her face. Any second now and there was going to be that telltale 'if I'm not mistaken, that smells like piss,' nose twitch.

"Sorry I was gone so long. I was waiting for the chemist to open, to get us fresh fit packs. But they only had a single left." I could tell that this, was going to be one of those days that lovers of cryptic crosswords would search four across and three down for.

"Are we going for a jog?"

"Well, I s'pose you could call it a jog." She smiled, as she knelt on the ground and reached into her handbag. "A jog through the streets of your mind."

At first, I thought it was a toothbrush. Well that's what the case looked like. Mind you, not too many toothbrush cases have a hypodermic needle inside them. I couldn't help but crack a half smile, as she showed me *the gear*, a little plastic bag with white powder inside, that was a far cry form the various guillotines and anal prods, that I had been imagining. Still, just as barbaric, in its own particular way.

Compared to the events of that morning, my queasiness about needles seemed like nothing. But my heart still quickened a little, after the spoon had boiled the liquid, and Jinx had drawn it into the plastic chamber.

"You wanna go first, baby?" she questioned, in a soft wet whisper, that promised something far better, than a thousand head jobs.

"Actually Jinx. I'd love to. But I can't. I have... the *worst* phobia about needles. I'm amazed I haven't passed out already. But, it's really nice of you to offer." No matter how I justified it, I still felt like a boy scout, who had found 50 cents and handed it in at the police station.

"Roderick! You wanna have some of this?" she queried, in a tone that already knew the answer. He must have been standing just outside the door, because within seconds he was slammed up against the skirting board, with the needle jammed up his arm. I didn't want to watch, but couldn't avert my eyes. There was something incredibly compelling about witnessing someone so desperate to escape, as they took the dice in their hands and flung them into the air. It was like watching that awful game show, *Pick a Box*, you can take life as it is, or, you can pick a box. Only thing was, in this case, there wasn't any chance of winning some wacky booby prize. There was a brief holiday somewhere amazing, or a very long one inside the box. Within seconds, Roderick's eyes were beginning to nod and I felt like I was David Attenborough, watching poachers tranquillise an elephant.

Next it was Jinx's turn, and of course, she couldn't use just *any* tourniquet, she had a special plaited leather one, with a jade stone hanging from it. And it was obvious that for her, the whole ritual was sexy. Fuck for three days until you can't walk sexy. She was the star of a raunchy film clip, and I was the camera. Not only did she sit opposite me with her legs spread, so I could see her big W munching on her panties as she pumped her fingers to swell her vein. She kept staring right at me, without blinking, as her eyes screamed 'Fuck me. Fuck me in the arse. Fuck me now.' At the point when the needle pierced and entered her, she exhaled, as if she had just taken a ride down the entire length of me. And if the expression on her face was anything to go by, I must have been hung like a humpback whale.

I guess I *should* have stayed with them for the next few hours, to make sure they were ok and didn't go to that great nightclub door in the sky. But there was the small matter of the mattress, and I thought, better to be a sod for going, than being a sod for making it sodden. Finally something went my way. Because it was a waterbed, the mattress was made of rubber and once I had soaked up the residual yellow tide with the pillowslips, I was out the door and down the Laundromat quicker than you could say, "Excuse me, could you make that two cups of OMO? It's a pretty soiled load."

By midday, I had picked up my car and returned the freshly laundered linen. Well, left it on the doorstep, rung the bell, and sprinted for my life. In a perfect world, I should have been happier than a gay Maori in a rugby scrum. But I wasn't. In fact I was sweating it, big time. Just after I had got onto the Tonkin Highway and slipped my Poo Brown VW into fourth, I made a *terrifying* discovery. I thought my groin was itchy because of some sort of reaction, you know a kind of piss-rot, so I snuck my hand down for a bit of a scratch, and got the shock of my life.

Generally speaking, I had no problem with crotchless nickers. Apart from when I was *wearing* them. My mind kept replaying an extreme close up of the needle, slashing its way into Jinx's arm and her blood doing its best impression of a lava lamp, as it giggled, flirted, mingled and melded with the cylinder's inch or so of contraband liquid. My hands were shaking, as I desperately tried to recall what had happened. *My* jocks were gone, and *her* knickers were on. What the fuck happened? I couldn't actually recall it but the only thing I could think of, was we did it. We *must* have. And I sure didn't see any used condom packets while I was playing housemaid. I could only conclude that I had unprotected sex with an IV drug user. My vomit, splattered the road with dot dot dot.

Surely, whatever it was that controlled the universe couldn't be *so* cruel as to kill two people in the same family by poisoning their blood, I thought, as my bravado took solace in the odds of this actually happening. But, she *shared* a needle with Roderick, and fuck knows what his sexuality was. Maybe, I couldn't get it up, on account of the vodka and VB. My mind was mid-way through playing a vigorous set of badminton with itself, where possibility would swoosh and float from one side to the other, when I was faced with a more tangible problem.

I was running on empty, and only had two dollars after my unexpected cleaning bill, and really wasn't in the mood to be pitied by a petrol station attendant. Unfortunately, the BP on the corner was my only option, and it *wasn't* self-serve. Nothing quite so humiliating, as Mr friendly BP man saying, "Fill it up?" and you replying, "Actually. Just make it two dollars worth thanks." The truly humbling part, was Mr BP didn't even bother with the charade any more. He would just say, "two or three bucks worth today?" Basically, I really needed to get a part time job. Mum and Dad helped out a lot, but I couldn't expect them to pay for my social life, as well as my food, board, lodging, electricity and everything else.

By the time I reached the top of the stairs, I'd decided to make joining the workforce, my number one priority — that was, until I saw Mum's face. No amount of Elna pressing could remove the sleepless night creased all over it. "So yer remembered yer ave a home ta come home to… Yer could have called."

"Sorry Mum, it got too late. I didn't want to wake you."

"There were no chance of that. I were up all night, with yer Dad," her eyes tried to make a stoic stand, but her face capitulated around them, "Poor bugger, must have sweat out 'alf 'is body weight."

"Oh Mum," I held out my arms, which she just managed to fall into, before the typhoon gripped her and a flying piece of debris became lodged in her throat.

"It's those new bludy pills, specialist gave 'im. They don't seem to do anythin' but make 'im irritable. He's got a short fuse at the best of times, but just lately, I can't say or do anythin'… I had to change the sheets, twice… I need to be strong, for his sake, but I don't think I can. Oh son. What am I goin' to do?"

"It'll be all right Mum. It'll be all right," I bluffed, as I stroked her exhausted shoulders. The truth was, I had absolutely *no* idea what any of us were going to do. She was right. Lately, Dad was more flammable than a Russian tanker filled with LPG. And yet, he was alive and although those pills were making his life hell, they were ruling out any possibility of him visiting there as well.

I made Mum a pot of tea, put her in her chair, and saw for the first time exactly how she must have looked at the age of nine, when her father died.

"It's not fair Stephen. It's bludy not fair," she sobbed, as tears streaked down the lines of her face. "Could yer go and check on 'im love?"

I hadn't even made it half way down the passageway, when I heard the most beautiful noise in the world. Dad's snoring sounded just like a model plane that was experiencing engine trouble, as it coughed and spluttered its way through the air. I was tempted to look in, but I didn't want to risk waking him. So I just adopted the foetal position next to the door, closed my eyes, and marvelled at his wonderful nasal symphony. I could have stayed there all day, but the lingerie biting into my groin got the better of me.

I had just freed myself from the confines of Jinx's crotchless bondage, when relief wrapped me in an enormous pillow and tossed me playfully into its cubby house. A used condom lay scrunched up and stuck to the inside of the knickers. I was in the middle of inspecting it, when Mum knocked at my door.

"Oh Stephen, I almost forgot, a bloke called Ronny 'ollywood called. I think it were Ronny, but I couldn't quite make it out. Line kept jumpin' about. 'is number's on pad."

19 tHE HUMAN tREADMILL, GREY POWER AND A BOttLE OF CORONA

His first name *wasn't* Ronny, it was Sunny, but his surname certainly was Hollywood. And the reason the line jumped about, was because he was calling from a mobile phone. The first one I had ever seen.

"Yeah, she's a beauty. Light, easy to use, portable." He smiled, as his eyes devoured every curve, line and crevice, of what appeared to be, about as portable as an average sized encyclopedia volume. "And the ringer? It's so loud, I can *even* hear it in my factory. I might be midway through a pour. You know, say 20 flamingos and 50 gnomes, and this little beauty; I'll hear it within three rings."

It was pretty safe to say, that Sunny had the gift of the gab, which was to be expected I suppose. If you owned a company called 'Stardust DJ's,' that 'Guaranteed you the best night of your life,' you'd want to be able to chat. I couldn't quite work out how the flamingos and gnomes fitted in though. His office, which was actually a converted bedroom at the front of his house, looked like a dentist's surgery waiting room, adorned with before and after shots of teeth. Although *Sunny's* office only had *after* shots, and they were all his. His teeth were so perfect, and that smile so rehearsed, it was obvious that the people standing next to him in the photos were only there to fill up the numbers. He took a big gulp of Coke.

"Now, your friend Tony tells me that you're pretty switched on, and a bit of a hit with the ladies. That's good. The bride and groom will be looking to you to guide their night, and everyone likes a good lookin' guide. I met my wife at a wedding. I'll never forget it. I had just done a seamless mix between *Endless Love*, the bridal waltz, and *Dancing on the Ceiling* (thought I'd pick up the tempo and rock 'em a bit) and there she was. Corrr, the way that dress clung... to her *wheelchair*! Ha ha ha! Only joshin ya. Na sincerely, she was a vision... If only I'd had mine checked! Ha ha ha ha ha! Sometimes you gotta stop me Stephen. S-t-e-p-h-e-n? Mmmm? Look mate, I'm gonna be straight up with ya. No disrespect to you, or your parents, but I think you should think, just think, about changing that name. You know, get something a little more *showbiz*. A little more razzle-dazzle. Colour, movement, that kind of thing. You want people walking out of that reception centre, thinking that for the last five hours, they've been an extra in a tinsel town blockbuster."

As the ferry pulled away from the pier, and I tried to (a) find my sea legs (b) work out how to remove the lids from the turn-tables and (c) go through the list of songs, selected by the boy who was *hosting* the Bar Mitzvah; I couldn't help but wonder precisely *how*, I was going to sprinkle a little *movie magic* on the assembled throng of 10 to 13 year olds. In the hours preceding my maiden voyage, I had toyed with the idea of painting my face like Marcel Marceau. If only I had. At least I would have had something to hide behind. I guess it could have been worse. I could have been pelted with bottles instead of biscuits, and the kids only had to wait 45 minutes before Sunny pulled alongside in a dinghy and gave me the power lead.

In fairness, I should really have told him that I didn't have a fucking clue about anything vaguely more technical than a kettle. But he was so keen for me to fit into the 'outfit,' as he put it, that I didn't want to derail his enthusiasm and found myself nodding all the way through his 10 or so minute sound system orientation-slash-demonstration. The ludicrous thing was, I actually came away from his carport thinking I knew exactly what I was doing.

Anyway, once I had that lead I was unstoppable. I must have played at least five songs before it was time to disembark, and two of those went all the way through without the brats jumping next to the console and bumping the stylus. In fact, I'd just slipped the theme from *Fiddler on the Roof* on, as Sunny came down the gangplank to help me with the gear.

"Beautiful touch, Stephen. Gold. Solid gold. I can tell, that you're going to work out just fine. In fact, I know it's a little early, seeing as you've only done one show. And we had the little mishap with the lead, but that was some boofhead called Sunny Hollywood's fault, not yours." He placed both his hands on my shoulders, and straightened his spine as if he was about to give his closing argument at a murder trial.

"Look Stephen. I can see, that you've definitely got what it takes, to be more, than just a DJ. If you want... You... Could be a great, *showman*." He swallowed, as if even mentioning the word, took his heart and squeezed it.

"It's stamped all over you. *You* rob a bank, they dust for fingerprints and they'll find, *SHOWMAN,* smudged all over the counter. So how 'bout, next week, we organise for you to do your first wedding?"

The door on the room that my sanity lives in, slammed shut. "Yeah, ok." His face lit up, like a trainer who'd just put two litres of untraceable anabolic steroid, into the cup favourite, "Sounds great." I said, not believing what was coming out of my mouth. The guy, was like an electric treadmill. Once you'd stumbled onto him, you didn't have a hope in hell of getting off. Anxiety picked the lock, "Actually Sunny, I was wondering if there was any chance of a few practice sessions during the week. You know, just to make sure that the, *show's,* totally ready."

"Did you hear that? The *show's* totally ready." He pointed his index finger at me and cocked his head. "Natural.

You've got it. Yes indeed. Great idea, Stephen… Do you know what sets a, true *showman,* aside from the rest?" Despite my forehead doing its best interpretative dance representation of pondering, my mind remained blank. "Dedication." He gave me another blast, from the index finger esteem-gun, "Right there!" before jumping into the other van and disappearing in a puff of black smoke. Well actually, a rather large cloud of it, that engulfed everything within a 30 metre range, as he waited for the lights to change green. And he's driving the *newer* van, I thought, as I wrestled the shift column into surrendering first.

Next to playing, talking and lifting, driving was one of the major parts of the mobile DJ's job description. And even though I'd avoided the 'Yellow Squid', as it was known by Sunny's other DJs, on account of it squirting ink everywhere every time you scared it by asking it to move, I had the pleasure of driving back to Stardust Central in 'The Rattler.' Named not because of its deadly venom, but its incredibly vigorous and violent vibrating. It was commonplace to have the rear vision mirror shake out of its housing at least three times in any journey, and William, one of the other DJs, swore he wore a kidney belt, every time he drove it.

Funny thing was, I was *kind* of enjoying it. It was certainly bumpy, very uncomfortable, and if you had a prang they'd be scraping you off the road with a dustpan and spatula. But it did have something going for it. Well, at least the bulge in my recently acquired rayon evening pants thought so. I had only left the Bar Mitzvah 10 minutes ago and travelled a few kilometres along Albany Highway, and there was a mongrel the size of a Rottweiler nuzzling up against me. Ok, maybe an adolescent sausage dog that was big for its age.

Regardless of how large my erection was, the fact I had one was pretty bizarre, considering where I was. I mean don't get me wrong, of all the 1971 Toyota Hi Ace Van front seats I'd seen, this one was right up there, in terms of sex appeal. What self-respecting man wouldn't be aroused by a caved-in cloth ceiling that patted you on the head every time you hopped in, and a ripped vinyl seat that revealed a pus coloured sun-hardened-foam that positively glistened in a mixture of Hungry Jacks sauce, dust, baked-on cement and residual DJ sweat? Not to mention, the couple of broken gnomes' heads, rolling around in the passenger foot-well, thrown in for good aphrodisiac measure. I have no doubt that every time 'The Rattler' pulled into a service station, there'd be a bona-fide, boner bonanza. Really, if I'm honest, I should have reported it to the right authorities. Any half decent RTA inspector would have ordered it off the road in the interests of Public Morality. It was chick magnets like that van, that were undoing the zippers on the fabric of society.

Basically, what I was suffering from was a terrible case of Coach-Bone. Coach-Bone, is a relatively common affliction that affects young boys and men, whenever they are subjected to a combination of loose fitting smooth silky underwear, pants or shorts and a vibrating environment. I'll never forget, one time at school we had an away fixture in Midland, which was a good hours drive. Anyway, this particular day, the usual buses didn't come and were replaced by antique double-decker ones instead. Honestly, I've been on roller coasters that gave you a smoother ride, and I wasn't the only one that thought so. As the journey continued, more and more school bags mysteriously migrated from the floor to boys' laps. By the time we arrived, every one on the bus was doing their best impression of a coat hook and the fixture had to start half and hour late because no-one would get off the bus. I don't know what the other guys used, but my deflation device was the thought of Mr Shrapnel sitting in a deer-stalker hat, scoffing hard boiled eggs on a hot humid day, as he explained the principles of algebra.

As the cat's eyes blinked past and the Rattler continued to do its thing, my mind wandered into the cinema, that's usually reserved for the five to ten minutes before I fall asleep each night. Mind you, ever since the crotch-less knickers fiasco, the projectionist had been on holidays. My selective memory kicked in, and I totally blocked the night at Jinx's out of my mind, preferring to concentrate on another night, a year or so earlier.

Of all of my friends, I was one of the last to jettison my virginity. I was 17 and I suppose I was waiting for the perfect time, with the perfect girl, in the perfect setting. Which makes the dodgy details, of the doing of the do, or indeed devious deed, decidedly more deranged.

I was spending the weekend with Andrew, one of my other dayboy friends. His mum and dad had gone off horse riding and had left us in the capable care of Bertha, Andrew's 83 year old grandmother, who was a dead ringer for Ronnie Barker in drag. As you can imagine, Bertha was hardly a vigilant watchdog. In fact, she had recently had a mild heart attack, and spent most of her time anaesthetised in front of the telly, as she dribbled on her chin and dozed in her armchair. Anyway, it was an unusually hot afternoon in late August, and we were feeling a little worse for wear from the night before's *activities,* and thought that some hair of the dog might be just the tonic we were looking for. So Andrew and Paul went off to the bottle shop, while I kept an eye on Bertha. It was my job to keep her busy, if she happened to wake up while the guys were gone.

As I sat there, slowly rotating my head to fine-tune the best possible angle for escaping her perpetual morning-breath, I watched the collar on her white lace shirt move less and less as a tide of drool engulfed it. It really struck me, just how *cruel* life can be. When it came to facial hair Bertha could have given Kenny Rogers a run for his money. It's a tragedy that she never got to see the casting directors of *Planet of the Apes*. But in her day, Andrew assured me, she was a beauty queen. Miss West Coast 1923 I think it was. I was in the middle of a large mental sweep of the other contestants, circa 1923, when I suddenly became aware of two rather magnified eyes, boring right into me.

"Can you smell that?"

"Oh, sorry Bertha… I was a million miles away. Can I smell what?"

"That, hussy, of a frangipanni tree outside the window."

Eager to placate her, I looked up towards the window and drew in a large lung full of air, "Oh? Yes… I think I can."

She shifted her weight in her chair and leant over towards me, "Of course you can. You're, its target. The *male* of the species. Primarily it's after male bees. But any males will do. So long as they've got a long hard *proboscis*-like-appendage."

I swallowed hard and wondered if this was Rhys Carlisle Karma.

Her gleeful lips slowly parted, revealing her butter-yellow dentures, "It's screaming to the world. Come take me. Come take, my hot, wet, nectar. Come slide, inside, my deep, pink, moist, fleshy canal and take it. Take it all."

"Is that right? "My hairline, sat three inches above my head, "Well… There you go." I was absolutely speechless, dumbstruck, catatonic, paralysed and stupefied; all rolled into one. Not only, at what she had just said but also at the slightly *uncharacteristic* way in which she had sprung out of her chair, pirouetted over the coffee table and landed with a rather, risqué, shimmy of her buttocks, on the couch. Where she now sat, well and truly pressed up, against me.

"You have no idea, how much honey, a woman produces at my age. All she wants is a little bee, to come and enjoy some."

My loyalties, ran faster than the words, out of my mouth. "Andrew and Paul have gone to the bottle shop to buy beer. They're underage. We better call the police."

"Don't be silly." She moved her face, so close, that her longest whisker poked into my cheek. "You boys buy beer all the time. I hope you won't think badly of me, but I pretended to be asleep to make them go. Now why don't you and I, have a little, drinky drop, to *loosen* us up a little?"

I went to speak, but my penis had withdrawn so far into my body, that it was lodged in my larynx and consequently stopped any sound from coming out. So I just nodded, reasoning that if we had a drink, one of us would have to move and that would mean a welcome reprieve from her deep drilling whisker, that had violated me all the way down to my cheek bone. At least that's what I thought. But Bertha was into the kitchen, pantry, and cupboard and back on the couch with two glasses and a flagon before I could say, "Cooking sherry?"

"Many a daytime dalliance, has had a sherry or two, to thank for its momentum." She said, as she heaved her considerable bosom, up onto my forearm, "One for you." She lifted the swollen glass to my lips and eased the sickly, sweet, fluid down my gullet, "Down the hatch…. And one for me… There it goes. Thank you, Fancy Man."

I was just about to begin protesting, when another glass appeared, followed by another and another. The amazing thing was, Bertha kept right up with me, shot for shot, until we had had eight glasses each. Then she decided, it was time to make her move.

I've got no idea how she did it. But somehow she managed, in *one* movement, to manoeuvre me away from the back of the couch so I collapsed onto the seat, swivel her hips around so she ended up on top of me, and, last, but certainly not least in the *impressive* stakes, remove her shirt and bra at the same time. As I lay pinned beneath her, for the first time in my life I seriously contemplated becoming a vegetarian. I honestly understood exactly how a cow feels just before it gets 250 000 volts, up the jatzie. She *picked* up her breasts, which were sitting on her lap, like two domesticated, extremely well fed Moray eels, and started to move them around, in a figure of eight pattern, like a parent does with a spoon full of baby food.

"Bzzz Bzzz Bzzz. Time for some honey, Fancy Man." She brought her left breast terrifyingly close to my mouth, whilst her right, gave me a quick jab in the eye and then she lifted them up and up, on one last enormous climb, that saw them peak a foot and a half above her shoulders.

"I've been a very naughty girl Fancy Man! Very naughty!!!" And then pulling a face, like she had just touched the slipper of God, she let them flop, like two enormous human bungy ropes, hurtling towards my face at the breast equivalent of terminal velocity. I tried to brace but there was nowhere to turn. Down, down, down they came. The nipples, letting off a minor sonic boom, as they pierced their way through the air. And then it went black. Pitch black, and all I was aware of were two wind tunnels, screeching like banshees past my ears, followed by a shuddering 'b – o – i– n - g' and then it was light again. Momentarily at least. I just managed to witness Bertha's enormous mammary missiles, as they came together and careered, into her unsuspecting jaw, before she toppled forwards and came crashing down on my chest, like an apartment block that had just been introduced to TNT.

After what felt like days, I realised that not only was she still on top of me, but she was on top of me, still. Totally still! Bertha wasn't breathing. The horny bugger's ticker must have given out on her, I thought. Now I was really in trouble. Somehow, I channelled five years of athletics training into one enormous effort and managed to sit up, with Bertha still straddling me. I would have liked to have got her flat on the *table,* but time was of the essence. There was no way I was going to have everyone return, to find one houseguest and one dead grandmother. I *had* to resuscitate her, there and then. I tried to secrete as much saliva in two seconds, as I possibly could, to act as a makeshift barrier cream and reluctantly pushed my lips against hers, to start mouth to mouth.

Fortunately, I had just got my life saving certificate, and the five quick breaths and one thousand two thousand three thousand routine, was still fresh in my mind. I told myself that she was just one of those plastic mannequins and all I had to do, was treat this like an exam. Which seemed to work quite well. So well, in fact, that I must have revived her. Well, if the tepid tongue, tenaciously, tearing at my tonsils, was any indication.

"Oh, give me another kiss, Fancy Man," enthused Bertha, picking up precisely from where she had left off, "Come on, whip it out. Whip out that scrumptious schlong."

"Mother! What are you doing?"

To my absolute delight, I turned around, to find that we were no longer the only two people in the room. I was saved. Andrew's father, Dr Fitzharding was home. Saved! Andrew's father, who was Bertha's son. Saved? And he was standing a few feet away. While his mother and I sat on the couch. In the missionary position. *Saved???* His *topless* mother, who as far as he was concerned, I had just been sharing a tongue sandwich with…

It all got too much, and despite my best efforts, my body started to shake little tears out of my eyes. Well, quite big ones actually. Dr Fitzharding approached; "Steady on there, Stephen old boy. No need for water works. Mother's just forgotten to take her lithium again. She can be a handful, without her medication. She doesn't mean you any harm. We'll just, put her fun bags away, get her off you, give her a pill, and every thing will be sweet as a nut." With that he led her away and left me to pull myself together.

I must have stayed in that shower for an hour, scrubbing and rubbing and scrubbing again. Honestly, my tongue looked like a broiled chunk of whale blubber by the time I had finished, and even then, it *still* felt disgusting and tasted of sherry.

Andrew and Paul finally got back, empty handed. Apparently, after an anonymous tip off from a concerned senior citizen, the police had been cracking down on bottle shops, so no one would serve them. Not that *I* cared, I still had half a flagon of cooking sherry sloshing around inside me. Not to mention three or four tablespoons of Bertha's spittle. That realisation had me back in the shower for round two in seconds, although this time I hurked my guts up everywhere. When I did finally emerge, Dr Fitzharding suggested that I should go for a relaxing stroll to settle my head and give Bertha's tranquilliser time to kick in.

Dalkeith was always beautiful. Not in the same way as the Doo. Instead of immense swirling oceans of blue sky and red dust, smattered with yellow spinifex, there were concise, geometric bands of colour; squares of green lawn, boxes of terracotta, triangles of slate, and stripes of blue-grey bitumen. The whole suburb was laid out like sushi, and everywhere you looked, you could see the thought and dedication that had gone into every detail.

Something, like the texture of a letterbox, would never have been left to chance in Dalkeith. I couldn't help but smile, as I tried to imagine *anyone* in the Doo giving a shit about the colour of their house, let alone whether their letterbox was rough or smooth.

I guess I must have been really tickled by this and probably still a little drunk, because unbeknownst to me, I was standing in the middle of the footpath and only saw her coming at the last moment.

"Get out of the way! You, bloody idiot…" Her mountain bike swerved to avoid me, as she locked up its brakes; "What, the bloody hell are you doing? You moro… Stephen?" a huge smile enveloped her. "You dick… I almost killed you."

My left eye scanned the outline of her face, while the right, took a direct hit from the late afternoon sun. I couldn't quite mould the collected features into a recognisable face, until she pouted. Then, I knew exactly who it was.

"Sammi Carrington-Browne. How the hell are you?" I gushed, ecstatic at how the day's rollercoaster, which up until now, had been ploughing along 10 kilometres underground, had just gone into a 90 degree rocket-powered climb.

"I thought you were away?"

Her voluminous blonde hair shook free from its helmet, casting me as an extra in its shadow.

"I, just got back last week.… I've, been in… Vienna for two years," she half whispered, in a tone that suggested she had just sealed a radioactive drum and didn't want to have to handle it again.

243

"Oh really?" I consoled, as my eyes flitted up and down the extraordinary length of her. Not that she was overly tall. She was about 5ft 9. But she was perfect. Absolutely perfect. Her face, was more symmetrical and mesmerizing than a Min-Min light hovering over an inland lake on a totally windless night, and her shimmering skin was wrapped so tightly around her taut body, that she was almost translucent. If anything, she had grown *into* her looks, instead of out of them, like a lot of her friends had.

Her marlin blue eyes looked up, as if playing out all the possible repercussions of speaking, before descending directly onto me; "I was actually there, on an Equestrian scholarship… it, didn't really work out… they said, I had a few problems with discipline." She gently exhaled, as she lowered herself into the bath of pity in my eyes; "But who wouldn't have, with 11 hour days and 5 am starts?" I blinked understandingly. "Speaking of working out, have you been hitting the gym Stephen?" She said, lightly grabbing my arm and caressing me, toward the side of the path as six jocks on racing bikes went flying past.

"No. I've just been buying smaller t-shirts."

Her smile extended even further, "So come on, tell me. Who are you seeing… Who's the lucky girl, this week?"

A wave of ignition, lambadaed up my neck, like it was a gas powered grill, "Actually, no-one."

"Oh come on…" I don't believe that, for a second."

"Well, I was going out with, Gemma Lloyd for a while," the light behind her eyes dimmed, "but, we broke up," and returned on full beam with fog lamps, spot lights and a couple of camping torches as well.

"Oh, I'm sorry to hear that," she muttered, with about as much honesty as you can muster, when you discover one of the bitches you hate most in the world, has been seeing an ex-boyfriend of yours.

"Well, I bet there are broken hearts all over Vienna," I countered, delighted that the conversation was going down this path.

"Only one… Jake Peterson." My heart sank, "He's supposed to be the next Ivan Lendl… Apart from the fact, that he's American… Not that I care… three timing bastard.".

I couldn't believe my luck, I had just bumped into the first love of my life, who I hadn't seen since we were 15-all, looked down at the floor and discovered we were standing on a *rebound* surface.

"Well, you're much better off without him. Any guy that couldn't see what an unbelievably good wicket he was on with you, is a total fuck head." Her hand reached up and etched my cheek.

"Why didn't things work out between us?"

"Well, let me see. It could have been the fact that when we started going out, we were so young our first five dates were in a humidicrib, or maybe, your parents not approving of my dubious lineage because I wasn't born in one of the three estates on your street, or maybe it was just that fucking boarding house, that incidentally I have to return to, in two hours."

"*Two hours*? You know, there's this really special place, just around the corner from here. I literally spent half of my life there when I was little. Would, you like to see it?"

she smiled as she arched her back and slowly rolled her sculptured shoulders.

"How can I refuse?" Sammi took my hand and led me down the grassy hill, towards the water. As our fingers interlocked, I felt a strange calm, take a ride up from my ankles like it was an art deco elevator.

The tide was pretty much in, so we took off our shoes and socks, dodging hundreds of bright, pink, jellyfish as they flapped with all their might against the beaching brine.

"It's a secret little park that no-one knows about," she giggled, as we rounded the small headland and her thumb traced seductively across my knuckles, "I couldn't begin to guess, how many times this little place saved my sanity during Mum and Dad's divor… Oh shit! No!"

Her face looked like it had been snap-frozen. I turned around, to find the park was filled with an enormous white marquee and a proverbial army of attendants, swarming around chairs, trestle tables, party lights, an ivy-covered archway and an enormous dance-floor.

"Jacinta Satchwell's wedding… fuck! They've turned my sanctuary into a theme park… How dare they?" If the rise in her pitch and the sudden return of her pout were anything to go by, I was about to witness, one of Sammi's infamous hissy fits.

"I don't know *what's* more offensive? What they've done to my park, or the fact I wasn't invited."

I decided to appeal to her reasonable side. "Oh, but aren't those medieval torches on the edges of the dance-floor, a *bold* touch? If her veil's too long, the groom could be doing the bridal waltz with a shish kebab. And a *beige* tent? I mean, slightly off white maybe, but beige? It's only a few stops up the line from missionary brown." *Thump thump thump.* The heartbeat in my ears, clapped out the seconds, as I waited for her to respond. "I mean, where'd they get it? A *hardware* store?" *Thump thump and strike.*

"Yeah." She took the bait. "And, what about those, huge, gaudy, kissing swans?"

I wound the reel in, as fast as I could, "Absolutely... to think that that, was once, a perfectly good hedge. It's akin to manslaughter. It's *shrub*-slaughter." Her humid sniggers, tickling my neck, signalled we were out of the danger zone. "Now I know this is a bit of a set back but I'm sure we can find another quiet park somewhere. In fact, there's *one*, just the other side of Victoria..." Her soft, wet, lips swallowed my 'Avenue' while her tongue, pushed me into that delirious state that I'd previously only known in the dream, where I hover in giddy-euphoria around the pointy pinnacles of the pines, at Cottesloe beach.

"Shh," she commanded, as she pulled me against her denim-clad crevice, like I was a slot car being clicked into its groove; "Follow me." She led me through the crowd, with such purpose, that no one seemed to notice us and with every step I took, my resolve, became stiffer and stiffer. She must have sensed this and slowed up, allowing my engorged member to ride up against her and seek sanctuary, in the deep valley between her muscular butt cheeks.

"Fuck, that feels, unreal," she panted, through the most deadpan of faces, as she brazenly batted and brushed, my bristling balls, between her ballerina's buttocks. I couldn't believe it. There were people hanging lights right next to us. Of course, she made it look like we were just sort of wrestling, as we walked. And every now and then, she would spin around and kiss me for a few seconds, before turning and grinding up against me again. I'm sure to anyone looking on, it must have appeared very sus. But, after a couple of minutes of Sammi's frisky friction, I didn't give a fuck. My cock had never been so hard in my life. It was throbbing with so much ferocity, I was scared that either it, or the zip on my jeans, was going to burst. Her lips, were the most delicious, divine, delicacy I had ever ached for. I wanted her tongue in my mouth again. I wanted to suck it, taste it, swallow it.

When we reached the top of the park and she gave my cock one, last, clench, I couldn't stand it any longer. I grabbed her shoulders, forcefully turning her around and went for her mouth, like a mongoose after a cobra. My whole being shook, with an infinite, indescribable and insatiable hunger. I was possessed and sucked so hard, that it felt like her lungs were now in my mouth. Then my hands, zeroed in on her unspeakably pert breasts that sat in her top like two helium filled, perfectly ripe peaches in a tissue-paper bag. My cock, inching even harder, as if it were attached to an endless ratchet. I had just about ripped her shirt off, when she grabbed the front of my jeans, gathering up my manhood as she went.

"Not here... We're not, there yet." Her voice, ripping my sanity straight out of me, as a once-in-a-hundred-year forest fire rifled through every vein in my body. My heart beat so fast, it became one deafening sound and my urethra squealed for relief, from the stifling anaconda that was constricting it.

I followed her into the thick foliage at the back of the park. Away from prying eyes, the dank ground's humus permeated the air with its acrid perfume, forcing my hand to slip down the front of her jeans and under the sopping, wet, triangle of her panties. Now it was my turn. Every step she took, was an earth shattering ride, on my teasing and tantalizing, clitoris-friendly fingers. They shuddered across the folds of her luscious lips, occasionally ducking into her sultry cove, sliding and squelching but never stopping. Sammi was so electrified by this, that not only was her love nectar trickling down to my wrist, by the time we had made it half way up the tree house ladder, she had completely removed her knickers and jeans.

As I looked up and saw the sun's last rays painting her puffy, pink, puckered, clam. I *totally* understood, why every important painting, road, technological breakthrough, gag, religion, sculpture, essay, bridge, play, athletic achievement, novel, profound thought and even mime routine; indeed, every single human breakthrough, achieved by a heterosexual man, had ever happened. I was staring straight at it. Well, for a short while at least. Its delicate scent and glistening ridges were far too attractive to just look at. My tongue slurped along its pleats, like a cartoon character licking a lollypop. Its milky marinade cascading into my mouth and down my chin. I could have licked it forever but Sammi had other ideas, as she drew me up the ladder, her pussy playing the Pied Piper's flute and me the rat.

"You know, when I was at Equestrian school, there was a kind of, initiation," she confided, as she sat me down on the floor of the tree house and knelt in front of me. "The schools credo, was 150%. So, every new girl had to… Only in front of the other girls," she paused, as her hands, slowly, undid her blouse, "this wasn't, an official, initiation…" she added, as her bra fell to the ground and revealed her bite size nipples, that looked like swollen almonds that had been dipped and roasted in rich molasses. "They had to, *deep throat*, a Corona bottle," she beamed cheekily, as her hands, tugged, at the button on my jeans; "And anyway, I may not have been good at the *discipline* but, God, was I good at the Corona bottle…" My rock hard projectile, completely disappeared, into the tunnel behind her lips; "Sa wha I mon?" I wanted to laugh but I couldn't. I had never even heard about, deep throat before, let alone experienced it, and here I was, standing in a tree house, with the blueprint for physical perfection, performing it on me. It was *way* too much. Even, concentrating on the image, of Mr Shrapnel in the deer stalker hat with the hardboiled eggs, didn't work. Well actually, it might have, but Sammi shoving her thumb up my bum, cancelled it out entirely.

On paper, I would have been horrified by the concept. I mean, the only thing I thought it was good for, was making more room for beans and the occasional gag in a lift. But Sammi's skilful thumb, was inside the aromatic aperture, before I could even think, 'Hold on! None of that Viennese funny business for me thanks,' let alone say it. And once she was in, my God, I shot my load with such force, that it made the Apollo space mission look like it was powered by rubber bands. Not that it bothered Sammi. She was loving, every drop, of my sizeable steamy storm. As I collapsed forward, she caught me in her arms and together, we lay on the matted, weathered carpet. My teeth were tingling like tympanis and it felt like the Virgin Mary was running a feather duster, up and down my spinal chord, vigorously polishing each vertebrae, with a high speed oscillating flick of her wrist.

As I lay there, cocooned, in Sammi's sweet, spring sauna, I suddenly became aware that my bolt-hard erection had decided to turn a blind eye to the litre and a half of semen it had just been a gangplank for, and, if anything, my turgid member seemed to be getting even harder. Sammi, was onto it in seconds.

"Ooh, someone's, still a little excited. Let's see if we can't *do* something about that..." She splayed her legs, to reveal, her now almost white-hot slit and Mother Nature did the rest. My cock, harder than a length of petrified wood, slid beyond her gates as she moaned, "Oooooooooooh!" and her lips let me in, bit by bit, like an abseiler, using their hands to inch down a rope; a rope, that lead deep inside her moist, tropical, velvet canal. Once she had taken me all the way to the hilt, she spent the next 45 minutes, fucking me, in every position known to the animal kingdom. Until finally, we both knew what it was, to have the chariot scene from *Ben Hur* being shot in the pleasure centre of your mind. I thought it strangely fitting, to have bid my virginity adieu while the band played *Addicted to Love* and the bride and groom greeted each guest, one by one, under the archway.

The raucous clank of the *Rattler's* handbrake, unceremoniously tipped me out of the tree house, and onto the driveway at Stardust Central. I must have been so entranced in my virginity re-run, that I had no recollection of the drive whatsoever. 'Shit, I hope I stopped at all the stop signs,' I thought, as I surveyed the vans already buffeted hull, for any fresh dents. Sunny had told me to let myself in and wait inside till he returned, so we could have a beer and a chat. But the last thing I felt like, was sitting down into the wee hours of the morning, listening to Sunny Hollywood's history of rock. So I conveniently forgot our little arrangement, until I was half way home and it was too late to turn around.

By the time I did get home, it was totally dark and for some reason the outside security light didn't seem to be working. So I trod, very gingerly, up the pebbled path, straining my eyes as I went. On any given night, there were dozens of orb weavers the size of a boy's hand, hanging in the night with outstretched fangs. I knew they weren't lethal, but they could give you a nasty bite, and the thought of walking face first into one, really freaked me.

I was jumpy but lucky, and by the time I made it into the kitchen, the stress of the day had really caught up with me, and I felt that all too familiar tingling, returning to my left arm.

"Yer makin' a cuppa tea lad?" I leapt so high in the air, that my feet almost collected the bench tops, and the tea bags fell onto the floor, like iron filings that had been strewn across a magnet.

"Shit Dad! You scared the crap out of me."

"Oh, I'm sorry son. I didne mean ta frighten yer..." He grinned, apologetically. "Did the Bar Mitzvah, not go, so well then?"

"No, it was fine. Why?"

"It's just, when a man asks for a cuppa and yer does yer best Rudolph Nureyov meets a trampoline, yer gets ta thinkin', yer could be under a bit of pressure."

I filled the kettle, "Don't worry about me, Dad. How are *you* feeling?" The fact that it was a bitterly cold night, and he was sitting in a pair of shorts, playing patience, told me everything.

"I *do* wurry son. I can tell yer, ain't been yerself, a late. Is somethin' troublin' yer? Yer know, yer can tell me *anythin',* don't yer?"

"Yeah, Dad, I know."

"Well, what is it then son?"

He was right, usually I could tell him absolutely everything, but whatever it was, wouldn't come out.

"Just 'cause I'm sick, don't mean I'm not yer Dad. I like, bein' yer Dad yer know. I'll still be yer Dad, even on my death bed."

"Don't talk like that, Dad. That, isn't going to be for a long, long, time."

"Well, I 'ope not son. But, we 'ave to face facts. Because of this, bludy leukemia, I won't be round, as long, as we would like. So for Christ's sake son, let me be yer Dad, while I can..." He nervously, twisted the pack of cards, in his hands, "Is, this about, yer bein' adopted?"

"Yes," I whimpered, acknowledging it to myself, for the first time also.

"Well c'mon then. Out with it. It's much better out, than in."

Instinctively, I took a deep breath, "I just, feel so, confused. Ever since Mum told me my other name was

Richard, I don't know where I belong anymore. I mean, I know who I am because I had the best teacher *anyone* could ask for, *My Dad*. But, where do I come from? What does my *biological* mother look like? Do I have any brothers or sisters? Are there any diseases that run in my other family? They're *big* questions Dad that most people know the answers to, and take for granted. I have no idea where I fit in, or where I came from." It all spewed out, with the honesty and uncensored clarity, that I only ever had in front of my Dad, and he sat and listened, like a priest taking confession. I could see pain in his eyes, but it wasn't the, 'Oh my son is rejecting me,' kind that you would expect. His hurt was compassion, and genuine understanding.

"Well, there's only one thin' to do. We *must* try and find, yer biological mutha… But, I am scared, for yer son. What if she wants nothin' to do with yer? 'Ave yer, thought of that? I mean, the 'urt from that, could be worse than now. And, I'm not just sayin' that to try and put yer off. Believe me, son, nuthin' breaks my 'eart more, then seein' yer like this. Are yer sure, yer wants to go, lookin'?"

"Yes Dad, I am" I whispered, through a steady stream of tears.

"Well, that's that then. We'll make inquiries, on Mundy. Now, stop yer waterworks and come and 'ave a game a pontoon, with yer Dad." His big arms wrapped around me like a towel, engulfing a toddler. And as I sobbed into his chest, I realised that tears weren't only running down my *cheeks*, they were running down my *forehead* as well.

20 DIGGING UP THE FAMILY TREE

True to his word, Dad *did* look into the adoption business on Monday and on Tuesday afternoon, we sat in the office of 'Separated at Birth.' A private detective agency that specialised, in reuniting the triangles of adoption, or so the brochure said. For a fee of $750, they promised to do as much ferreting about as was necessary to find your missing relative, and they boasted a success rate of about 85%. Which sounded impressive enough, but as we sat waiting for the 'detective', I couldn't help but feel a little unsure. I guess, the fact that we were sitting in a couple of cotton director's chairs, and the desk in front of us was actually two card tables butted up against each other, didn't really instil a lot of confidence.

"Prob'ly just a, tight arse," Dad reassured. But when the sleuth responsible for such a serious search saunters in, in a crisp, fluorescent lime-green, linen safari suit — that would have been a bold choice when it was fashionable, let alone 15 years after its use by date — the alarm bells can't help, but begin to chime. And when he opens his mouth to speak, and out comes what could be best described as a loud whisper, punctuated with a great deal of lisping, so in effect you have a kind of 'lhisper', the alarm bells drown him out completely.

"Thorry to keep you waiting. You muth be Gerry, we thpoke on the phone, and Thephen. I'm Julian Parker. Lovely to meet you both."

"And you." Dad and I chorused, as we lent further forward in our chairs.

"That's a, lovely loud suit," I complimented.

"No prizes for guessin' what that's, compensatin' for," Dad added, under his breath.

"I juth had to thend off a faxth, about another over theath cathe I'm working on. Thith oneth in Thcotland and it lookth like, it's going to have a happy ending. Which, I'm glad to thay, happenth more often than not, but I do have to warn you, that it'th not alwayth the way." His eyebrows bowed in respect, "Thometimeth, a birth relative doethn't want to be contacted. They *can* feel, that the adoption chapter of their life is clothed thut. I wish I had a crythtal ball, tho I could thee which thearches will thuccceed and which oneth will fail. But thadly I don't. If you *do* want to protheed, I promith to do everything in my power, to find your Mum and then it'th up to her. The ballth in her court. Tho to thpeak. But if she doethn't want contact, its againtht the law for me to give you her adreth. Now, you do, underthand, what I'm thaying?"

A slightly shell-shocked Dad, nodded his head, "Stephen and I, 'ave discussed the possibility of, 'er not wantin to, know 'im. What do yer think Stephen, it's yer decision, d'yer still want to look?"

Despite Julian's message and the bizarre way in which he delivered it, I had absolutely no doubt whatsoever that I wanted to go through with it. I knew in my heart that my mother would want to see me. And I was totally convinced, that whatever it was that controlled the universe, couldn't be so cruel as to hand me another dose of rejection. I'd already had to deal with growing up in the Doo and not fitting in, going to boarding school and not fitting in, finding out that I was adopted and Dad getting leukemia. So as I saw it, the odds of her rejecting me again, were so low, they weren't even worth calculating. And besides, the thought of finding her, and finally knowing, really knowing, where I came from and where I truly fitted in, was so intoxicating, I would gladly have surrendered half of my life span just to know.

"I couldn't be surer," I stated, with the conviction of a Calculus Professor answering what's two times two. "I would like to start as soon as possible." Julian stuck out his hand and dabbed me on the shoulder, "I thintherely hope, it all workth out. Now, did you bring along a copy of your original birth thertificate?" Dad handed it over, "Right, we'll thart with that then. Yeth, here we are. Motherth name… Kim Bathinger," His mouth turned up at the corners, "Only kidding. I'm thuch a prankther. Claire Limb. Good. Very good. What I'm going to do, through my athothiate in the UK, ith go through the electoral roleth and marriage and death regitherth in that part of the country. Which I can thee is Nottinghamthire ith it? Yeth it ith. Right, well we'll do that in Nottinghamthire and then once we find her — Thorry *if* we find her — Which I'm confident we will, then I'll make contact and we'll thee if the's interethed in correthponding with you."

He may have been a little odd to look at, and a little hard to listen to, but he did seem to be genuine, and he took very fastidious notes about everything, including what little we knew about my birth mother. Dad explained to him that at the time, he had been told that she was quite young and unmarried, but that was about it.

Trepidation sat quietly on the back seat, for the majority of the drive home. Even though Dad had been wonderful, and so understanding about the whole thing, now that the wheels were in motion, it felt as though the search had a life and will of its own. And two or three more large scoops of uncertainty had just been sprinkled through our lives.

In true Dad fashion, he took it out on the road.

There had never been traffic lights in the Doo, and it sure did show every time he hopped behind the wheel. For a start, just about every green light we ever approached would go amber, usually because Dad was expecting it to and consequently he would ride the brake, every time we approached one. When it did go amber, he would plant his foot in order to speed through the intersection. The only problem being, a second or so into his deft dash, he would reconsider and slam on the brakes, which usually brought us to rest a half-a-car to a full-car length into the intersection. From which point, Dad would curse and swear and get beeped at, until eventually when the lights went green, he would plant his foot and repeat the whole ritual again, at the next set of lights.

We had just pulled up, in our second cloud of singed rubber, when I decided, that at least for the sake of the tyres, we should chat.

"You know Dad, even though I've started this search, it doesn't, in any way, undermine the great job you and Mum have done bringing me up. I mean, even if I do find my biological mother, it's not like I'm going to move over there and start my life again. I would never want to do that. You are my Dad, and Mum is my Mum, and nothing will ever change that. Together, you have given me the best start in life I could have ever dreamed of. And I love you both, so much. You know that don't you?"

"Yes son but it sure is nice, ta 'ear yer say it." He looked out at the road, like a surfer studying the swell, "I won't lie ta yer and say it's, easy, though. A tiny part of me, can't 'elp but feel like we, 'ave som-ow failed and not dun a good enough job. And that's why yer need to go lookin'. I know it's daft. But sumtimes it feels that way." A glove of knitted fear grabbed me by the throat.

"Oh Dad, please don't think that. I am so, so, lucky that of all the people in the world that could have adopted me, I hit the jackpot and was chosen by you and Mum. I thank God every day… Well I would, if you hadn't brought me

259

up to be an atheist," Dad's rosy cheeks quivered, as a big belly laugh rumbled through them.

"I sincerely hope, 'e uses sum of that muney we just gave 'im, on some new clothes and a maybe a megaphone or speech lessons, 'e were straight out a *Carry On* film,"

"Couldn't you just see, Kenneth Williams in that suit," another set of big belly laughs, rolled over the steering wheel, and this time I joined them.

For the first few days after the initial meeting, every time the phone rang I'd rush to pick it up, hoping like hell that there would be a sibilant mouse squeaking on the other end of the line, with wonderful news from a far away land. But alas, the call didn't come, so on Friday I phoned him and got an answering machine that said,

"Theparated at Birth, is thorry to announce, that due to illneth we will be clothed for four weekth, from the 30th of Theptember. Any inconvienienth is deeply regretted." I left a message anyway and a couple of hours later, Julian's aunt rang, to tell me that he had had a melanoma removed, but the doctors were confident they had got all of it out, and he should be back at work as planned in October. Which left me feeling like a New Years Eve pyrotechnic, that due to a faulty fuse, had failed to fire and consequently had been put back in the shed for next year. The reunion that was so close I could almost embrace it, would have to wait at least another month. Which, I suppose, did give me a bit of time to concentrate on some more, immediate issues.

21 HERE COMES THE BRIDE

I was so impatient to get on and find my birth mother, that I almost forgot the other important meeting on the horizon. The one with Saturday's bridal party. Sunny's voice crackling down the mobile brought it clearly into focus.

"Look mate, about Saturday's show. I'm sure you're gonna be fine mate but I just thought that maybe your idea, about a couple of hours of practice, might come in handy. The turntables *can* be a tad tricky, but they're much less likely to bite if they're used to you patting them."

"Yeah! ok Sunny, I couldn't agree more. When were you thinking I should do it?"

"Well, the wedding is tomorrow night. So that really only leaves, this arvo."

"I'll be right over." My voice quavered, as the reality of being totally responsible for the entertainment, on the most important day in two people's lives; *tomorrow*, crashed down on top of me. The pain in my arm, which pretty much resided there full-time now, ripped up my bicep and into my head. My neck locked up and it felt like someone was cutting my breastbone open with a chainsaw, as sweat poured like a monsoon out of my palms, "Oh fuck. FUCK! I don't want to die. Make it stop. Make it stop!" I pleaded, as my ability to breathe jumped into a lifeboat and left me to sink into the couch, where I lay on the verge of passing out… until eventually I realised it had passed by.

Half an hour later, my now *dry* hand, crawled into a fist and banged firmly on Sunny's front door. It was the fifth, in a series of knocks and I thought it very strange that he should invite me over, and not be home when I arrived. Eventually my knuckles tired of thumping, and I took a walk around the side of Sunny's house to see if there were any clues out the back. As I traipsed past the three DJ vans and a collection of speakers, lights and record boxes, I couldn't help but wonder what the neighbours thought of all this mess. I mean, don't get me wrong, I wasn't knocking it. After all, it was going to be my bread and butter. But it must get a little annoying, with vans coming and going in the middle of the night, and a mountain of sound gear greeting you, every time you look out of your window.

Mind you, it's fucking lucky they can't see out the back I thought, as my head peered in disbelief over the gate. Sunny's house was in one of those strange suburbs that back onto an industrial area, and in his case must have sat right on the edge of it. Because what was green lawned suburbia (albeit a little messy) out the front, was a full-on grey cement-scape factory, out the back. There was of course a little bit of fenced off back yard that sported a Hills Hoist, and an above-ground swimming pool, which was totally devoid of water, and overflowing with weeds, garden refuse and chunks of multicoloured clay.

Unsure what to make of this, I made a beeline for the bigger of the two sheds. As I came closer, what started out as a muffled haze of noise, cleared into the unmistakable chorus of Chris De Burgh's, *Don't pay the Ferryman*. And it was just as the song squawked; "Beware that hooded old man, at the rudder," that my eyes asked my brain to clarify that the image they were sending, of Sunny Hollywood dressed in a black hooded robe, holding what looked suspiciously like a rudder, while he hand painted a red hat onto a particularly large garden gnome and demanded; "Come on! Pay up! We're almost there," was in fact, Sunny Hollywood, dressed in a black hooded robe, holding what looked suspiciously like a rudder, while he hand painted a red hat onto a particularly large garden gnome and demanded, "Come on! Pay up! We're almost there." Which my brain confirmed was indeed the case. I didn't know what the fuck I should do, and as Sunny hadn't seen me, erred on the side of caution.

Once outside the shed and obscured from his view, I gave my knuckles another go. "Sunny? Sunny? You there mate?" It took every cubic millimetre of my self-control, to get that out of a straight face, "Sunny?" Fortunately, it took a couple of minutes for Sunny to respond. Which gave me time, to gather up a mental picture, of every horrific death, disease, car crash and horror story I could think of. *Anything*, to stop what I knew was almost inevitable. I had spent my last three years at Perth Grammar trying not to laugh in people's faces, but I had become so good at it, and developed such a reputation for it, that occasionally even the teacher I was laughing at would join in with me.

"G'day Stephen. Have you traded the Volkswagen in for a Porsche? I wasn't expecting you for another half an hour."

'Fuck, by then, he would have been playing the *lady in red* and *dirty dancing* with the gnome,' my mischievous brain interjected, while I involuntarily spluttered through my nose, bit down hard on my tongue and kept my eyes staring at the ground.

"Well, come in then. Let me give you the guided tour." My feet followed him into the shed, while I did my best, to look in every direction, other than that, of the hooded old man at the rudder.

"Here it is. The artist's workshop. You got ya, kiln over there. Ya, clay mixing station over there, and ya drying and painting section just here." A half chortle snuck out of my nose, which I quickly dressed up in the disguise of a sneeze.

"Admittedly, it doesn't look like all that much, but six and a half percent of WA's annual gnome population is manufactured right here, by yours truly. We *also* produce your garden-variety flamingo, which we've started to export to Florida. They're not that big over here but the yanks go crazy over them. Probably got something to do with that *Miami Vice* show. But that's a relatively new venture for us. It's really about these little buggers down here… Well Stephen, what da ya think?" Crunch time. I could hardly *not* look at him after such a direct question. My head, slowly moved up, like a camera shooting the opening crane shot in a schlock horror film. The soundtrack, in my mind at least, consisted of one partially trained mobile DJ chanting, 'Please have lost the rudder. Please have lost the rudder.' When the frame finally did come to rest on Sunny, it found him smiling expectantly, resplendent in an old pair of tracky dacks and a flannelette shirt, which my propensity for the particular, quickly pointed out was almost an identical replica of the cast uniform, in *The Texas Chainsaw Massacre.*

"I've gotta hand it to you, Sunny. It's a very *impressive* operation." I admitted, shaking my head in fabricated awe. "And you run the *whole* thing yourself?" I asked, eager to keep my words to a minimum.

"Absolutely. Right down to boxing 'em up and shipping 'em out. I know it looks like a big job, and me missus is always at me to put someone else on. But ya see, the thing is Stephen, if I *did,* how would I know whether or not whoever I hired, was makin' 'em to my standard?" It was a good question but it wasn't the only thing that had me thinking. Something had happened to Sunny's voice. It was as if slipping on that flannelette shirt had erased his rich cultured grammatically correct accent and replaced it, with a whiney clipped one, that had spent a lot of time leaning against bars. The cylindrical steel variety.

"Some people might think, 'Well, what does it matter, it's only an ornament that's going to bake in the sun *and* make it a bit harder to mow the lawn.' But I don't look at it like that Stephen... I haven't told many people this, but I've got a feelin' you'll understand, where I'm comin' from... Ya see... They're not *just* gnomes, Stephen... they're little people. Each one an individual, with a totally different personality and every time I make a gnome, I conceive a life and I give away, a tiny, part, of meself. Admittedly, that's three thousand six hundred and fifty bits of me each month, but I didn't say they were big bits."

"No, just tiny bits. Microscopic bits." I offered. Astonished at myself, for turning up the dial on the Sunny treadmill, yet again.

"Exactly! You know Stephen. It's almost as if, there are two sides to Sunny Hollywood. On the one hand, you've got your smooth, sophisticated, outgoing life of the party that everybody loves, side. And then you've got, your quiet, shy, reflective, introverted, delicate side, that I share with me gnomes. All that loud showbiz stuff, is all well and good and a large part of me, but *these* little fellas with the red hats, complete me Stephen."

To my utter amazement, I didn't even crack a smile. Fuck knows I should have. But there was an honesty and truth in Sunny's voice that you might hear once in a lifetime, if you're lucky. If anything, I almost felt jealous. Well at least initially. However, his decision to pat one and then kiss it lightly on the forehead, pushed me off the precipice and undid the safety catch, on my deadly derision trigger. My DJ career was surely over before it began, because I knew now, that I had passed the point of no return and was *doomed* to laugh in his face. He had shown me, the beautiful, decorative, ornamental skylight, into his soul, and I was about to take to it with a mallet.

As if controlled by my autonomic nervous system, my right hand moved with military precision into my deep jeans pocket, where it opened its vice like fingers, grabbed hold of my testicles and proceeded to squeeze them so hard, I became dizzy. Sunny mistook the groan of discomfort I emitted, for a religious experience — a deep and appreciative wonder, for everything gnome — and silently left me to contemplate *the little buggers,* while he went indoors to get some records. By the time he returned, I had negotiated the release of my left testicle and spent the rest of the afternoon attempting to mix records, while my right one remained in clamped solitary confinement, as Sunny stepped up into the stirrups and brought another 58 little red faces into the world.

The Mitchell Reception centre took its name, funnily enough, from the Mitchell Freeway, that roared past it like a butane flash from a flamethrower. Why someone would want to have their unique and sacred bond, celebrated, next to a wonderful metaphor for the busy pace of modern life and the toll that it exerts on everything, including the family unit, was beyond me. I mean, if the statistics were right, a third of those cars were being driven by divorcees.

Sunny had said that the Mitchell's staff were second to none, and so far he was right. Nigel, the drinks waiter, had come straight up to me and asked if he could help with the gear. As it *was* my first time, I didn't really want to impose and had almost said "no." But as my arm wobbled under the weight of the Rattler's back door, I was glad I hadn't.

The console that lay before me made the Bar Mitzvah one look like a toy you'd find in a Kinder Surprise. Not only was it a metre and a half longer, it was upholstered in a rich, maroon Berber, that must have weighed as much as the three sheep that produced it. And the front of the stand was littered with little lights, that when lit up, spelt *Stardust*. At least, that was their default setting while you played background music. Then, when you got them dancing, there was a special luminous orange switch you flicked, that made the *dust* flash on and off, intermittently.

Once set up on the corner of the *dance-floor,* my fingers rummaged through the record boxes, desperately trying to get a feel for where all the different kinds of music were kept. When it came down to the sweaty business of toe-to-toe combat, or 'boogie-time,' as Sunny called it, I would have on average, three minutes; to choose my next song, find it in the box (that held at least four hundred singles) put it on the vacant turntable and cue it up so it would start precisely where I wanted it to. Then, it was just a simple co-ordination matter of *lifting* your mixing finger, which released the stationary disk, onto the spinning turntable as the other song died away, cut out or subsided into applause, if it was a live track.

Which admittedly wasn't a quadruple bypass, but it still carried with it, a considerable degree of difficulty. Especially, when this whole series of tasks were (a) performed under the effects of the, Fuck what comes first, the cutting of the cake or the bridal waltz, hangover and (b) completely alien to you. And speaking of alien, that's what my *fingers* looked like within 20 minutes of setting up. The practice session the day before had gone quite well, but I thought I better cram in another one, just before the guests arrived. The thing was, the often frantic flicking and fumbling through the filed field of cardboard sleeves, had started ripping the quicks right out of my fingers. And consequently, that crucial moment when the guests first walked into the room, or onto the *set*, as Sunny called it, was accompanied by a large burst of crackling hiss. Due in part, to one particularly savage paper cut and one particularly old Richard Clayderman record, that staged a mutiny one and a half songs into a 10 song side. Of course, the seasoned DJ, like the seasoned guitar player, would have had methylated-spirit-hardened fingers, and would be standing behind his trusty console, ready to rectify the tinkling ivories that weren't. As opposed to crouching between two industrial fridges, running your hand over a chemistry labs worth of decomposing matter as you *chase* The Mitchell's last remaining bandaid, like Stevie Wonder, reading a particularly flattering and descriptive, brail review, of his most recent album.

Anyway, by the time the bride and groom had arrived, and were ready to make their entrance, I was standing in position; albeit with beer-soaked pants clinging to my legs, a throbbing right index finger (doing its best to join the rest of the Stardust sign's light team) and a great deal of old fashioned terror, traumatizing my trachea.

"Deep breaths, mate." I muttered, as I brought the once gold, now dull bronze, microphone to my lips. "Ladies and Gentlemen presenting, Mr and Mrs Bosnich!" Despite the Parkinson's disease, that had set up shop in my hand,

I was *just* about to release the record, when I realised that no one had responded to my announcement. "Probably because the fader was turned down." I grizzled, audibly. I pushed it right up and tried again, as the Parkinson's expanded into my whole body, "The bride and groom!" Boomed out of the speakers and this time there was an expectant murmur, which in turn cued my finger, which in turn cued the music, which in turn cued the bride and groom.

I guess in the anxious moments that followed, I was so busy staring at the record, willing it to keep spinning that I didn't even look at the newlyweds. Well, not properly anyway. I did kind of clock them peripherally, as they made their way towards the bridal table. Sunny had *stressed,* that it's very important *not* to keep the special couple waiting, once they had made it to their seats. As soon as they had sat down, I was to put the Clayderman back on, so they could relax and I could wait for the MC to approach me and tell me when he or she wanted to use the microphone. So I was sticking to Sunny's game plan when things came a little, unstuck.

The Bosnichs, made it to their table quite quickly but when they got there, they didn't sit down. In fact, as their table was circular, their guests were scattered all around them and they were very keen to chat to as many of them as they could. Which would have been just fine had it not drawn my attention away from the record, so I actually looked up and saw them clearly. This, added to the fact that their entrance had milked The Carpenters, '*We've only just Begun*' of its entire 3 mins and 4 seconds, was compounded by me having *forgotten* to turn off the microphone, and finally the bride and groom's remarkable resemblance, to a stone fish and ferrel bush pig, respectively. All of which conspired to make me say in a very startled and disparaging tone, into a live and very loud microphone, "Jesus Christ!" The whole room looked up at me, with daggers in their eyes. I wrote my mouth a blank cheque, "We give you thanks... oh... Jesus, up above. Thanks for this," I desperately scanned the room, "beautiful, reception, centre? Because it's, quiet... praise the Lord. Even though it's almost, in the middle of Perth's busiest freeway... And... and... praise the Lord... if you think about it. That's what," my eyes sprinted across the running order, "Yelena and Bryce have just turned onto... the freeway of love." My tongue found its rhythm, "And I'm sure, as anyone who knows them can tell you, their deep and abiding love and respect for each other, will be the perfect vehicle, to whisk them safely and comfortably through God's glorious kingdom. No matter what bumps, blind corners and roundabouts come their way. You won't find these two in a cul de sac. So, dear Lord, we give you thanks, for this very special day, in this very *special* place. Praise the Lord. Amen." My left hand, allowing a second for dramatic effect before slowly fading up Sade's, *Your love is King*.

I was just about to pat myself on the back, when a portly and affable looking gentlemen, came over and did it for me, "Very nice work Mr DJ. Very nice." Strangely enough, his tone seemed considerably less straight than his appearance, "Thought of that yourself, did you?"

"Mmm." I nodded. "You know, just kind of gauging the feeling in the room. I… I, hope it, wasn't too over the top," I added humbly.

"Over the top? No! Not at all. I'm sure every atheist bride and Muslim groom wants to hear an unsolicited, evangelical sermon at the beginning of their reception."

"Atheist and Muslim?" I bluffed. "It says on my sheet, that they are devoutly Christian. Oh no. I'm really sorry."

"Don't worry about it. They won't. After all, you weren't, actually addressing them. You were addressing, Yelena, the groom's mother who's apparently marrying Bryce, who would be me, the bride's father. Oh, and just to finish off the trifecta, his family are traditional Croatians, who amongst other things, are anti-abortion. It's a shotgun wedding. They've known each other, for about, eight weeks. And as you can possibly imagine, I'm just tickled pink about it… Anyway, I'm the MC."

"Oh. So I guess, we'll be, working together."

"Lucky us," he grinned, before taking a big swig of champagne and heading off to the bridal table, to reassure the happy couple that I wasn't a plant from *Serbian* Candid Camera.

There isn't really a great deal of room behind a DJ console, but on this occasion, what little there was, was far too much. I think, what I was craving, was something about the size of one those urns cremated people are housed in. Even that, would have been a little large. I felt so stupid and under-prepared. Why didn't I just tack on a, "For what we are about to receive make us truly thankful. Amen" after the "Jesus Christ." Oh but no, I couldn't pass up the opportunity to *talk* my way out it. Unfortunately, brevity had never really been my strong point, and that was particularly true, when I was whipping myself. Don't get me wrong, the wedding had started appallingly, but it probably wasn't a third as bad as I thought it was. The older I got, the harsher I seemed to be getting with myself. Mind you, there seemed to be a lot of it about that night. If you closed your eyes and felt the atmosphere, you could have been forgiven for thinking you were at a boxing match.

A thick current of animosity, seemed to be hanging around like a spoilt child that wouldn't go to bed. Thankfully, Nigel appeared with a large glass of Emu Export.

"There you go, Stephen. You've *earnt* that. I've seen some debuts in my time, but that takes the pavlova. 'The freeway of love.' And what about the cul-de-sac? I think that, was the one bit that Jabba the Hut - I mean bride - understood. Hilarious!" And speaking of the bride, it wasn't long before I discovered that her resemblance to Jabba the Hut, was a lot more than skin deep. Sade had given way to Sinatra's *Nice and Easy*, and I was settling into my second Emu Export, when I became aware of a clicking sound: I jumped to my feet, crapping my dacks that there was something wrong with the equipment. Not that I would have had a fucking clue what to do if there was a technical issue, but thankfully there wasn't. The problem actually lay with the bride, who was clicking her fingers to get my attention. When I did finally trace the noise, to her large, podgy paw, she rolled up her finger and gestured me over.

"Ya got any Barnsey?"

"Yes, I think so."

"Well put it on, this stuff is shit."

"Oh, ok, if that's what you want? It's just… um.. It's just usually people like laidback, background music, so they can chat over dinner." I quoted straight from Sunny's manual.

"I don't give a, shit, what you think. I want Barnesy and I want it, now," she insisted, with a dismissive flick of her head, that almost dislodged her 10 centimetre tall tower of a tiara. She genuinely thought she was a princess. I mean, I know it was her wedding day, and traditionally brides can be a little difficult, but did she *really* need to sit on a cushion and have one of the staff fluff it up every 10 minutes?

I tried to disguise the anything but subtle shift from swanky Frank to screaming Jimmy, by keeping the latter's level relatively low. But the bride wasn't having any of that.

"Turn it up, ya fuckin' moron," she barked, like a blue heeler trying to round up a sheep. I could tell that I was rapidly becoming the Princess' pea, and I wasn't too happy about it. But luckily, she must have found someone else to pick on, because she left me pretty much alone after I buckled to her Barnsey lust.

By the time the speeches started, I'd ingested just enough amber fluid to have completely covered my usually razor sharp judgement, in eight layers of industrial strength bubble-wrap. Mind you, compared to Bryce I was as sober as a nun. As he staggered over towards me, he was hitting his glass with a knife, so hard, cracks had appeared down the length of it, and it was ready to shatter in seconds. So I immediately handed him the mic.

274

"Laies and gena mon…" He bellowed, with the diction and finesse, of someone who had recently had a serious head injury, "Could have I your… um… attention, please." A raised eyebrow heralding a belch, "Burp…. For, those of you, who don't… know me, my name is … Bryce… Keene… and contrary, to the *rumours* being circulated by our wonderful DJ… who likes to play *rock* music, when people are *trying* to talk… I am not, the groom… I am *actually,* the father of the bride… I've been asked… *told*, to keep this brief tonight… very brief. I'm wearing briefs as it happens. But I won't show you them cos I'll get in… Shh Shh. Right, get it together Brycey. I won't go on and on. No I won't… Because that would be… Where were we? Yes, righty, ho." He glanced down at the card in his palm. "I am not going to pretend, that Cheryl marrying someone, that she's only known for a couple of months, is ideal… Ideal? It's a bloody joke!!!" He slurred, as his legs gave way underneath him, and he fell back, onto the console. "Steady on. Steady on. I might be old, but I'm quick," he warned, as he lifted his fists and sized up the potted ficus next to him… "Where was I? Oh yes, I won't go… No I've done that. Um? Oh yes, it's a Joke!" His eyes squinted, as if for the first time in his speech, the room was actually coming into focus. "But, I have to respect, my daughter's, choice. That's what being a parent is all about. Respecting, dodgy decisions, that you don't necessarily, agree, with and know are totally, fucking, wrong! Hey watch it. Watch it," he spluttered, as he let go with a couple of left jabs, into the defenceless foliage, before turning back, transformed, with the pious face of a choirboy. "And so, without any further ado, I would like to welcome, Drago, into the family." And with that, particularly warm outstretching of the hands, he dropped the microphone onto the dance-floor and staggered off to the bar, like a sea lion wobbling along a diving board, while the rest of the room, sat, in stunned silence.

Instinctively, I pressed play, thinking any noise would be better than the deafening screams of gutted expectation. I was wrong. Jimmy Barnes screeching, "The rising sun just stole my girl away," only served to underline the situation, in the audio equivalent, of flashing neon. Not to be denied on her wedding day though, the bride appeared to take it in her stride.

"Right, come on then, we're cutting the cake," she snarled, as she looked over in my direction, "Play, the cake song."

"Your decree, is my reason for living," I muttered under my breath, as I picked up the mic and launched in to my second attempt, at announcing for the evening.

"Ladies and gentlemen, if you'd like to shift your attention, to the area on my left," I thought about personalising it but decided generic was the safer option, "the bride and groom, are about to cut the cake."

Their chosen song, ACDC's, *It's a long way to the top if you wanna rock and roll*, accompanied the knife, through the marzipan and deep into the fruit cake.

Keen to wrestle back some semblance of control, I took the bold step of moving things along. "Ladies and gentleman I would now like to ask," Oh what the fuck, I thought, "Drago and his precious, *cargo,* to dazzle us with their ballroom brilliance, as they take their first dance, as man and wife."

The *delightful* couple, made their way to the dance-floor but just before they arrived, Jabba decided she better show me, exactly, who was calling the tempo of the tune, by bending over to adjust her shoe, *prior* to commencing her waltz. This should have just served to make me re-cue the record and show me once and for all, that she was the boss. But her demonstrative display actually pushed one of the laws of physics, a little *too* far. As she cascaded forward in her dress, the hundreds of buttons, that were effectively stapling her into it, exploded, leaving her hindquarters on show for the world to see, like a pig's carcass draped over a butcher's shoulder, as it's carted across the High Street. The rest of the night blurred into a bizarre blend of beer, bad break-dancing, and Bosnich brawls.

22 YORKSHIRE PUDDING

As I leaned into the last bend that turned into Sunny's street, I eased the Rattler into neutral and coasted down the road and up onto the driveway. Disengaging the transmission *did* make the rusty old van a little quieter, but only a little, and I'm sure most of the street's occupants still would have thought a low-flying passenger jet was buzzing their neighbourhood. Having been robbed of the post-Bar Mitzvah chat, Sunny had been very definite that I was to drop in after the wedding, and let him know how it went. But the truth was, I just wasn't up to it. I mean as Sunny-driven as Sunny's conversations were, they still involved a lot of listening and prompting, and *oohing and ahhing,* which was tiring at the best of the times. But after six solid hours of being a bride's whipping boy, a UN peace keeper and a holding tank for seven or eight beers, all I wanted to do was go home and sleep.

Sunny's porch light flicking into life, signalled that that was going to be out of the question. He must have really been hanging out to bond because the light went on so quickly, it almost pre-empted me.

"Oh, g'day Sunny. How's it going mate?" I said, trying to muster my mettle for the imminent marathon. I looked into his eyes with a, come on then, give me your best-shot expression. But the sullen lacquer on Sunny's face told me all was not well. And it suddenly hit me, as if a bride that was that much of a bitch, would just walk away without at least a *bucket* of blood and a *kilo* of flesh. I felt what little energy I had, free fall inside me.

"Come inside. Stephen," Sunny said as he ushered me through the door, "I'm afraid, I've got some bad news mate."

'Oh well, it was good while it lasted,' I thought. 'I probably haven't got the right knees for all that lifting anyway.'

When I got inside, Sunny's wife met me with a glass of water. Fuck, this *is* serious, he's not even going to introduce us.

"It's your Dad mate. He's been rushed to hospital."

A sober wind of dry ice swept through every cell in my body.

"Is he all right? When?"

"Your Mum rang about 20 minutes ago. They're at The Mount Street Hospital."

"Fuck, I've gotta go."

"Do you want me to take you?"

"Oh, thanks for the offer Sunny. But…"

Thirty seconds later, I was burning down Albany Highway, at a hundred k's an hour in Sunny's V8 Commodore.

"It's really nice of you to do this Sunny… Fuck, I hope he's going to be ok."

"He will be mate. The Mount's the best hospital in Perth. It's totally state of the art."

"If he dies I… I can't even…"

"He's not going to die Stephen. They'll get some drugs into him and he'll be fine."

"The drugs are half the fuckin' problem," Sunny looked non-plused. "He's got leukemia Sunny and all the drugs they give him fuck him up."

"Do me a favour Steve. Reach into the glove box. There should be a… medical chest in there. Can you see it?"

It was so dark in there I couldn't see anything, but I did feel something cold, hard and lumpy.

"You mean this?" I asked, of the gnome-red clay box that sat on my lap.

"Yeah that's it. Open it up." My finger nails scraped along its bumpy surface, until they grabbed hold and the lid came away to reveal a bottle of Chivas Regal and two shot glasses. "My emergency back up. Just in case I don't have enough *show,* in my *biz.* Don't tell the other guys, they'll think I've lost my nerve. It's our secret ok?"

By the time the Commodore skidded into the ambulance bay, we had had a couple of shots each, which if anything just acted as a surrogate jacket, as I'd accidentally left mine on Sunny's couch. He offered to come in with me, but this time I was adamant that I should go alone.

The massive double glass doors parted with a surreal 'phttt' sound, that not only heralded your entry to the nurse on the desk but also, subliminally informed you that depending on your ticket, the hospital was both a transit and departure lounge.

"My Dad's Gerry Briggs, he's just been admitted."

"Oh, yes Mr Briggs. He's in room 305 on level three."

"Is he all right?"

"I think he's being assessed by the doctors now."

Fear flung me down the incredibly plush corridor to the lift. Even in that strung out, hysterical state, I couldn't help but notice how much the place resembled the pages of an interior design magazine. It was as if some doctors and nurses had hijacked a Five Star Hotel. The lift's antique call button sat perfectly in its modern rendered cement wall, and the lift itself threw back its doors in welcome, as soon as I was within a centimetre of pressing the button. Within seconds it had Chaise Lounged me up to the third floor, and the rosewood door of Room 305. The door swung in, and revealed what looked like the set of a Science Fiction film. A complex matrix of bottles, pipes, bags, monitors, tubes and charts, that all converged in and around the frail, withered figure of a man, aging ahead of his time. Set amongst all that impersonal technology, it almost felt like I didn't know him. But then my eyes skimmed across his back and up over those all too familiar chicken wings, that jutted out of it, like two tiny spinnakers trying to drag him into calmer waters.

As I rounded the Roman column at the foot of his bed, I discovered the doctor was extending this theme, into the procedure department as well. Even in an age of organ transplantation, heart bypasses and neurosurgery, occasionally medicine must still resort to a dirty big horse needle and a generous dollop of elbow grease. For one epic nanosecond, I witnessed the sacred fluid that housed my Dad's incredible brain, trickling into a plastic syringe, like left over bacon fat being drained into a used milk bottle. And even though the sight of this made the pain in my arm so severe that my thumb started to twitch uncontrollably, I stood my ground and maintained my composure. This wasn't about me, it was about my beautiful, beautiful, Dad.

To be honest, I don't think at that point Dad even knew that I was there. After all, he was lying on his side facing the wall, while a six-inch hollow nail punctured his spinal cord. Even though he had suspected Meningits and was in excruciating pain, he didn't make a sound. In fact, Dad rarely complained about anything. The closest he came to it, was when he would say, "When I were six, I 'ad to walk five miles along railway line, to fetch a bucket of water, every day, so we could cook and wash. And compared to that, everythin's a bloody brilliant day at beach."

Somehow I didn't think that that rule applied today. Finally, after what felt like 10 minutes, the doctors removed the needle.

"I am sorry about that, Mr Briggs. I know it's not pleasant but now we'll definitely be able to find out what's wrong. Can I give you anything more for the pain?"

My father's normally buoyant and boisterous bark, could only manage, a frail, "No," that instantly unravelled my bravado and simultaneously hit the claustrophobia and gravity buttons, forcing me into the hallway, stooping, progressively as I went, until I spiralled down like a wounded bird, onto the cold hard floor. Where I sat, long enough for my left buttock to absorb enough ambient temperature, that it went hard and numb. I could hear Dad's voice in my head, 'You'll get piles son, yer better get up,' but I couldn't. Grief held me in a catatonic bear hug.

"Are yer all right love?"

Mum wrapped her weary arms around me, like a wren protecting its chick. I tried to be strong for her but the only strength I could find, was enough to shake my head.

"It's all right Stephen. He's going to be ok."

My words were drenched in tears, "They ask... asked him if he wanted anything for the p... pain... And he was strong and said 'no'... But he... he sounded like he... was a... a... little boy. And I wanted to help him but there was noth... nothing I could do." Mum grabbed hold even tighter and muffled her sobs, into my shirt. From the way her chest was shaking, I realized, that I had gone too far and quickly grabbed myself by the scruff of the neck, 'For fucks sake mate, *now* look what you've done. She needs to lean on *you*, not the other way around. She's been married to him since she was 18, you, insensitive, fuckwit. For Christ's sake, pull your useless fuckface self together.'

"I'm sorry Mum. I shouldn't have told you that. You didn't need to hear it. Come on."

I tried to stand up, but stumbled under the weight of the both of us.

"Come on Mum. It's going to be ok. Dad *needs* us doesn't he?" Her sobbing stopped.

"I mean, I don't know why? We both know he's a stubborn old ox and he's not going to let some stupid disease, that sounds like it should be a dessert, bother him." I adopted the voice, of a pompous waiter; "Actually madam, the chefs just put the finishing touches, on a magnificent, meningitis. Superb, with a little cream." Mum's twinkling smile broke through the gloom that was clouding her face. And together we returned to Dad's bedside; a groggy half turn of his head, his only acknowledgment. "I'm here Dad. I'm taking care of Mum, so you just concentrate on getting better. All right?" But Dad didn't answer.

We spent the next *week,* sitting in that hospital, drinking tea in the dark, while we held Dad's floppy, pethidine-filled hand. Despite the spinal tap's grisly mechanics, the results certainly were worth it. Dad had contracted bacterial meningitis, which meant he could be given antibiotics. It was still a very serious condition to have, especially on top of leukemia. But thankfully, courtesy of the gods from Pfizer and the phenomenal constitution of a man reared on mushy peas and Yorkshire puddings, Dad joined us for the drive home.

And the good news continued when we *got* home. Amongst a million other messages on the answering machine, there was one from Julian Parker saying that, "I have thome exthiting newth for you." Which was pretty weird, considering *he* was supposed to be in hospital as well. For a second, I wondered if all this hospital stuff, was some kind of sign, that I should join the Red Cross and go save the starving millions in Africa. Then I remembered, that I was a middle class Australian, and these kind of fantasies were bound to float in and out of my consciousness, as I tried to define some sort of meaning, from my plentiful and over-abundant leisure time. I wonder if the starving Sudanese, have the time or inclination, to play esoteric, philosophical, chasie with themselves? Probably not, I thought, as I sipped on my homogenised and pasteurised chocolate milk, while my finger tapped out Julian's number.

"Hello." A voice, slightly deeper than I was expecting, answered the phone.

"Hello, it's Stephen Briggs calling. Is that Julian?"

"Yeth Thephen, it ith. I thound like a drag queen don't I? Big night, lath night. It wath my birthday. I athked my doc, if a few drinkth would effect the chemo and he thaid 'no,' tho I got on it."

"So, are you feeling better then? I mean, apart from the hangover?"

"Thuprithingly yeth. Apart from, the thumping, in my head." Now the pleasantries were out of the way, I expected him to continue and tell me the good news but it wasn't forthcoming. Probably just the hangover, I thought.

"Jul…"

"Look Thephen, there'th been a bit of a development."

"Yeah, you mentioned on the machine. Exciting news, you said."

"Yeah that'th right… At leatht wath. … You know how I told you, I had another cathe in the UK? Well I wanted to finish that, before the chemo thtarted and anyway

285

while I wath talking to my man over there, I mentioned your cathe and ... he found your mother."

My heart burst out of my chest, like an orchid unfurling in the morning sun.

"That's unreal!"

"Hold on, Thephen. Before you go danthing around the houthe. I left that methage, before, I'd had a chanthe to contact her... look, I'm thorry. But her firth rethponthe, wathn't too pothitive. In fact, Claire thaid, she dothn't want to have *any* contact with you."

"Oh... I see... But... that was only her initial response, right?"

"Yeth that'th true..."

"And, it, must be a... shock, when someone, comes looking?"

The line hummed.

"I mean, she could change her mind, couldn't she?"

"Yeth, she could Thephen but I've got to be honetht with you, I don't want you harbouring any falthe hope. She was... pretty emphatic."

As my heart returned to the rather mundane task of pumping blood around my body, I felt myself begin to slip into a depression, with the momentum of a cruise ship sliding down the slipway at its christening. Had it not been for the casual touch of my father's hand, as he went to boil the kettle, I'm certain I would have disappeared into an ocean of quicksand that never would have released me. Even though he hadn't been there to hear my conversation and had no idea who I was talking to, his instinctive, gentle love and reassurance reached out and saved me once more, as it had done countless times before.

23 SO MUCH TO SAY

Despite my best efforts, the knockback from my biological mother *really* hit me hard. To be in effect, rejected *twice*, shook me about like an antique Faquari Rug that had been left on an Egyptian washing line during a sandstorm. The very fabric I was made of began to fray at its edges. Julian said that he would contact her again, a couple of months later, which he did, but her story was the same. 'No. No contact whatsoever.' She did give him a little more information though. She said it came down to her family. She had a husband and four daughters, and they had no idea that I existed, and she didn't want to disrupt her daughters' studies with such a disturbing piece of news. 'Their *studies*! What about my fucking *life*!' I kept thinking to myself and repeating to any nightclub punter who would listen.

It kinda pains me to admit it, but after the second 'No-Go conversation' with Julian, the world I would wake up to every morning became less vivid Panavision and more dull black and white. The last thing I wanted, was to be some cynical world -weary middle-aged adolescent, wandering around wearing a faecal waistcoat and a permanent expression of tart indignation. But the truth ain't always pretty.

It wasn't my fault Dad was sick. It wasn't my fault I'd been an unwanted baby who had been put up for adoption, it wasn't my fault that I had been sent away to boarding school, and it wasn't my fault, that my biological mother, had told me, in the nicest possible way, to go get fucked. But fuck me, it sure *felt* like it was. I couldn't help but think, that there was something, intrinsically wrong with me. And tragically, somewhere along the line, I became aware that a frozen family pack of 'McCain Oven Fries,' had been stapled to my shoulders and was accompanying me on every single one of my travels. Even when I was drinking or fucking, doubts would crowd along the sidelines of my mind, heckling my every move.

And as the next few years came and went, I found myself in not so much of a rut, as a corrugated road. Occasionally I would manage to drag myself, in a Herculean act of optimism, out of one enormous corrugation. But when I reached its summit, I would lose my footing and tumble straight into another, heading in the same direction.

Over the months after the meningitis episode, I tried to spend as much time with Dad as I could. Some nights, I would forgo Limbo all together, so I could *get up* at six, rather than *get home* at six, and spend the morning turning earth, planting seeds and reaping my father's rich, resilient, harvest. I did of course continue clubbing and D-Jing. In fact, one usually led to the other. I would routinely get shit faced at work for free, before heading out into the night, to drink and dance away my pain. And as there was no shortage of pain, there was no shortage of drinking and dancing and no shortage of hangovers. It was, while attempting to evade a particularly nasty one of these, that I had a truly unsettling experience.

I had read somewhere, that if you concentrated hard enough, it was possible to meditate yourself out of the holocaust that was, the day after a night on the piss. My first couple of remedies, namely bacon and eggs followed by a vigorous spot of masturbating and 20 pages of 'The Godfather' in the bath; had failed miserably. So I decided to steal a chapter from the mysterious book of the east. Amazingly enough, I had actually attended, a Siddha Yoga seminar a few weeks earlier at Uni. That is to say, a cute girl in my theatre class had attended and I went along, to attend to her attending. Anyway the forum, was chaired by this lady who was apparently a deity, as far as these Yoga people were concerned. Not that she really did that much chairing, it was more chanting. In fact, most of the two hours were taken up with chanting the rather innocuous phrase, 'Om Namah Shivaya' over and over again. Which, if I'd been told about third hand, instead of witnessing myself, would have had me derisively stuffing mung beans up my arse and firing them across the quadrangle towards Byron Bay, not that that's strictly where Siddha Yoga comes from, but it's in the general direction. But the *incredible* thing was, every single person in the room, sang out that phrase in perfect harmony, no matter *how* difficult the deity made the melody. And there must have been 1500 people in that auditorium. Five of which, were second row rugby players, who spent three hours a week *trying* to learn the melody of the first phrase of their team's song. Which was incidentally, 'Give us a U. U. Give us an N. N. Give us and I. I. What have you got? UNI!'

Armed with my new phrase, and the knowledge that it could at least assist the rugby team in the change rooms, after the game, if not on the oval, I decided to try and apply it to the atomic testing that was being conducted between my ears. Initially, I must admit, I did feel a little stupid lying in a bubble bath chanting words that had no meaning to me, as loudly as I could to be earnest, and as quietly as I could not to get busted by Mum or Dad.

I'm not sure exactly when it occurred and indeed my recollection of the whole experience is pretty hazy. But somewhere around the twenty-minute mark, things got a little bit *strange*. For a start, I saw something really bright glowing, even though my eyes were shut and the light was turned off. Then, after a bit longer, the light was not only in front of me it was also inside of me, in my pelvis, moving up towards my head. Then I was asleep but still sort of awake, and there weren't *any* lights, or anything *weird* at all. In fact, it felt like a totally ordinary day that had been plucked from my life... I was just lying on my bed, staring out the window and coming to terms with the fact... that my Dad was *dead*.

When I came to, I got the fright of my life. For a start, I was not only *in* the bath, but I was *floating* in the bath. My hands and bottom, weren't resting on anything. They had totally ignored the laws of physics and were literally suspended, in the water. And most distressing of all, I was crying, like totally fucking bawling, so much so, that there was a knock at the door.

"Yer right, lad?" came Dad's curious voice, from the hallway.

"Yeah, I'm fine thanks Dad. Must have nodded off." I explained, as the door opened slightly, "Got the shock of my life, when I woke up in the bath."

"'ow many beers, did yer 'ave last night then? One or two, too many, by the sounds of it."

"You could be onto something there Dad," I smiled a little too eagerly, desperate not to let him see any hint of the harrowing chord that was still resonating in my ears.

As the towel did one last sweep across my body's damp, forgotten, little crevices, my rational mind finally started to regain the helm. 'It was, just a stupid dream. You mix 15 beers, eight B52s, a couple of vodkas, a kebab and a half baked notion of some religion that claims it's not a religion, and spends it's time maniacally muttering a mantra, that emanated from time immemorial, and you're asking for trouble, aren't ya? I mean, *Om Namah Shivaya*, probably translates to '*I'm a little teapot short and stout*' or, '*Give me all your money you gullible western fuck.*' But the truth was, no matter how I explained it away, the dream's vile taste, kept tapping at my door all day. Like reflux, from a dodgy two day old hamburger. And a week later, as I gathered up my wallet and keys so I could pay Dad a quick visit on the way to that nights wedding, I inexplicably found myself picking up the phone instead. Dad was back at the Mount Street hospital for his monthly, 'top up,' as he called it, of chemo. I knew I was going to see him in half an hour, and yet, I *still* asked the ward's head nurse, to put me through to his room.

"'ello."

His voice, sat so high in his throat, it sounded like he was 100 years old.

"Dad?"

"'ello son. 'ow are yer?" He asked, like he'd just run a marathon.

"I'm ok. I'm on my way to see you. I just wanted to check, if there's anything you need."

"A new fuckin' body, if yer can manage one," he said, without any trace of his usual humour. Something was wrong. Dad very rarely swore, and never ever complained.

"You don't sound yourself, Dad. What's wrong?"

"I've picked up, some sorta virus. I 'aven't, bothered telling yer muther. Yer know 'ow she worries."

"What, like a cold?"

"Is it 'ell. I wish it fuckin were. I'm sittin 'ere, wearin' a nappy and I've been shittin' blood, for the last three days. There can't be much left to shit."

He wheezed, with his short fuse, audibly burning.

"It's got somethin to do, with them shingles, I 'ad last year. Ohh!" His guttural groan, swallowed the receiver. "Fuck, it 'urts, so, much. Ohh!"

"Dad? Dad?"

"I'll be all right, son. I'm just feelin'… bit sorry for meself."

"Dad get the nurse. Get them, to give you something."

"She's *been* in. And specialist, 'e said, it should be gone, by tomorrow."

"You sure?"

"It'll get better. Fuck knows, it can't get worse."

I heard tears, drip down the back of his throat.

"Don't yer, go worryin' yerself lad."

"Of course I worry Dad! I don't, understand." My voice was beginning to waver. "So you've got, the sores again?"

"No, not on the outside of me. They're *inside* me. Ohhhh."

His pain-racked yell, tap danced across my nerves, in six-inch stilettos.

"Fuck, son, I don't know 'ow much more, I can take of this," his soft pleading sobs, stabbing me in the chest.

"Oh Dad. I love you so much. You are the most wonderful, kind and funny man, that I have ever known. I am so lucky, that you picked me, to be your son."

"And I'm so lucky, I 'ad yer. I do love you, Stevie." His voice, only just managing to blub out my name before he started to bawl, like a newborn baby being cut from its umbilical chord. Without acknowledging it, we both looked up and saw the enormous wave about to crash down, on top of us.

"Don't be frightened, Dad. You just lie back, and relax. You've done, so well, Dad. You've fought, it, for so long. You don't, have to fight any more. You just lie back and relax. Lie back and relax. I love you. Mum loves you.

Everyone, who's ever met you, loves you. You are so loved. So..."

"I've gotta go Stevie, it's like, I've got to do a great... big... fart." and he hung up the phone.

Thirty-nine minutes had elapsed, by the time I had picked Mum up from the shops and driven her to the hospital. And when we saw his specialist, waiting to greet us at the front door, it was obvious that my conversation with Dad, had been my last. Well, at least the last one he'd be able to speak in. In a macabre twist of fate, the technology that had kept Dad alive, was having the last laugh of all. If you were going to have a brain haemorrhage, the Mount Street Hospital, was certainly not the place to do it. Because, what would surely have *killed* Dad anywhere else, had only managed 98% of the job. The other two percent, lay hooked up to a ventilator in ICU. As we sat there talking to him, holding his hands, narrating the photo album of our family's life and praying that he would wake up, I could only imagine, that this must surely be hell.

After six agonising hours and dozens and dozens of tests, my beautiful Dad was pronounced brain dead. The machine was switched off, and after a couple of involuntary twitches, he was gone.

24 THE BLACK CURTAIN

The following Thursday, Mum and I sat at the front of Bowra and Odea's crowded funeral chapel. We knew that Dad was popular, but never could have imagined just *how* popular. People had flown in from all over Australia, and the amount of love in that room completely swamped its modest capacity, so much so that a number of people had to stand in the corridor, while others still, chose to stand in the garden and watch through the large window. And everywhere you looked, the crowd was dotted with white lawn bowling uniforms, that gave the congregation, through my tired, broken-hearted eyes, the appearance of a big blue sea, brimming with beautiful white caps. Dad would have loved that I thought, it would remind him of his days in the navy.

Not being a religious man, my Dad had only met the priest, when the priest came to bless his body, and consequently, the 'representative of the cloth's' brief eulogy, was what you would politely call, 'adequate' in a very *generic* kind of way. But I couldn't blame him for making it sound impersonal. He didn't know who Dad was. So I decided that someone should speak, who did.

"Ladies and gentlemen… We have come here today, to say goodbye, to the most beautiful man I have ever known. A man, that profoundly effected, everybody that knew him. Because to know Gerry Briggs, was to know one of the wonders of the universe. His love, his wisdom, his compassion, his generous nature, his incredible sense of humour. When *he* made you laugh, it was like there *was* a God, and he was shining his light all over you, through Dad's eyes. He was my beloved mother's husband for 41 years, and I can't even begin to understand or fathom, what she must be going through. He loved you, so dearly, Mum. From the cup of tea he brought you every morning, to the kiss he gave you at bedtime… I'd like, if I may, to tell a little story that sums up the extraordinary spirit, that *was* my father."

I furiously sand-bagged my eyelids, in vain.

"I'm sorry… Its never really struck me, before today, just how ugly the word *was* actually is … Twenty three years ago, Mum and Dad wanted to have a baby, and unfortunately they weren't able to, so they decided to adopt. And one day, they went to an orphanage, to meet a little boy. The thing was, the orphanage had no money and not too many clothes. So when they arrived, the little boy was wearing a *pink* dress. When they were asked, if they liked the little boy, they said, 'Oh yes.' When they were asked, do you think you could get used to having him around, they said, 'Oh yes.' And when they were asked if they wanted the little boy, Mum said, ' Oh yes.' And Dad said, 'We'll take the little boy, but I'll be buggered if we'll take the dress. I'm not having, no transvestite, in my car.' So Dad took off the dress, took off his own shirt and jumper, we're talking Yorkshire in February, wrapped the little baby in it and drove home, for two hours, half-naked. He gave selflessly from the first day I met him, and he never stopped. He would often go without material things, so his family, could have the best of everything in life. And I will *never* forget that. Up until last week, he was still wearing a t-shirt from 12 years ago, and our junior soccer days... But unfortunately, we have *run out* of days Dad... And now, your brave fight and your wonderful life, are over. Tread gently into the sky and don't look back, because the world has lost all its beauty and is nothing but a barren, hollow rock without you standing on it."

I can honestly say getting up to speak that day, was the hardest thing I have ever done in my life. And watching Dad's rose coloured casket trundle down that narrow pathway of stainless steel rollers, until it disappeared behind the black curtain, was a very close second.

I had never been to a cremation before, and I prayed that the unique scent, hanging in the air like a black chiffon veil, was that of a cheap, fast burning, cigar. Just in case it wasn't, I hurriedly moved Mum towards the back, where a special seat was waiting so we could personally say goodbye to everyone who attended. A line of biblical proportions filed past. Each person wearing their solemn, gutted expression on their face, like a legacy badge on their lapel.

The mixture of emotions you feel at a time like that, is astounding. It's almost as if every colour, every smell, every sensation, every feeling, every thought, every observation, every intuition, every meaningful experience you have ever had, consciously or subconsciously, is laid out on an enormous pallet, and smudged, into the cracks of your soul. One second I would be suffocating in the belly of a whale, as I contemplated never being able to make him a cup of tea again. And then the very next second, I was surfing on the wings of a Condor, as I proudly basked in the *joy* he had given, to everyone in that room. I think I was somewhere between the two, when I saw a fluorescent suited hand, reaching toward mine. How, did Julian Parker know, that Dad was dead?

"I'm tho thorry, Thephen."

He reached into his jacket and produced an envelope.

"Thith, ith, totally unethical. But, it doethn't look like I'm going to get better and I want you to have it."

In the surreal psychedelic sideshow, that is farewelling your father, I thanked him, put the envelope in my pocket and didn't give it a second thought. It wasn't until the following month, when I stood in the same jacket, in a very different setting, that I remembered it was there. I didn't open it, mind you. I had something else to take care of, before I did that.

25 DAD'S LAST WISH

Mum and I were *travelling* as well as could be expect-ed. In fact, someone at the airline had heard about Dad's passing and moved us up to first class. Which did make the flight more comfortable, but unfortunately the bigger seats weren't big *enough,* to fill the void of flying up north, without him.

Paraburdoo, was just as I remembered it. Hot, red, covered in spinifex, teeming with flies and absolutely, deliriously, beautiful. When I got off the jet, I lifted up my arms to embrace it, like a grandmother I hadn't seen for ages. I filled my mouth, with its delicious warm dry air and rolled it back and forth, across my tastebuds as I breathed it in. I would never be so arrogant as to assume to know how Aboriginal people feel about their land, but on that occasion, I think I had at least a semi-solid inkling.

Twenty minutes after we had placed our feet on the sticky bitumen tarmac, Charlie Crabbe came waddling up to meet us.

"G'day Jean."

He gave Mum a big hug.

"G'day Stephen."

His rough callused hand scraped across mine. Charlie had never been one for many words, and today was no different.

"Did you want to head into town first, or just get on with it?"

"I think Dad would have preferred to make a start. But it really depends, on whether there's *any* around. The sun wasn't quite up when we came in to land, so we couldn't see."

"Oh yeah, there is. I saw a decent bunch of them, over Kelly's Pool on the way out here."

I looked at Mum. She gave me a nod, and handed over Dad's bowls bag.

"Well, let's give it a go then." I smiled.

I'd kind of hoped, that Mum would have been able to come as well. But I knew she was terrified by the whole concept of being in something that small, and the fact it could only hold two people, offered her a perfect escape slide.

I think it had started its life as a tiger moth, then became a crop duster, and now was used for the odd bit of survey and joy-flight work. To be honest, I doubt that

Charlie even had a licence. Not that he couldn't fly it. He could certainly do that. I'd seen him fly it at all sorts of things; like the annual Paragala fete and the walkathon. Once, when he'd had a few too many homebrews, he landed it on the oval during a footy game against Tom Price, to protest about the umpire's one-eyed whistle.

Its hard, unforgiving seat was an evolutionary galaxy away from what I had just been sitting in. In fact, when you compared it to the sterile efficiency of a passenger plane, it all appeared very organic. I mean, we seemed to be doing the same speed just before take-off, as we were when we turned around in front of the hangar. But just when I thought I would have to get out and push it that little bit faster, we lifted up into the plush panorama of the Pilbara sky. I've got to admit, that I was a little nervous for the first few minutes, until I realised that the wings weren't actually *flapping*, that was just the wooden bird's equivalent of the slack you find in an old car's steering wheel. Once over my initial jitters, I couldn't help but marvel at the wonder of flight, and the shrinking tarmac, as we sliced our way through water's, invisible cousin.

As a sign of respect for Dad, Charlie flew us in a large circle around the town. We weren't up that high, so it was possible for me to look down and clearly see all the roads, easements and trails of my childhood, laid out like a 'This is Your life' aerial snapshot. When we'd completed the lap, Charlie took us right over our old house and back yard, dropping so low, I could almost smell one of Mum's Shepherd's pies. I gave Kimba a wave and for once in my life, made absolutely no attempt to hold back my tears.

The engine was so noisy, that I could cry out loud, all I liked. Which would have been a bloody long time but for the immense mass of billowing, black, commas-from-God that reared up on each other's backs, to greet us. Charlie's description of the storm clouds had been as *understated* as usual. I'd hate to see what he would call a cyclone, I thought, as I gripped hold of the bag in one hand and the plane in the other.

"Straight into the biggest, blackest one, we can find, Charlie!" I shouted, "There, over on the left."

Charlie banked us around, while I prepared myself, to execute Dad's final request.

I knew that he liked the Doo, and he loved his mates and his time living up there. But I didn't, really understand, the depth of his feelings for the place itself. Because my father, one of the proudest Yorkshiremen you could ever hope to meet's, last wish, was, "… that me ashes, be carried by me son into the sky. Where they will be sprinkled, into the curved canopy, of a colossal cumulonimbus cloud, from where, I will rain down on that steamin' 'ot ground; coloured red, yellow and brown and the tiny flecks of me spirit, will bring nourishment, to every little thing, that calls Paraburdoo, its 'ome." And with the plane jumping about like a ride at the show, I reached into his bowls bag, grabbed the urn holding his ashes, and seeded the surliest storm cloud I could see.

As my dad's dust disappeared into the black void and I looked out at the infinite red horizon, a half-smile forced its way across my face. I realised dad had got me this far, and now the rest… was up to me.

303

Made in the USA
Charleston, SC
26 December 2013